Far From the Sodding Crowd

By the same authors

Bollocks to Alton Towers
Uncommonly British Days Out

The Framley Examiner
The book of the website of the newspaper

Historic Framley
In association with Framley Museum

Far From the Sodding Crowd

More Uncommonly British Days Out

ROBIN HALSTEAD
JASON HAZELEY
ALEX MORRIS
JOEL MORRIS

MICHAEL JOSEPH
an imprint of
PENGUIN BOOKS

MICHAEL JOSEPH

Published by the Penguin Group
Penguin Books Ltd, 80 Strand, London WC2R ORL, England
Penguin Group (USA) Inc., 375 Hudson Street, New York, New York 10014, USA
Penguin Group (Canada), 90 Eglinton Avenue East, Suite 700, Toronto, Ontario, Canada M4P 2Y3
(a division of Pearson Penguin Canada Inc.)
Penguin Ireland, 25 St Stephen's Green, Dublin 2, Ireland (a division of Penguin Books Ltd)
Penguin Group (Australia), 250 Camberwell Road,
Camberwell, Victoria 3124, Australia (a division of Pearson Australia Group Pty Ltd)
Penguin Books India Pvt Ltd, 11 Community Centre,
Panchsheel Park, New Delhi – 110 017, India
Penguin Group (NZ), 67 Apollo Drive, Rosedale, North Shore 0632, New Zealand
(a division of Pearson New Zealand Ltd)
Penguin Books (South Africa) (Pty) Ltd, 24 Sturdee Avenue,
Rosebank, Johannesburg 2196, South Africa

Penguin Books Ltd, Registered Offices: 80 Strand, London WC2R ORL, England

www.penguin.com

Published in 2007
1

All photographs are the property of the authors, except those of The Valiant Soldier, pages 57–60 (kindly
supplied by John Parr) and The Centre of Britain, page 122 (kindly supplied by Michael Mann).

Printed in Great Britain by Clays Ltd, St Ives plc

A CIP catalogue record for this book is available from the British Library

ISBN: 978-0-718-14966-6

www.framleyexaminer.com

A NOTE ON THE TYPEFACES
The chapter headings and photo captions are set in Johnston Underground, a typeface
designed in 1916 for London Transport by Edward Johnston to a commission by Frank Pick.
The body copy is set in Bembo, cut c. 1495 by Francesco Griffo at Aldus Manutius's print works for the first
edition of Cardinal Bembo's *De Aetna* and revived by Stanley Morison for the Monotype Corporation in
1929. But you probably knew this already.

THE CITY OF EDINBURGH COUNCIL	
C0024888109	
Bertrams	02.06.07
DA650	£14.99
KL	PL2

Contents

Where they all are

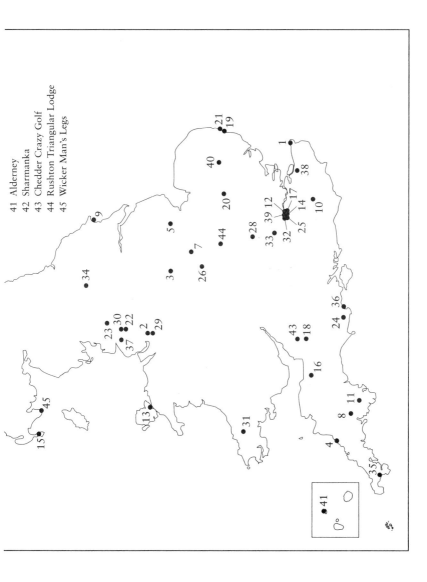

41 Alderney
42 Sharmanka
43 Chedder Crazy Golf
44 Rushton Triangular Lodge
45 Wicker Man's Legs

Introduction

We've been here before. Perhaps you came with us. If not, here's the story so far.

In 2004, we wrote a book about some of the plucky and brilliant underdogs of British tourism, hoping we might taste some of the true spirit of the nation, and that we would get some nice days out with a Thermos. We were looking for places that were modest, eccentric, free from costly dazzle and which would let you enjoy yourself quietly at your own pace; examples of Britain's admirable desire, noted by George Orwell, to 'choose [its] own amusements and not have them chosen from above'. An uncommonly British day out would be spent in a converted factory shed full of locally produced pencils, rather than wasted in a sticky two-hour queue for an internationally standardised Mach Speed Corkscrew Galacticoaster. We called the book *Bollocks to Alton Towers*.

Plenty of readers seemed to understand the criteria, and recommendations began to trickle in (pouring in would have been uncharacteristically showy, so thank you all for your admirable restraint and good taste). In addition, our eyes were now attuned to spotting these odd little attractions. Everywhere we turned, we noticed more and more strong contenders, places that had been overlooked for *Bollocks* just because we didn't know where (or how) to look properly. The forty-odd attractions that made up the first book were, as we'd predicted, merely the tip of the iceberg.

This time round, we decided to call the book *Far From the Sodding Crowd* because it seems to sum up something essentially good about all these places. It hints at a wilful refusal to follow the herd, a determination to wander off the beaten track in pursuit of idiosyncratic pleasures.

'Far from' is a euphemism, rich in understatement. 'The minister's position is far from secure.' 'Fans were far from happy at the team's 6-0 defeat.' 'Pat Coombs is far from alive.' It does the same job as a roared fratboy 'NOT!' but in a bowler hat. Its implications are clear, but it veils them delicately, with a wry smile, allowing the listener to intimate the extent of the minister's insecurity, the fans' unhappiness, the much-loved comedy actress's deadness, without actually saying it and risking offence. In that, it's very British.

'The Sodding Crowd' is obviously the line of boiling cars snaking into Chessington World of Vomit, filled (oddly) with representatives of that same ninety-six per cent of the nation (according to a widely publicised Mothercare survey) who think theme parks are a rip-off, but still go, spending £1bn a year at these undemanding nowhere-holes. The Sodding Crowd is also that broad, undistinguished swathe of us at whom an increasing chunk of our culture is now aimed: the sawn-off-shotgun target of 'customers' who, if treated individually, would be revealed as sensitive, discerning, interesting people with wildly varying tastes, but whom, unfortunately, it's easier to treat as a fat demographic slice and spray with thin gruel from a firehose.

A mainstream attraction will usually, and deliberately, underestimate its visitors to attract the largest number of people. It's a Catch-22. To pay for the razzmatazz of a state-of-the-art international-calibre leisure attraction, the owners will have to fork out for flashy presentation and questionable gadgetry. To make that investment back, they will then need to attract more ticket buyers. So, to broaden the attraction's appeal, more tinsel is poured over the place, which costs money, which requires more visitors, and so on. These attractions bellow and whine, 'Please don't be bored,' 'Love me! Love me!' We may fall for it, pressured into brief knee-jerk enthusiasm by the sugary allure of duelling suits of animatronic armour in the Great Hall and exploding lions in the Majesty of Africa exhibit but, if pressed, we'd admit it makes us slightly uncomfortable. Being told to love something makes us mistrustful and we find reasons to hate it.★

Although most of us accept that there's nothing necessarily great about an internationally branded leisure-format day out, you may wonder whether a visit to Leicestershire's biggest collection of pincushions† is a tempting alternative. Isn't this sort of attraction far from the sodding crowd for a reason? If it were that great, wouldn't it have all the trappings of popular success: three-hour queues, three-figure ticket prices and nowhere to park?

If we're honest, one of the reasons for including certain attractions in these books is that they do sound so unpromising that for a moment we're convinced 'there can't be one of those'. Sometimes we go as a personal challenge to enjoy it. But, trust us, we've never been disappointed. These places may not take the easiest path to tempt in the casual visitor, but that's what makes them such surprising, exciting, invigorating places. A tourist attraction is designed to make money. But if it's off-beam theme isn't

---

★ So probably best not to read this book then. Why not pretend we hated simply everything featured in here, and then you'll be free to make up your own minds?
† We made that one up. Don't get overexcited. Unless you plan to start one, in which case, have our heartiest encouragement and send us a brochure.

drawing huge crowds, you can be sure the owners and curators must be in it for something more exciting than mere profit, otherwise they'd check the accounts, close their pincushion museum and turn it into a supermarket. Something about the place must be pretty good, we'll wager, if the owner is willing to stick to their guns (or paperweights or cuckoo clocks).

All these places have something to say: often too much. Considering that many of them are engaged in a very niche discussion with a very niche audience, a surprising number struggle to find enough space for all their exhibits. Again and again we'd be told, 'This is only a small sample of what we've got – lots of other stuff is packed away in a warehouse.' You may remember the Millennium Dome,* which was designed back-to-front. Not an exhibition, a show or an attraction, but a space: a great big nothing to celebrate the arrival of three zeros. But imagine if it had been planned the right way around. Imagine if a roof had been thrown over a hundred travelling versions of places like those in this book: a giant Cabinet-Of-Curiosities picture of Britain and its myriad passions. If the Millennium Dome had been full of apples, fans and shells; clowns, clocks and coracles; bubblecars, gas ovens and bags of George Best crisps; wouldn't that have been a more engaging and joyous celebration of Britain than the McDonald's Our Town Story?

The British have an unspoken social agreement that there are only three unthreatening topics for discussion: television, sport and the weather. These are the things we have agreed we will have in common with people we meet (strong views on religion or politics, for instance, being considered unforgivable bad manners). But hobbies can break that conversational taboo. At these small attractions, you'll find that the curators, like all of us, will happily talk about their passions (which happily also happen to be their jobs). So listen and learn. You never know when it will pay to become a dilettante polymath. Next time you get into a taxi driven by someone who's only interested in coracles or pork pies, you'll be able to join in and make some sort of warm human contact.

Enthusiasts and eccentrics are often regarded as 'sad'. And yet the one thing that chess nerds, stamp collectors, Gilbert and Sullivan geeks, trainspotters and other ostensibly 'sad' people have in common is that they're

---

* Doubtless, by the time you read this, the Millennium Dome will have some new corporately sponsored name, yet another otherwise reputable company having painted their logo on it like a sailor leaping out of the lifeboat and swimming desperately towards a sinking frigate, screaming, 'Let me get on!' You can rebrand it all you like, but we're the kind of people who call a Post Office Tower a Post Office Tower.

visibly happier than the rest of us. They have a third place to exist. Home. Work ... and where's your third place? What? You haven't got a room full of antique thimbles? Making this book, and spending so much time in the company of the passionate and sharing their passions, was like stepping into that parallel notional world where BBC Radio 4 is set. We bumped into maniacs, romantics, visionaries, wildly different points of view, the honeycomb of detail that obsession inhabits, things you didn't know, stuff (even the most trivial stuff) you'll remember for the rest of your days. We were blissfully lost for a few months in the sheer blimey-ness of life.

Sometimes the delights of an attraction took a bit of thought, or a little time to reveal themselves. Of course you're not interested in paperweights ... yet. Expecting everything to jump and dance and sing and entertain you without any effort on your part is part of a dangerous modern tendency to infantilism. Not all days out are going to be like sticking a 10p in the slot and watching the puppet Sooty band jiggle about in the machine near the stairwells at the Co-op.* The sort of infantilism employed to sell brightly coloured things to adults overstimulated by advertising is only tangentially related to the behaviour of actual children (who are more complicated than that). Real children are open, wayward and interested. They will never stop asking 'but why?' until it's been explained. Adults are more resigned to not understanding things. Most of the places we recommend don't work unless you can find some reserves of childish glee, and summon up a child's openness to new experience.

The oft-heard parental story of the child opening a gift on Christmas Day, discarding it and playing with the box for two hours isn't a tale of woe about how much the parent spent on a flash toy that went unappreciated: it's a joyous acknowledgement that children (and, for that matter, big children) can get as much (or more) satisfaction from something into which they have to invest some imagination as they can from something which spoon-feeds them unrealistic levels of expectation.

These unique, slightly more demanding attractions also lend their town, village or region a modicum of identity in an increasingly homogenised and franchised world. As we explored, often going to corners of the country we'd never visited before, we built a mental map of a secret Britain of distinct, individual places: a map laid over the usual map so that, while High Streets from Thisborough to Thatbury remain indistinguishable,

---

* If you didn't have one of these near the stairwells at your local childhood Co-op, there is bound to be a no-win no-fee solicitor who can get you compensation.

odd attractions shine like lighthouse beacons so you know where you are. Lincolnshire, for us, is now Bubblecar Country and, though similarly flat, will never be mistaken for Norfolk (an area we now know as Dad's Army Museumshire).

A visit to a tiny attraction is a wonderful opportunity to exercise the sunny side of the brain. The glass is half full (as, very often, is the tourist attraction). It's not particularly intellectually rigorous to decide something's crap and stomp around like a bored thirteen-year-old. Instead, try to see the good in it. As any decent psychologist will tell you, no, everything isn't just shit, and yes, it is just you. A certain frame of mind is the only tool you need to get the most out of one of these visits. Their greatness is always there to find, but usually it's not dashing about, letting off fireworks. Fascinating pearls will turn up in the forbidding oyster shells of dusty display cabinets, and valuable truffles can be snouted from the undergrowth of arcane ephemera. We're delighted to report that we have included every attraction we visited, and there was something inspirational and tremendous in all of them.

One of the precious myths of our culture is that the small man can defeat the big monster, whether it's Beowulf battling Grendel, Robin Hood taking on the mechanisms of state taxation or Tom Baker twatting the Daleks armed only with a bag of jelly babies and a scary smile. When we see a big thing, we don't feel a need to celebrate it, because we know everyone can already see it. We like to cut it down to size, so we look for the chink in the armour of the seemingly invulnerable behemoth and have a pop. And, when we see a tiny underdog, we do the reverse and look for its strengths. This levels the playing field and, if there's one thing the British love, it's a level playing field.

So let's drag the weighty roller of fairness over the lumpy cricket pitch of tourism one more time, turn away from whichever one-size-fits-all leisure pustule has erupted from the grounds of your local stately home, and spend a day surrounded by delicate, gentle, charming, mind-broadening delights. Pack a picnic and follow whatever brown sign leads farthest from the sodding crowd.

Far From the Sodding Crowd

Margate Shell Grotto

...the mere asking of a question causes it to disappear or to merge into something else.

E. M. Forster, *A Passage to India*

At the end of Margate not yet lapped by the advancing waves of gentrification is the unfussy modernist frontage of the Margate Shell Grotto. It

could be a provincial theatre box office, the chunky white curves as unremarkable as the polystyrene packing from a new television. Margate was one of the first seaside towns to attract visitors from outside the genteel bathing classes, built from the holiday pennies of donkey-back cockneys, on foundations of lettered rock and newspaper chip cones. Just down the road (pending the developers' hovering wrecking ball) is Dreamland amusement park, home to Britain's oldest surviving scenic railway, a Grade II listed proto-roller coaster from the birth of come-one come-all seaside tourism. That this place should have a shell gròtto, whatever that might be, sounds just right.

The Shell Grotto has been open for over 200 years, has two streets named after it, and yet it still feels like a secret. You'll have to ring the doorbell to get in, as if it were a members' club, which isn't far from the truth; the gift shop behind the plate-glass windows seems so sweetly unprepossessing that only those in the know would ever cross the threshold expecting more. At the rear of the shop is a small museum, but new visitors are advised to bypass it, as it lets slip some of the grotto's best secrets. Best to treat this area as dessert, and not spoil your appetite for the main course. Pay your entrance fee, and sneak out the back door, down into somewhere so bizarre you'll eat your bucket and spade.

A chalk-sided tunnel slithers into the ground, gently undulating to and fro in a series of tantalising blind bends. Before it was fattened for tourists, this entrance passage was only four feet tall and double its current length, really cranking up the anticipation for stooping visitors clutching anxious candles. Eventually, with the crafted shock of a well-arranged orchestral stab, the last turn of the tunnel opens up, flooding with pearly light.

You can be sure of shells.

You find yourself in an exotic pagan temple: millions upon millions of cockles, mussels, oysters and whelks eerily studded into the walls in coiling abstract patterns, forming suggestions of roses, skulls, animal faces, crosses and ankhs. The shimmering shells make the corridors glow like an ancient ossuary. Indeed, such is the shock of stepping from the gloomy tunnel into that first shimmering rotunda that, for a moment, the walls seem to be made of human bones. It's the sort of place into which Ray Harryhausen would unleash a stop-frame-animated phalanx of duelling skeletons. Right up to the gothic points of the ceiling arches, and as far as you can see, there is the pale, subterranean gleam of endless calcium. It is alien, unsettling and magical; the last thing you'd expect to find under a Margate street. It's either been transplanted from the other side of the world or trawled from the distant shores of some nameless architect's broken mind. In the next six months, unless your soul is utterly dead, you will have a dream set here. In the serpentine knots of these mysterious, opalescent corridors, every surface slathered with crustacean Artex, you could really snag a cardigan.

The grotto is constructed from long, sensuous curves, suggesting something pre-classical, maybe even prehistoric, and somehow feminine. On the far side of the main circular passage, as the jewel in its ring, a dome is open to the sky, reconnecting the grotto's claustrophobic bubble with the world above. The dome used to have a wooden lid, defeating the object somewhat. This was replaced with disco-era orange perspex, which can't have helped much either, but the current owners have sensibly opted for a transparent skylight; in a damp, underground cave full of fish skeletons, you

want as much fresh air as you can get. A serpentine passage leads from here to a square chamber known as the altar room, home to the only straight lines in the grotto, a few mystifying sacrificial alcoves and a slightly less haunting ceiling and east wall made of dull concrete. The wall is the work of the Luftwaffe, damage from the grotto's brief tour of duty as 'the most unusual air raid shelter in Britain' (*Thanet Gazette*), but the original vaulted ceiling was, barely believably, cemented over to allow an extension to the school above, leaving a brutal grey firebreak in the enveloping shells.

The grotto is an overwhelming experience. Light from the dome aperture and sensitively placed bulbs glitters off the pearlescent interiors of the upturned shells. The shells are mostly mounted wrongside-out to take advantage of this effect, but

there are occasional splashes of colour. Originally, as a reconstructed panel in the museum illustrates, the grotto would have been a riot of harlequin cockles and Technicolor winkles, but a dusty carbon coat from a century of gas lamps has turned the grotto into a pale ghost of itself.★

Questions will be leaping around your brain, poking their tongues out. What was the grotto for? How old is it? Who built it? Your guess is as good as anyone else's. At the front desk you can search in vain for an authorita-

---

★ In the past, sacred spaces trumpeted their separateness from the drab, brown world with riots of colour. Now that cheap dyes have made the world as garish as a French backpacker's wardrobe, we mark our holy places by keeping them pure, minimal and understated. The grotto's accidental paleness helps it look sacred to modern eyes.

tive guidebook; the only likely contender is so impenetrable that even though the pages are printed in the wrong order, it took years for anyone to tell the grotto's owners (there's now an erratum sticker on the frontispiece). Carbon dating is impossible, as all those sooty gas-lamp deposits muddle the sample. When English Heritage commissioned a survey into the age and purpose of the site in 1999, they concluded that, er, they didn't know. What fun.

The grotto never cropped up on any maps and local residents had no idea it existed until 1835 when local schoolmaster James Newlove, who was renting the property above, announced he'd stumbled upon the grotto by accident. Newlove claimed one of his workers had dropped a spade down the skylight of the dome chamber while building a duck pond. Newlove sent his young son down on a rope to investigate (an act that would surely have scarred the child for life, but shoving small children into confined spaces, often carrying a chimney brush, was what passed for good parenting in Victorian Britain). This press-friendly yarn is, like the grotto, slightly fishy. Newlove's children later said they'd played in the grotto long before this date, and maybe the duck-pond yarn was a canny way of postdating the 'accidental' discovery of a valuable moneymaking attraction until Newlove had purchased the land on which it stood. Whatever the truth, within two years the weird underground structure was open to the public as a lost pagan temple, pulling in holidaymakers keen to follow their efficacious promenade with a romantic dash of voguish pre-Christian culture.

It's a magnificent puzzle. If the structure was a folly constructed by Newlove himself, how did he get away with it? Fakes are usually uncovered sooner or later. From spiritualism to the Cottingley fairies, someone eventually gives the game away. One of Newlove's necessary army of workmen would surely have found his tongue loosened in a local pub and, in a tight community, it's unlikely a team of builders could have escaped notice as they dredged the seashore for four million shells and poured them into a hole in the ground near the main Margate to Broadstairs road. Follies are built as public declarations of wealth on large estates, but the Shell Grotto was

tucked beneath unremarkable farmland, nowhere near a major house. Even if Newlove had built it as a moneymaking novelty, there must have been easier things to attempt, a small pier perhaps or a what-the-butler-saw machine. Maybe he wasn't the builder, but merely discovered a pre-existing faux-ancient structure, a meeting place for some forgotten secret society. Many find it unlikely that an ambitious construction job such as this could have gone unrecorded less than a couple of hundred years ago, but Liverpool has begun digging up the similarly baffling and undocumented Williamson Tunnels (of very recent vintage)* so maybe it's another gorgeous and inexplicable lost wonder from Great-grandma's day. We could do with more of those.

The appeal of the mystery hasn't dimmed with time. Children (already excited that they're in a secret den) love the chance to have a guess, their answers as plausible as those of their parents. And grown-ups aren't immune to the temptation either. If Occam's Razor is the logical process by which the correct answer to a problem is the simplest possible one, places like the Shell Grotto encourage what could be called the Occam's Beard approach, where the preferred answer is the one that is the most unkempt and shaggy. In the absence of a simple solution, taking your mind for a walk is part of the fun. Enthusiastic amateurs and diligent scholars have all had a try, concluding the grotto is without a shadow of a doubt the work of the Knights Templar, Phoenician refugees or Sir Isaac Newton. Fancy a go?

No sooner have you spotted something you think identifies the purpose or age of the place, than the grotto dances away again, giggling through a conch. The most thorough and encouraging recent study has uncovered repeating geometric patterns and cadences of equinoctial sunlight that could point to the grotto's use as an ancient pagan solar calendar. Although this solution might cause countless New Agers to throw their wizard's hats in the air, it's just as likely the solar patterning is a clever folly based on seventeenth-century ideas about Stonehenge (cue pointy hats landing back on Mother Earth with a bump). The exotic designs are 'almost entirely of India, Egypt and the East' according to one book, but nineteenth-century Britain was obsessed with pillaging the imagery of Empire, so that's no clue.

---

* See the popular Penguin book *Bollocks to Alton Towers*.

Pointy arches? Could be gothic revival, except the Assyrians were turning out drains this shape as long ago as 722 BCE. A big modern-looking shell heart? Dead giveaway, except the shape dates back to the Cro-Magnon era, leaving you none the wiser. Whether ancient temple, Victorian joke or some sort of lost hellfire club from the years between, it's gleefully maddening.

The age of the grotto could have serious repercussions for its future. Though it's a listed structure, it badly needs repair (and proper academic investigation) but the relevant authorities are reluctant to entangle themselves. English Heritage seem oddly embarrassed about the idea that it could be anything mystical and strange, no matter what its age, preferring to classify it as a seaside folly. But the bickering is self-defeating, and misses the point. Even if, as English Heritage's mildly dismissive official description states, the grotto can only be dated to the year of Newlove's discovery (an assertion for which there is as little evidence as there is for it having been built by aliens or Michael Foot) it's one of the most impressive purpose-built tourist attractions in the country; one that would have required a level of dedication more usually expended on a cathedral.

Sensibly, the current owners don't take sides. Sarah Vickery, a former travel journalist, and her partner, Colin Bowling, just want the place to survive. Sarah fell in love with it as a girl and couldn't pass up the chance to buy 'her grotto' when it came up for sale. They loosely agree the grotto is old, and probably had some sort of ritual purpose, but leave it to visitors to make up their own minds – a wonderful and liberating sensation if you're used to poring over drily instructional display boards telling you exactly what to think.

The grotto is simultaneously haunting and homely. Who hasn't brought back or been given a shell-encrusted knick-knack from the seaside? It could be a lost pagan shrine or have 'A Present From Margate' picked out in the shells – it wouldn't matter. It's still magical, mysterious and (once it's in your head) impossible to forget. If we want to keep mementos of our social history, and we can see the value in preserving piers, pavilions and pleasure beaches, there's surely even more of an argument for saving this unique, antique tourist attraction. There aren't many seasides with one of these buried beneath them.

The Shell Grotto, Grotto Hill, Margate, Kent, CT9 2BU
01843 220008
www.shellgrotto.co.uk

Cuckooland

Sumer is icumen in,
Lhude sing cuccu!

Anonymous, 'Cuckoo Song', thirteenth century

At some point, a sufficiently large collection of things will choose to emerge from its secretive cocoon as a beautiful museum, stretch its east and west wings and take flight. The placing of pots full of souvenir pencils near the front door or rolls of 'I've seen the ashtrays at Nantwich' stickers are key signifiers, but the adoption of the word 'museum' is usually the only way to excuse the size of a collection that has run out of control. Either open your lovingly gathered clump of vintage washing machines to the paying public, or run the risk of being sectioned as a twin tub-obsessed lunatic. Collecting isn't seen as a worthwhile pastime for a grown adult, whereas being a curator is absolutely fine.

Brothers Roman and Maz Piekarski jointly curate Cuckooland, and their awesome collection is approaching its third decade as a fully fledged museum. Having flown their original nests, around 550 very old-school cuckoo clocks adorn the walls of Tabley's Old School House near Knutsford.* Roman proudly announces that every single one was made within the same twenty-five-square-mile area of the Black Forest, the true home of the cuckoo clock. No dilettantes these; a strict self-imposed rule like this is the hallmark of any collection that has a desire to be taken seriously. The expert Piekarskis have dedicated the remainder of their working lives to completing this collection, despite it already being the largest of its

---

* We managed to drive past it twice by mistake. Cuckooland is crying out for one of those brown tourist road signs but Cheshire County Council don't give them out to attractions where visits have to be pre-booked.

kind in the world. They consider themselves custodians rather than owners of their beloved flock of clocks. With a combined total of no wives and no children between them, the clocks are their family – a family that predates them both and that will, in time, outlive them.

The Piekarskis' house is a magical Roald Dahlish place that will appeal to a certain sort of imaginative youngster, so hats off to the one admirable child who recently held their birthday party at Cuckooland instead of going to McDonald's.* The bloke from TV's *Flog It* said it was the best collection of anything he had ever seen, and not only has the bloke from TV's *Flog It* been around a bit, the bloke from TV's *Flog It* is contractually obliged to know what he's talking about. The value of the collection doesn't bear thinking about. Almost every clock here would see a frenzied battle of the bidders were it to go individually to auction. Not that any of them will be sold if the Piekarskis have anything to do with it, as they have made plans to ensure that the collection will remain together when it ultimately has to leave their hands. Quite right too. When the clocks are seen together the

Cuckooland

---

* McDonald's don't take pre-bookings so they are allowed to have a brown sign. We passed one in Carmarthen and nearly crashed the car in disgust. In the great ledger of life, the name of someone from the council went down firmly in the 'twat' column for that one.

effect is simply startling; separate them and they may as well not have bothered to collect them in the first place.

The clocks date back to the 1750s when the Schwarzwald's own Franz Ketterer is believed to have come up with the very first Kuckucksuhr. Farm workers in the Black Forest had been making basic clocks for over a century, primarily in the winter months when the snow

reflected much-needed sunlight onto their otherwise poorly lit indoor work (and when there weren't as many gateaux to harvest). Cottage, or rather chalet, industries sprang up, with different villagers specialising in carpentry, clockmaking or wholesale. Initially the clocks were made with the face mounted on a simple wooden shield that sat in front of the clock mechanism. The more familiar, ornately carved, full-framed variety, came later, influenced by the nineteenth-century house-style designs of Johann Beha, a man who turned a humble clock into a home fit for cuckoos to live in.

Black Foresters also made trumpeter clocks (smartly dressed little

An alarming clock.

feller pops through door, toots on trumpet, then trundles back to bed for another hour), but it was the cuckoos that really took off. Previously it was the traditional 'wake up' rooster that had been the clock world's big bird. Crowing cocks featured on showpiece timepieces in some of Europe's major cities, but ultimately, with only a set of bellows and a pair of tiny organ pipes to play with, a 'cock-a-doodle-doo' sound was harder to replicate than a 'cuck-oo'.* Be thankful that the system's

---

* The cuckoo-clock cuckoo traditionally cuckoos at the A and F below middle C.

restrictions ruled out parrot clocks ('POLLY WANTS ELEVENSES'), woodpecker clocks (that get ruined every time the big hand points to XII), or seagull clocks that pop out and steal your chips. If only the roadrunner – another member of the cuckoo family – had been indigenous to central Europe then we might have been listening to a series of cheery MEEP MEEPS! every sixty minutes.

Cuckooland is home to the International Cuckoo Clock Keepers' Society (TICCKS) because Roman and Maz founded it themselves. There are 450 members, including Sotheby's and Christie's, but the brothers are keeping schtum about any other famous fans. It's like trying to get information out of a pair of clockwork Freemasons. The brothers Piekarski have developed a reputation in the world of cuckoo clocks as high as any of the Black Forest technicians. They have given lectures at the Bavarian School of Clockmaking – now known as the marginally less charming Furtwangen University of Applied Science – and worked on the cuckoo clock on show at Dove Cottage, William Wordsworth's former Lake District hideaway. Both of them began seven-year clockmaker apprenticeships in Manchester in their mid-teens, and the Germans now positively welcome their advice. They have even struck up a relationship with Beha's descendants, who still live in the family cottage.

Their foreign contacts alert the brothers should any valuable, rare or unusual items come on the market. Alongside the trumpeters, there are also clocks painted as human and animal faces with pendular eyes shifting from left to right to left, queasily following you around the room (providing your movement around the room is limited to shifting slightly from left to right and back again). There are even gratuitously large 'grandfather' models, which lead one to ponder just how big these clocks could get. Think about it. A cuckoo the size of a light aircraft springing out of St Stephen's Tower and hooting the hour using a ship's foghorn would certainly liven up the start of the *Six O'Clock News* on Radio 4.

The Piekarskis' showstopper is the clock made in 1860 for the royal palace at Baden Baden. It has intricate figures clambering all over it, including a dapper chap dangling from the pendulum like a Black Forest Harold Lloyd. It can't have been an easy task to fill a room with so many cuckoo clocks that you barely notice a massive chunk of wood measuring six feet from pendulum to belltower, but the Piekarskis have done it, giving a royal masterpiece equal status with the rest of their clock family. There's no favouritism in this collection and nothing is singled out, no matter how grand its origins.

Cuckooland gets itself plenty of press coverage twice a year when its curators are pictured turning the hands of their hundreds of clocks backward or forward an hour. They have only tried to synchronise them once, for midnight on a New Year's Eve; it was an impossible assignment thanks to the clocks' analogue movements. It's as well that they didn't succeed. That many cuckoos going off together twelve times in succession could probably shatter most of Cheshire's windows. Not that Roman and Maz mind noise; while working on clock repairs their chosen listening is hurtling punk rock.

Music plays a significant part in Cuckooland for its guests too. Many of the clocks provide a tinkling musical accompaniment for the call of the cuckoo, and to top it all the Piekarskis have acquired a small number of impressive fairground organs. A business diversification for some of the old clock-making families, the fairground organ's mechanism, you may be surprised to discover, is based on an early cuckoo clock. Hearing one of them sound its trumpets, piccolos and glockenspiel at full throttle in such a confined space, you will definitely appreciate all that linden wood around the walls that keeps the decibels at a non-deafening level.

A collection as focused as this leaves you reeling. It seems so unreal that days later you'll find yourself wondering if it might just have been a dream, terrified that if you even mention it to the people you think you went with, they'll look at you blankly, and shake their heads. You will simply never have seen a collection (and that means a collection of anything whatsoever) on this scale. These heroic places definitely do exist, and it's the committed narrowness of their focus, and diligence in pursuing it, that contrarily give everybody such a remarkably diverse choice of attractions to visit.

Cuckooland, The Old School, Chester Road, Tabley, Cheshire, WA16 0HL
01565 633039
www.cuckoolanduk.net

Papplewick Pumping Station

In Britain we've always made more fuss of a ballad than a blueprint.
Engineering Council advertisement

Those born when it was all fields around here all too often accuse the younger generation of taking things for granted. Cars, television and phones are cited and, apparently (tchoh!), the younger generation don't know they're born. Yet the accusatory list rarely includes the one thing that has really softened up our cushy lives, the innovation that the affluent, modern Western world least appreciates: a clean water supply. Every time some nerk drills through a mains pipe a couple of roads away, and trying to fill a glass from the tap brings you nothing but an empty splutter, all hell breaks loose. Shops sell out of bottled water within minutes and everyone starts unscrewing the living-room doors and making them into little dens or building nests out of fruit tins. The sky might as well have fallen in. We go to pieces without fresh water, so we ought to show our thanks. How quickly we forget. Only a century or so ago, we were building industrial cathedrals in honour of its supply: places like the Papplewick Pumping Station in Nottinghamshire.

Pumping stations were a frontline weapon in the Victorian war against disease. A new, healthier populace was able to pooh-pooh the threat of cholera, typhoid and polio, thanks to advances in sewage management led by Sir Joseph Bazalgette's pioneering work in London.* The Public Health Act of

---

* Sir Joseph was the great-great-grandfather of Peter Bazalgette, the man behind such enjoyable televisual sewage as *Big Brother*, *Ready Steady Cook* and *Ground Force*.

1875 ensured a water supply and loo for every dwelling, and people were finally able to drink water that didn't contain a detectable soupçon of next-door neighbour's bowel movement. Pumping stations provided the power to keep this new hygiene cycle in motion, supplying clean water at one end and moving sewage away at the other. The Victorians couldn't live without them.

Papplewick Pumping Station is in unbelievable condition for a working building dating back to 1884. This is the result of both a striking restoration job and the preservation plan hatched the moment its steam-powered pumps were retired in favour of an electric station. During its eighty-five years of use, the station staff would never have believed it would one day become a thriving tourist attraction.★ Then, the only people to see it in operation were the fourteen employees who kept the pump engines and boilers rumbling, and any visiting

Hot pumping action.

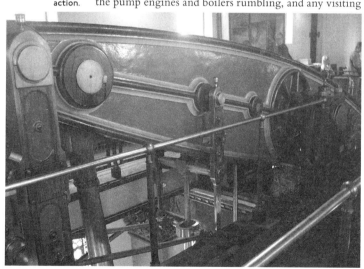

★ Another unlikely industrial tourist magnet, Sellafield Nuclear Power Station, has its own visitor centre. We trust that it will carry on providing a festive glow with its 'Come and meet Santa Claus at Sellafield' offer as it did in the run-up to Christmas 2006.

bigwigs from the Nottingham Waterworks Company. It's surprising how many visitors Papplewick gets today, given how remote the place is; despite the giveaway 120-foot red-brick chimney, you'll need a map to find it.

Over a steam-cooling fountain and fishpond, the exterior of the engine room rises up like a church: its central slatted roof vent resembling the bell-tower and its gigantic chimney looming overhead like a steaming steeple. It's clear that the pumping station's designer, Marriott Ogle Tarbotton,* had a lot of fun with the plans. The neat red brick used throughout the site gives it the complexion of a small country estate. Architectural flourishes such as the carved wooden porch and the terracotta fishscale motif between the engine-room windows surprise with their decorative delicacy, like gleaming brasses on a hardworking shire horse. Papplewick is by turns flamboyant and functional, grandiose yet gritty, showy but sturdy. It's elegantly engineered, and would have been an utterly (and literally) heart-warming place to work.

The interior of the engine room, the pumping station's own thumping ticker, looks more minster than machine room. Thrifty Victorian restraint meant that the station's construction came in under budget, allowing Tarbotton free reign to plough the surplus into lining the inside with elaborate ornamentation. The idea of such an underspend lining anything other than shareholders' pockets would be unthinkable today. The images on the stained glass of the arched windows running the length of the building may borrow their fish, lilies and other watery imagery from Papplewick's pond, but they are reminders of the business at hand: this is the hub of the freshwater revolution. The central cast iron columns

are clad in detailed metalwork and finished with golden ibises. Papplewick could have been purely utilitarian, a Meccano-fetishist's fantasy, an oilrig in motion, but it's a secular cathedral of engineering.

The heavy machinery, built by the Rolls Royce of engine-makers, James Watt & Co., positively bellows for attention. The two beam heads and pistons are picked out smartly in red paint and gold trim, while the engine cylinders sport honeyed mahogany cladding and the enormous

---

* They don't christen 'em like that any more.

rolling flywheels are finished in British Racing Green: bold colours that evoke the unswayable pride and confidence of Imperial industry. Next to each flywheel is an incredible spinning device that looks like two ballcock floats from a brass toilet, attached to a heavy pair of compasses. These are Watt's Patent Governors, which would surely make at least the quarter-finals of any competition to find the most Victorian-sounding contraption ever conceived.

Make sure you visit the station on a day when it's in steam. While the engines serve no practical purpose today, their pointless pumping brings the place dynamically alive. The rhythmic hubbub of Papplewick at full pelt was the pulse of life, the engine house a big iron heart keeping the region healthy and vital. Its heaving and sweating parts are all the more exhilarating for being within easy reach. Don't wear your Sunday best to Papplewick, as the pumps are not only immaculately restored but immaculately greased. Chances are you won't want to get too intimate with the machinery anyway. When the engines begin to pick up pace it's like watching a single-minded, steam-driven giant robot repeatedly failing to climb out of a hole. You'll be grateful for the four columns spanning the middle of the hall that, aside from supporting a pair of thirteen-ton beams, appear to prevent the roaring behemoth from uprooting itself to march lopsidedly down the road towards Nottingham.

The outbuilding opposite the café tells the history of Linby Colliery, which supplied Papplewick with fuel. Here you can view three films on the history of the pumping station (provided you can hear it over the outbuilding's other exhibit – Linby's imposing steam-powered coal winder). One of the films, a 1969 documentary, goes into the sort of detail you get in the instructional video that comes free with a pair of hair clippers: very useful on the off-chance you need to operate a Papplewick Pumping Station in an emergency. Behind the outbuilding – and included because children need to let off steam generated from not being allowed to ride on the pumps – there's a great adventure playground with the unique centrepiece of a Watt's Patent Governor roundabout.★

On 25 June 1969, around the time the documentary-makers were double-checking they'd included absolutely everything, and a month before Man set Armstrong foot on the Moon, Papplewick's pumps shifted their last drops of water. They had been working twenty years longer than expected. The concealed electric pumps that replaced them may well reach the same length of service, although it's hard to imagine people going out of their way to pay them a misty-eyed visit. The same miniaturisation of technology that allows us to carry our entire record collections around in our pockets also prevents us from seeing how it works. The concept of an electrical current passing from A to B will never be as exciting as watching huge clouds of steam puff from a 120-foot chimney or getting a handbag caught in a rotating flywheel. Ironically, even the fountain at Papplewick, divorced of its original power source and purpose, now requires a shock of electricity in order to spurt. Still, Papplewick Pumping Station stands as a reminder of a noble age when our priorities were very different; when we so revered our industrial machinery that we built it grand houses in the country.

Papplewick Pumping Station, off Longdale Lane, Ravenshead, Nottingham, NG15 9AJ
01159 632938
www.papplewickpumpingstation.co.uk

★ Seriously, if we'd been a quarter of a century younger and not so full of pork pie, you'd have had trouble keeping us off it.

Witchcraft Museum

The dust of exploded beliefs may make a fine sunset.

Geoffrey Madan, *Livre sans nom*

Boscastle's Witchcraft Museum is so full of charms, amulets and totems that it ought to be the luckiest building in Britain. It certainly needed

protection on 16 August 2004 when a freak storm sent nearly half a million gallons of water crashing through Boscastle, threatening to destroy the museum and everything else in its path. When shocking news footage showed an avalanche of cars, flipped like tortoises and cascading towards the sea, alarms howling, it was the Witchcraft Museum they were wailing past. The village has recovered with great tenacity, a community determinedly pulling itself back together. Two years later, the only evidence that an horrific natural disaster happened here is a tidemark in the upstairs bar of the Wellington pub and piles of building materials where the grockles of the National Trust haven't quite got round to finishing repairing their bits. Though the Witchcraft Museum was sloshing head-deep in sewage for several days, and parts of their Wise Woman's Cottage exhibit were later found washed up on a Welsh shore, over ninety per cent of this collection of magical artefacts, delicate manuscripts and all, survived.* It's enough to make you believe.

The Witchcraft Museum was founded in 1951 by legendary occultist Cecil Williamson on the Isle of Man, after the residents of Stratford-on-Avon, where he'd originally attempted to set up shop, made it clear that

---

* One of the few buildings to be completely destroyed was the much-loved old Christian bookshop next door, with which the museum curators had perfectly cordial relations. If there is a decent Church of England god, he's not putting his protection where you'd expect.

Shakespeare's home town wasn't ready for the world's largest assemblage of eye of newt and wool of bat. We're still not quite comfortable with witchcraft in Britain, and before it found a welcome home in Boscastle, the collection was driven out of premises in both Windsor and the Cotswolds by concerned citizens diplomatically setting it on fire and leaving dead animals on the doorstep. The museum finally settled in Boscastle in 1960. It seems most at home at the edges of the country, out of sight.

The collection is currently cared for by a passionate team led by the magnificent Graham King. A successful photographic engineer, King changed his life by selling the house and Jag in order to walk the old drove roads of Britain. In 1996, when he heard that the Witchcraft Museum was up for sale, he walked all the way down from Hampshire to buy it, arranging to exchange the deeds at midnight on Halloween, much to the annoyance of the solicitors.

The Witchcraft Museum doesn't let kids in unaccompanied, not because it's a PG-rated scare ride but because it's a densely packed attraction and small, hyperactive people tend to just dash from one end to the other, not registering anything beyond the copy of *Harry Potter* near the entrance. King likes parents to take their offspring through hand-in-hand and chat about the exhibits. The museum uses its space cleverly and atmospherically; enormous mirrors render the quarter of a stone circle whole again, and the corridors are filled with ghostly incantations courtesy of a homemade CD.

The collection is skewed towards British artefacts, recording a parallel folk history that's slipped between the cracks of our cultural memory. The exhibits are as exotic as voodoo paraphernalia, making you examine grey old Britain through new eyes. Every inch of the lovely Victorian showcases (donated by the Natural History Museum amongst others) is filled with eye-opening weirdness: a collection of moles' feet (for toothache), dozens of mandrake roots gnarled into human forms – even a Ouija board produced by family-friendly gamemakers Waddington's.

Since witchcraft has little time for the familiar pruderies of mainstream religion, there's some vigorous, earthy rudeness, designed to delight both smutty children and authors of lighthearted travel guides. How can you resist the chance to see a set of terracotta tits, Joan Long's magical 'fanny stone' and a big rock cock? This last fertility charm was donated to the museum a few years ago, because, according to the display caption, 'no one in the village now believes in its properties', an admission of how recently it is that these beliefs have faded from popular acceptance. There's a good smattering of spine-chillers too, familiar from their (often erroneous) usage as horror-film props. It's hard to resist a shiver at skulls with daggers thrust through the eye sockets, button-eyed hand-stitched 'poppets' and, most strikingly, the staring, goat-headed mannequin of the horned god Baphomet. Enthroned in one corner of the upstairs gallery, he ought to be no scarier than the benignly beaming model of Ganesh in your local curry house (the staff here know the model affectionately as Old Horny), yet his appearance can't help but unsettle anyone conditioned by centuries of propaganda about 'satanism'.

The Witchcraft Museum sits smiling on the anthropological fence, making no particularly hyperbolic claims as to the efficacy or otherwise of its artefacts. Historians, folklorists and interested sceptics will get as much from the collection as the most fervent Wiccan. Like Oxford's Pitt Rivers Museum* (described by Graham King, with a grin, as 'the second-best museum in the country'), Boscastle's collection tells an important story, one that many people today might be embarrassed to hear: that a very short time ago, our world seemed very different, run by older, more peculiar rules that made allusive, not literal sense. Leftovers of that pre-Newtonian mindset still lurk in the corners of the most coldly rational brain. From wishing someone good luck, to finding anything remotely interesting in *Deal or No Deal*, our enquiring minds are hardwired to look for patterns in nature and believe we can affect them by our behaviour.

The psychologist B. F. Skinner performed a famous experiment in which pigeons whose food was dispensed at random intervals seemed to repeat whatever physical tics they had been performing when the food last dropped, as if attempting to skew the pure chance of the feeding cycle. Skinner's experiments are a tempting allegory of much human behaviour. Think of the sportsman who insists on wearing a certain lucky garment before taking the field, or the UFO nutcase who wards off alien mind control with his tinfoil hat (a space-age variant of carrying an amulet against the evil eye). Witchcraft is an attempt to influence the otherwise unaffectable. Faced by a hostile environment, battered by the vagaries of blind chance, who wouldn't seek charms, potions and elaborate interventions?

The Witchcraft Museum's collection of these totems is both huge and hugely entertaining. One cabinet gathers together items discovered walled up in houses. These charms were meant to protect (or curse) the property and are found when renovation work is undertaken on old buildings. Again, it may seem peculiar to finish off a construction job by popping a

---

* See your well-thumbed copy of *Bollocks to Alton Towers*.

pig's skull, a jar of pierced hearts or a dried cat into the wall cavity, but plenty of modern homes hang a horseshoe over the door or feng shui the sitting room for similar reasons. One person's magic is someone else's religion. The difference between protecting a child from evil by putting an amulet in her cot and doing the same thing by ritually splashing her with holy water might merely be cultural familiarity. Just as a language has been described as a dialect with an army, so religion might be seen as folklore with bigger buildings. Treating witchcraft itself as a religion is a relatively

A devil of a beard.

modern invention (largely popularised and codified by Gerald Gardner, who was, until 1954, the Witchcraft Museum's 'resident witch') but the museum encourages you to see these artefacts as expressions of the same human impulse for intervention, faith and ritual you accept every time you go to a church wedding.

One of the museum's jobs is to mark centuries of misunderstanding, intolerance and persecution. A chart on one wall honours the names of those known to have been killed as part of the suppression of witchcraft. Exact figures are hard to come by, with Wiccans and interested parties pushing the totals into the millions, while more cautious historians estimate that the peak period for European witch trials cost around 50,000 lives (mainly women) of whom about 500 were British. Whatever the truth, the wall's roll call is tragic and shameful.

In a humidity-controlled cabinet in the museum is an original 1591 edition of King James I's witch-baiting milestone *Daemonologie*. The book caused a sensation, and much violence. Suddenly 'witch' was the equivalent

of 'paedophile' or 'terrorist' today: a word with a burning fuse attached. Matthew Hopkins, a failed small-town lawyer who turned self-appointed 'Witchfinder General' in 1644, was one of the most high-profile persecutors, feeding off the panics that recast trusted village wise women, herb-toting midwives and lonely schizophrenics alike as agents of the devil. Hopkins's fees (the equivalent today of £3,500 to turn up plus the same amount per witch discovered) almost bankrupted many frightened towns, who found that their streets were indeed full of witches, all identified by an overpaid consultant on commission. As Joseph McCarthy understood in 1950s America, puritan communities love to blame their own moral ambiguities on an unseen enemy within, and the nation's Roundhead heartlands, torn apart by the Civil War, proved rich pickings for wily operators.

Hopkins drew out witches by a blend of Guantánamo-esque torture (enforced standing, sleep-deprivation, starvation) and transparent trickery. One artefact on display in the museum is a retractable pricking pin of the type used by Hopkins to prove that frightened old women felt no pain when stabbed in their demon-suckling 'third nipples' (usually perfectly normal post-menopausal growths). The church, to its credit, played no role in the hunts, understanding how traumatic and destructive these scares were for the community, occasionally intervening on behalf of the accused, themselves often God-fearing, churchgoing Christians. An intelligent pastor would sometimes suggest a 'Witch Weighing' to placate the masses: if a suspected witch was unable to fly and make herself lighter than a Bible, she was innocent, a move that must have saved many lives.

The contemporary pamphlets in the museum's library are quite terrifying, neighbours bandying accusations of witchcraft about to exact crude revenge on one another, confessions conducted at hysterical pitch (a man at one trial claims to have had sex with some sort of giant mouse). These may seem like faintly comic relics from a credulous past, but for thousands of women worldwide this sort of persecution is still very real. Between 1985 and 1995, South Africa's Northern Province saw at least 200 lynchings at the instigation of hired witchfinders; in India, the same number of witches is disposed of every year; and a single witch-hunt in the Congo in 2001 had a death toll of 800. Britain's own witchcraft acts were only repealed in 1951 at the instigation of Winston Churchill, himself a believer in spiritualism.★ The museum answers many questions about anti-witch sentiment, tracing the origins of propagandist images such as the pointed hat (an item of clothing symbolising wickedness that had formerly been forced onto persecuted Jews), the cauldron (traced to a 1489 woodcut), and the black cat. Witches' 'familiars' (animal helpers) were a British idea developed by Matthew Hopkins, amongst others. Clearly it must have boosted his hit rate to be able to wander into a village, sniff the air for the whiff of cat food and yank out some pet-owning spinster to face trial.

Sensitivity and paranoia about witchcraft, from all sides of the religious divide, affect the daily running of this beautiful museum. Churchgoing visitors taunt the nice lady in the ticket booth that she is an 'abomination', covens of Californian Wiccans object to the displays of curses, and Graham King gets personalised hate mail and literature from the sort of glassy-eyed pillocks who think Christ's message of love is best expressed by cutting out pictures of thy neighbour and pasting them into threatening collages. With

★ The last woman to be convicted, Helen Duncan, is regarded as a martyr by some witches, who believe her wartime seances contacting the dead of sunken battleships (in advance of official notice of loss) were seen as a threat to national security and morale. She can't have been popular with the authorities, but the section of the 1735 Witchcraft Act under which Duncan was tried concerned fraud, not knowing the unknowable. Duncan was certainly not above the usual theatrics of the spiritualist trade; she had been fined £10 in 1933 after Peggy, her child spirit guide, was grabbed at by a sitter and turned out to be a white linen vest. 'I'll brain you, you bloody bugger,' said Duncan at the time. During her trial, one supporter wryly questioned how Duncan could be imprisoned for being unable to prove that she could intercede between mankind and the divine, while the Archbishop of Canterbury was free to walk the streets and earn £5,000 a year.

admirable good humour, the museum pins up the best of this foaming correspondence, lovingly laminated.

A gentleman of infinite charm and enthusiasm, King is a hero far beyond the limited scope of this book. Parked outside the Witchcraft Museum is a Land Rover, a replacement for one dredged from the heaving floodwaters in a knot. It is decorated with a broomstick and pentangle logo and bears a coastguard's identity plate to go with the high-visibility jacket that hangs inside the museum door. King is Boscastle's deputy coastguard. He raised the alarm for the 2004 deluge and for the first terrifying hour he was the only uniformed official on the scene. It is partly his doing that one of Britain's worst natural disasters claimed no fatalities.

He is also a passionate folk singer. Two days after the flood, he and a small group of friends, their homes and businesses in ruins, kept their regular date at the wrecked Wellington pub. They waited until the media had gone home, then gathered round to sing the traditional songs they love so much, songs which speak for ordinary people in hard times. Particularly moving was a traditional sea ballad whose chorus ends with the lines, 'No matter what you've lost / be it a home / a love / a friend / Like the *Mary Ellen Carter* rise again.' For centuries, the practices recorded in Boscastle's Witchcraft Museum were woven deeply into British rural life. Through persecution and misunderstanding, the passage of time and even plain embarrassment, they have been distorted or forgotten. Thanks to the museum, these relics of British folk history are not swept away, but celebrated. Like the *Mary Ellen Carter*, and Boscastle itself, they rise again.

The Museum of Witchcraft, The Harbour, Boscastle, Cornwall, PL35 0HD
01840 250111
www.museumofwitchcraft.com

Witchcraft Museum

Bubblecar Museum

Motoring, if you'll just pull over and let the pun pass, is approaching a crossroads. As Britain becomes more cluttered with cars, the brakes are being applied to our endless desire to travel in bigger and more ludicrous vehicles. Chelsea tractors, those petrol-pigging ego pantechnicons, are undergoing a collapse in popularity more commonly suffered by pop stars caught downloading Romanian child pornography. Meanwhile funky microcars like the Smart and the G-Wiz are becoming a familiar sight, and an educated guess says we're going to see many more of their ilk in the future. But, as the Bubblecar Museum shows, these revolutionary little vehicles, small as a coffee table and using about as much petrol, are nothing new.

The bubblecar – or minicar or whatever else you'd like to call it* – had its heyday between 1950 and 1965. Examples date back as far as the birth of the motor industry (Sherrin's Electric Bath-Chair took part in the first London to Brighton run in 1896), but it was post-war belt-tightening that would contrive to make the bubblecar the backbone of austerity motoring. Materials and money were scarce, the purchase tax on cars was sixty per cent and the average 1950s car did an embarrassing fourteen miles for every rationed gallon of petrol. However, a very small car used few materials and cost little. If it had three wheels, instead of four, the purchase tax was the

---

* The cognoscenti say 'minicar'. The curators of the Bubblecar Museum prefer 'bubblecar' because it annoys the cognoscenti.

same as for a motorcycle (twenty-two per cent) and, though it got the same petrol ration as a family car, it could clock up a remarkable 80mpg. Owning a bubblecar was a no-brainer.

Mike Cooper got his first bubblecar in his twenties. He and partner Paula now have around fifty-two of them in their ever-expanding museum, and plenty more in the wings, awaiting restoration. Entering, you're greeted by the sunny sight of Sir Jimmy Savile's Isetta 300, customised in custard yellow and sporting an orange roof light (because, for reasons best known – and probably kept – to himself, Savile wanted it to resemble an AA rescue vehicle). There's even a message from Sir Jim. 'Took it to a garage in Manchester for a check. Forgot about it for nine years. Woke up one night, remembered it, phoned the garage to see if it was ready.' We trust the garage had fixed it for him, because only a fool would say no to iron-willed ex-wrestler Savile if he rang in the middle of the night asking for his car back. The collection resembles a petting zoo. You can wander amongst – and, if you're very nice to Mike and Paula, experience first hand – lots of small, friendly, Smartie-coloured specimens with names like Frisky and Bamby.* Do try at least one for size. Sitting in a Messerschmitt with a friend is like sharing a dry bath. It's only slightly roomier than your skin. It's hard to believe that over the years the bubblecar has been the intimate rendezvous for many an intimate rendezvous, but the curators assure you the vehicles have been used for backseat trysts as often as any other car beloved of young people. God knows how either of you (we're assuming a threesome is out of the question) get your knees trembling in such a perilously small space but apparently it's something you don't forget.† Perhaps the memory is regularly jogged by chiropractor's appointment cards or the unexpected honk of a horn.

Just looking at any of the Bubblecar Museum's kooky ducklings, it's no surprise they have a *Carry On Canoodling* history, because they're obviously meant to be fun. There's a difference between driving and motoring. Driving is slumming it slowly past a fatal accident on the M4 in shattering, clattering rain. Motoring is bowling along the seafront or bimbling around country lanes with a silly great grin on your face and your latest squeeze

---

* The Eeyore in the zoo is the Casalini Sulky, a name that starts well, but ends rather boggily and sadly.

† We tried to find out the sweaty details. Really, we did. No one was prepared to be indiscreet enough to explain to us just how you make the beast with two backs in a three-wheeler. The only clue we can offer is that, according to our source, it's a good job the steering wheel is on a telescopic column. Make of that what you will.

clinging lovingly to your elbow. Fun, fuss-free motoring is what bubblecars are for. These cute compacts don't have enough luggage space for you to pack up your troubles.

The cornerstone of the bubblecar's success was its status as a symbol of social mobility. Owning one was how a low-income family could graduate from motorbike and sidecar combo to proper car (even if it was a three-wheeled one with an engine as powerful as a cough). This step-by-step journey from aspirant low-income pedestrian to pukka middle-class motorist is marked out in stages by

Bubblicious.

the range of cars produced by Lawrie Bond's company. Owners would move from one model to another as their incomes and families grew, starting with the frog-nosed Bond Minicar and ending with a saloon-sized SuperBond that could have parked alongside the Morrises and Triumphs outside the shops without being rumbled as a three-wheeler. Bond was the Henry Higgins of bubblecars, smuggling council-estate flower girls into suburban society balls undetected.

Bond – like many bubblecar-makers – was an aviation engineer who saw a period of hectic activity come to an end with VE Day. He turned his talents to micro-travel, and came up with an aluminium, 197cc runaround for himself and Mrs Bond (which could be lifted comfortably off the ground by the two of them and did a stunning 100mpg). Two years later he pulled out all the stops with the De Luxe model – which had a windscreen wiper. The bigger Bonds were uncharacteristically wide (giving them that saloon profile). Take a peek under the bonnet: most of the space is taken up by space. The single wheel sits squarely in the centre, with an engine mounted to it, as if a motorised unicyclist had spotted the gap and parked there. The yawning gaps on either side allow the wheel enough give to be steered hard each way, so the Bond could execute its trademark turning-on-a-sixpenny.

The name most associated with three-wheelers, Reliant, was set up in 1935 by Tom Williams, a talented engineer who worked for Raleigh until they gave up making minicars to concentrate on things with even fewer wheels. In time-honoured fashion, Reliant's beginnings were in Williams's garden shed. Production was interrupted by the Second World

War, but returned with vigour and led to the company swallowing Bond (its biggest competitor) in 1969. A year later, Reliant launched the maddest, most triangular, most tangerine car the world has ever seen: the Bond Bug.

Even if you don't think you know a Bond Bug, you do. For some reason this car – of which only 2,270 were made – has become an immediately recognisable classic. It's more or less how a Lilliputian would see the Red Leicester from Gulliver's lunch-box: a big, Flymo-coloured wedge. 'Something new under the sun' was its launch motto. No kidding. There's never been anything quite as garishly bonkers as the Bug. It caught the public imagination, but never caught on. Even the revised 700ES – which came fitted with (oh, the luxury) a heater – couldn't save it from the terrible fate of cult status.

Whenever people are short of cash, the bubblecar will flourish. They are things of unadorned functionality, thrown away when they go wrong: disposable cars in the same range of colours as disposable lighters. That's why it's so glorious to see a flotilla of them sitting pretty here in Lincolnshire. This is a preservation project for vintage cars that weren't expected to last this long. Mike Cooper always goes for a dig around any old sheds he passes in case there's a forgotten gem rusting away inside under a pile of grass clippings. The scouring has turned up some proper rarities. The international hall has a Velorex, a utilitarian Czech oddity made by covering a tubular steel frame in a tightly stretched skin of vinyl. This one is currently missing its vinyl and so resembles a giant toad skeleton made of communist bicycle parts. (The glove compartment appears to be a paint tin screwed to one of the crossbars.) Then there's the AC Petite – one of five left anywhere.★ And the Sinclair C5, that little victim of large market forces, stashed quietly in the museum rafters above the only Snuggy left on the planet.

Outside the museum is a British icon you can't believe no one got round to inventing before, a tearoom in a double-decker bus. The tea is excellent and the air is thick with bikers' conversations. Tucked away in an elbow of the main road, the Bubblecar Museum has a tang of the roadside café about it. It hosts miniature petrolhead rallies and open days, and is a favourite haunt of biking types of all ages. It's always a delight when a *Wild One* gang roars across the gravel and, on removing their helmets, reveal greying locks, bifocals and dentures.

The class-busting legacy of the bubblecar may even have been the impetus for that British design classic, the Mini. Alec Issigonis, the Mini's designer, recalled Leonard Lord, head of Austin, complaining, 'Goddamn these bloody awful bubblecars. We must drive them off the streets by designing a proper miniature car.' After a visit to the Bubblecar Museum, it would be romantic and sentimental to say we'll never see the like of any of the exhibits on our roads again, but, in all probability, these are the kind of things we'll all be driving in a few decades. You may giggle at the Reliant Regal when Nicholas Lyndhurst chugabooms round the corner in it, but you're better off laughing from inside a microcar than laughing at it from the outside. If the Bubblecar Museum is any indication of what the future holds, we're in for some terrifically good fun.

Bubblecar Museum, Byard's Leap, Cranwell, Lincolnshire, NG34 8EY
01400 262637
www.bubblecarmuseum.co.uk

★ AC – Allard Clipper – is famous for the Acedes, a powder-blue three-wheeler, famously *the* invalid carriage to be seen in during the 1960s and 1970s.

St Peter's Seminary

Beauty in distress is much the most affecting beauty.
Edmund Burke, *A Philosophical Enquiry*

There's a photograph of Terry-Thomas taken shortly before his death. He's in a wheelchair, knackered by age and illness, the ton of charisma packed tightly into that gap-toothed face blunted by time and eroded by exhaustion but stubbornly shining through the wrinkles and wreckage. It's shocking, yet undeniably him: torn apart by Parkinson's disease, he remains fabulous, gleeful and terribly Thomas.

Like the veteran stage cad, St Peter's Seminary has a personality so vigorous that it defies the shabbiness of its condition. It is a virtuoso example of modernism, a RIBA architecture award winner, a grade-A listed treasure, Scotland's best post-war building and – easily its greatest accolade – the Twentieth Sexiest Person, Place or Thing in Scotland.* Yet, when you break cover in the woods above Cardross and behold this much-loved, magnificent, barely middle-aged masterpiece for the first time, you

---

* In a top-hundred list published in the *Sunday Herald* – above Gleneagles (65) and Kirsty Wark (22), but below Lulu (12) and Franz Ferdinand (7). Naturally, Dudley Watkins's cartoon bombshell Maggie Broon came top.

come face to face with a helpless ruin.

Designed at the turn of the 1960s by Izi Metzstein and Andy MacMillan, two young architects working for Gillespie, Kidd and Coia, St Peter's was built as a teaching seminary for a hundred wannabe Catholic priests. The buildings, opened in 1966, were unashamedly modern and Le Corbusian: tiered, cantilevered, curved; concrete, wood and lots of glass. The main building had barrel-vaulted ceilings, shallow, reflective ponds abutting huge plate-glass windows and a stunning granite altar dwarfed by a semi-circular wall adorned with a soberly funky cast mural. The whole place was breathtakingly bold.

It was also breathtakingly cold. The underfloor heating wasn't up to much (not helped by skyscraping oil prices) and you couldn't get within six feet of the windows in winter for fear of freezing your rosary beads. Buildings flooded, ceilings leaked and the classroom block was invaded by an unfortunate fungus. Obviously, not ideal, but this wouldn't have been the first time that a clerical building had housed its inmates in conditions of contemplative austerity. A bigger problem was that it was obsolete by the time it was even in use. Just before St Peter's opened, the Second Vatican Council decided that priests ought to be taught in the community – on the job, as it were – not in isolated locations, surrounded by dozens of other trainee diocesan clergy. Even at its peak, St Peter's wasn't half-full, and in 1981 it closed. Two years later, it reopened as a drug rehabilitation centre – an experiment that lasted until 1987, when it closed again.

It would be poetic to say that, since then, the seminary has gradually and gracefully been consumed by the forest creeping up and over and into it, like Sleeping Beauty's castle. The truth, sadly, is that St Peter's is more of an old rugged cross: an emblem of suffering. Far from yielding gently to the forces of nature, it has been relentlessly (and, in some cases, systematically) ransacked. You've never seen such wanton vandalism.

In one night, 104 sinks (and their 208 taps) were torn out by some unidentified and thorough looters with access to a ready market and a very big van. The kitchen block no longer has anything left but its walls – even the pitched, curved roof is gone. The interiors were once bounteously timbered; only a very few panels remain. Whole staircases are gone. Every fitting, furnishing and fabric has been ceaselessly smashed, kicked in, ripped out and wrecked. The wondrous chapel, the centrepiece of the seminary, is a shattered mess of its former self. Even if you're the most fundamental atheist, there's nothing very satisfying about seeing DAVE'S RAVES sprayed on the altar steps or DON'T FUCK THE POPE plastered in huge red letters across a study wall. Let's get the bollocking out of the way now: the custodians of St Peter's – which was graded as an A-listed building in 1992 because of its international importance – have disgracefully and egregiously neglected it. They should be ashamed of themselves.

Basic efforts have been made to fence the building off from intruders, but these inadequate measures are a mixed blessing. Although the seminary is under constant attack from neds and twerps, its protected isolation also makes it a haven for architecture students, photographers and naturists, who have variously studied, captured and sunbathed stitchless on top of it. ('The moss on the roof is as soft as fur,' says one non-textile.) In 1972, St Peter's was immortalised in Murray Grigor's short film, *Space and Light* – a gentle, crystalline paean to its brave design. (At lunch one day during filming, a priest told Grigor that the architects were 'much influenced by Le Courvoisier'. You can almost hear the hiccough.) Grigor latterly won a £30,000 award from the Scottish Arts Council to remake the documentary, shot for shot, to document the building's decline.* A great idea but, like Robert Ballard finding and filming the remains of the *Titanic*, potentially a post mortem almost too poignant for words.

The seminary has many high-profile pilgrims. Award-winning artist Toby Paterson has painted it. *Prospect* magazine dedicated a whole issue to it. The Royal Commission on the Ancient and Historical Monuments of Scotland published its biography. The BBC featured it on *One Foot In the Past, Restoration Nation* and *The Culture Show*. Jonathan Glancey and Gavin Stamp eulogise it. People who know more about architecture than you do about your own reflection say St Peter's is a masterpiece. A trust has been established to fight for its survival. It could scarcely have better references,

---

* He also co-produced another celebration of a Scottish icon, Billy Connolly's *Big Banana Feet*.

and yet it looks like the Royal Festival Hall after a nuclear strike or something from the background of *28 Days Later*: a bloody great mess.

So what's to be done with this skeletal wreck? Suggestions have been made to convert it into flats, a hotel, a conference centre – it would even make a decent addition to the golf course next door (you pass the fourth hole on the path up to it, just before a bridge with the portentous WELCOME TO HELL scrawled on it). However, these suggestions have amounted to nothing and, frankly, St Peter's seems destined for years more nothing. One realistic and sympathetic scheme for the seminary proposes that it be stripped back to its superstructure and left. The bones of the place are in great shape, so clearing the smashed pipework, rotting floors and punctured ceilings would reduce it to a *bona fide* ruin, like Fountains Abbey or Malmesbury Abbey – or, for that matter, Machu Picchu, Angkor Wat or the Acropolis. Understandably, some of the seminary's approbators regard this as a cop-out. But, given its

Britain's youngest ruin.

dreadful state of repair, leaving it as a ruin might be the only viable option (apart from demolition). And, anyway, with a few more decades of inertia, only the superstructure will remain. Meanwhile, there's the crushing inevitability that this once consecrated building will be subject to further desecration.

As it is, Britain's Youngest Ruin is already enormously evocative. Having been 'the wrong building in the wrong place at the wrong time' (as it was described by the development director of the Archdiocese of Glasgow), St Peter's deserves a decent future as something. Surely even the stunted, cul-de-sac mind of the modern developer would feel some shame turning it into a Radisson or a Premier Travel Inn? Standing here in the verdant woodland, you can't help but conclude that St Peter's would be better off as a radiant ruin rather than a soulless ghetto of philandering middle managers.*

Left as a ruin, the radiance of St Peter's is in no doubt. The combination of destruction and decay has carved through the seminary's careful shapes like waves hollowing random but ravishing caves into a cliff, changing the planned play of light and space in beautiful and unexpected ways. With so many roofs missing, the place is drenched in glorious, jagged parallelograms of sunlight. The window frames are surprising flashes of lime green against the weathered concrete, and the only 'cell' (one-man dormitory) left anything like intact is a lone horn blast of peach orange – that tart, garish shade beloved of swinging sixties interior decor partworks. Echoes of its working life are discernible among the devastation: a piano, exploded like a dropped melon at the foot of a staircase; the precious stone altar, still standing, but with bites taken out of the corners as if ravaged by concrete rodents; the rusting guts of a washing machine, still intact in the basement, waiting hopefully for more dirty habits.

St Peter's is among the very finest cultural specimens of its era – and

---

* One of the architects, Andy MacMillan, agrees. 'I rather enjoy the idea of everything being stripped away except the concrete itself – a purely romantic conception of the building as a beautiful ruin,' he said.

they include Concorde, *Strawberry Fields Forever* and George Best, so it was a pretty good era. It has as much swagger, magnitude and cheek as any of its contemporaries. You should be picnicking and snogging here. Instead, you're being fenced out while it festers. And that's not right. It's downright contradictory: you're discouraged from getting near because someone else has first dibs on wilfully mistreating it. This tangle of broken palisades, eroded warning signs, collapsing woodwork, violated masonry and execrable neglect is steadfastly holding its ground, refusing to be vanquished, unrepentant. When Scotland's Best Building wakes with the blest in the mansions of rest, there will be stars in its crown. Until then, you're probably going to be hearing a lot more about St Peter's Seminary. It is far from ready to meet its namesake.

St Peter's Seminary, Carman Road, Cardross, Dunbartonshire

Pork Pie Pilgrimage

You wait all day for a pie and 3.14159 come along at once.
Hadleigh Carport, *How May I Fascinate You?*

Steak and kidney pies are grand. We go mad for a chicken and mushroom pie. Even a minced beef and onion has its place. These, though, are hot pies, and if you want hot pies, you'll have to look elsewhere. Melton Mowbray in Leicestershire is the town that gave us the best cold pies in the world, and so this is where we propose to proudly present Britain's only Pork Pie Pilgrimage.* It needn't be a particularly religious pilgrimage, depending on how reverently you feel about pork pies (deeply, in our case) and the length of the stroll isn't going to trouble your shoe leather either.

Why the Melton Mowbray pork pie? If you need to ask the question, then it's crystal clear that you've never eaten one. The Melton Mowbray is the ultimate example of the holy trinity of golden-baked pastry, coarsely cut chunks of succulent pig bits and sweet bone-stock jelly, all acting in perfect porky harmony. If the Melton Mowbray pork pie were an animal, it would be a majestic, roaring pork pie lion. And it would be the mighty king of the pork pie savannah, preying mercilessly on sweeping herds of those weedy, pony-and-trap little pork pies that litter Britain's garage forecourt chiller cabinets. Its pastry isn't gravelly, its jelly isn't chewy and its chopped, greyish meat hasn't been minced, cured and turned a point-

---

* The Pilgrimage is, uniquely for this book, our own invention. We looked for one, there wasn't one, so we made one up – partly inspired by Waltham Forest Council's entrepreneurial spirit in devising the Beckham Trail (see *Bollocks to Alton Towers*).

less lurid pink. And, because of that, the makers of the Melton Mowbray pork pie want to protect it so that only they may use the name.

Champagne, Parma ham and Roquefort all have a protected regional status so that outsiders can't claim to be making something they're not. Europe is peppered with these designations, which the French call *appellations d'origines contrôlées*. In the UK there are already thirty-six products that have been granted special status, amongst them Newcastle Brown Ale, Arbroath Smokies, West Country farmhouse Cheddar, Jersey Royal potatoes and Cornish clotted cream.★ Should the Melton Mowbray pork pie join them, it will be the first composite food to be added to the UK list.

This regional ownership system can work against our food producers as well as in their favour. In 2005 a cheese-maker was informed that her business could no longer use the term 'Yorkshire feta', following complaints from Greece. This hardly seems fair when Yorkshire never gets cross about people from Devon and Dumfries claiming that their nan makes the best Yorkshire pudding.

Defra has hooked up with Melton to help smooth things along and, at the time of writing, the piemen are at the final stages of a ten-year wait, having foolishly imagined that the matter would be done and dusted within six months. Despite appeals from manufacturers who make their non-native Melton Mowbray pies outside the proposed 1,800-square-mile exclusion zone, it is looking like a dead cert to go through. Defra also has several other cases under consideration, including Cumberland sausages, English lamb and the Cornish sardine.

The first place of worship on the

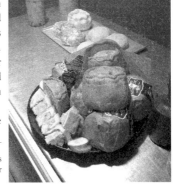

A pile of perfect pies.

★ If the free tissue to mop up your dribble has fallen out of this volume please contact your bookseller.

Pork Pie Pilgrimage is the Melton Carnegie Museum. Every town seems to have a museum whether they have enough history to fill them or not and, boy, some of them don't half go on. There are some excellent examples, however, and the newly refurbished (and cute as a button) Melton Carnegie

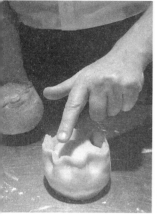

Museum is a model for them, succinctly covering the key facts without outstaying its welcome. It gets straight down to business. Through the main door, sharp left and there it is: a big wooden pork pie hanging over your head. Crowd-pleasing, yes, and that's absolutely fine, the town is right to be proud of its world-renowned product.

There's a traditional pork pie oven and a fleeting history lesson that covers the pie's symbiotic relationship with Stilton (an already protected East Midlands foodstuff); the cheese-makers fattened up pigs by feeding them the leftover whey from the manufacturing process, providing the piemen with a ready supply of plump meat. The rest of the museum covers the heritage of the local area, and throws in a couple of first-rate educational anecdotes concerning men riding their horses where they really shouldn't have. Now write out a hundred times, 'A horse ridden up the stairs of your house may not always wish to come back down again.'

Victorian Melton was known as the centre of English fox-hunting and the wealthy would travel across Europe to enjoy a spot of blood sport. Pork pies were the ideal food to be carried across country on horseback, the pastry casing being durable even when bumped against roiling jodhpurs for a few miles. Previously the pork pie had been seen as commoner's chow, with veal or beef considered more suitable pie fillings for toffs. When the visiting aristocracy decided that they too fancied a bite of the people's pie, the ready availability and superior quality of the Melton Mowbray strain gave it the wings to rise above any snobbery.

From the Melton Carnegie Museum it's but a short walk to Leicester Street, where you can see the blue plaque that commemorates pie pioneer Edward Adcock. This heartfelt tribute from the Melton Mowbray Pork Pie Association is mounted on a wall at the site of Adcock's nineteenth-century bakehouse, just next to what is now USA Chicken.* His were the first

---

* You may pass some people doing a Spicy Chicken Wings and Regular Fries Pilgrimage but do feel free to snub them.

Melton pies to explore the world outside. Thanks to the hunters bigging it up back home, the pie had become the very thing in the smart gentlemen's clubs, and an arrangement was made to carry the porky treats down to London on the regular mail coach from Leeds. Such was the reputation of Adcock's pies that it was a decade before anyone successfully challenged his export monopoly.

The final port of call (until the council gets round to building the proposed pork pie-shaped seat in the town centre) is the Melton pie's most famous retail outlet, Ye Olde Dickinson and Morris Pork Pie Shoppe. The half-timbered and whitewashed building is the temple of the master pie-makers, where you will be able to enjoy a fifteen-minute demonstration of the art of hand-raising pork pies. It is best to book ahead, and if you can get an eighteen or more-strong gang together, there is also the option of shelling out for the far more in-depth Pork Pie Experience. This lasts for a couple of hours and by the end of it you'll have made your own pie which will be baked and jellied for you, to be collected from the shop the next day.

Hand-raising has nothing to do with the way that the pork was reared; rather it's the act of manipulating the pastry casing up the side of a glass bottle or a wooden dolly to give it its shape. Red-wrapper Dickinson and Morris pies are sold in stores throughout Britain and they are scrumptious enough – but the white-wrapper pies are hand-raised, and they are only available in this one shop. Knowing that someone has lovingly crafted your own pie gives it a piquancy that's strong enough to taste.

The Melton Mowbray pie must be cooked on trays with no support, meaning that it bows out to the sides, bulging like one of the stomachs it intends to fill. Be warned, however, that, as you are shown the process of turning the raw ingredients into a bakeable pie, your attention may wander to the temptingly ready-to-eat slices at the front of the teaching area. The urge to grab the slices and make a run for it is to be resisted. All good things do eventually come, even to those who hate to wait.

Stephen Hallam, the hands-on managing director of Dickinson and Morris, is a baker. He is not a butcher and he is most definitely not a cook. A cook is able to finely tune a dish right up until it hits the plate; Hallam's pies need to be perfect from the moment the lid is sealed. The seasoning mix is tried and tested and top secret. Hallam appears to be winking as he claims not to be able to remember the two very specific types of white pepper used in their own particular blend. (He might have some in his eye.) The gloriously tickly afterburn left in the throat by the pie would be too ferocious were it not for the month that the ground pepper mixture is made to stand in the naughty corner to consider the potential consequences of its behaviour. Preparation and patience are key to the craft of the pie. Like a decent bottle of red, a Melton Mowbray should always be chambréd for at least an hour before one commences the stuffing of one's face. The pie needs to be relaxed in its last moments on earth or the flavours won't come through properly. This is also true of Scotch eggs.[*]

Melton Mowbray has yet to cash in on the trend for 'wedding cake' pork pies, which are rapidly becoming a Yorkshire thing. A company in Leeds is prepared to make massive three-tiered 'growlers' (a Yorkshire dialect word for pork pie) if your big day needs fattening up. Wedding days aren't the only celebrations that can be enlivened by a slab of encrusted pork. There is a Leicestershire tradition that encourages a Christmas Day breakfast of pork pie and a glass of spirits and this may explain the average 5,000 pies per day that Dickinson and Morris sell through their shop in the peak period running up to the festivities. (Not the most suitable week to choose to make your pilgrimage then.)

Stephen Hallam is on a mission to maintain the high quality of Melton Mowbrays. He believes that the protection that an *appellation d'origine contrôlée* offers will help to fight off the unnoticed incremental denigration that would end up ruining the good name of the pies forever. As the man himself says, at a time when it has never been easier to take on calories, it has never been harder to lose them. He shouldn't worry. Once in a while it's okay to pig out.

Melton Carnegie Museum, Thorpe End, Melton Mowbray, Leicestershire, LE13 1RB
01664 569946
www.leics.gov.uk/museums

William Adcock's plaque, Leicester Street, Melton Mowbray, Leicestershire

Dickinson & Morris, Ye Olde Pork Pie Shoppe, 10 Nottingham Street, Melton Mowbray,
Leicestershire, LE13 1NW
01664 482068
www.porkpie.co.uk

[*] Based on our extensive research. Oh, and sausage rolls.

Yelverton Paperweight Centre

A poor life this if, full of care,
We have no time to stand and stare.

W. H. Davies, 'Leisure'

There are places that cast a spell over you. Outside, you can't believe you're going to get much out of your visit. Inside, once you've adjusted your eyes to understand what you're seeing, a fantastic new world offers previously unimagined small joys. You dash to and fro, lapping it up, suddenly alive to the wonders of some unconsidered corner of existence. Then, a couple of days later, back in the drab reality of your everyday life, cradling a smoggy pint in some dingy urban pub, you wonder if it really happened, or whether it was some strange dream. Did you really spend an afternoon staring at paperweights, convinced they were the most beautiful things in the world? It was lovely, and now it seems impossible. It's as if a hypnotist had made you fall in love with a brick.

Before stepping into the Yelverton Paperweight Centre you could be forgiven for thinking that anything could be a paperweight. Surely there won't be glass cases filled with reverently curated heavy objects, grabbed at arm's length from around the office and bathed in dignified lighting? But paperweight collecting is a popular worldwide pastime, and it has its own high standards. Calling any of the paperweights here 'a paperweight' is like calling the ceiling of the Sistine Chapel 'a ceiling'. There's little evidence to suggest that these glorious glass globules were ever used to hold sheaves of paper down on the dropped leaves of escritoires in draughty garrets. A paperweight

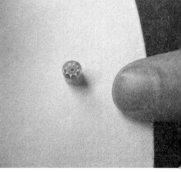

A tiny bit of
paperweight
(actual size).

isn't defined merely by its function. Every one is a valued ornament with a history. Like the stone you once picked up on a beach in Devon that you're now using as a doorstop; it's not a doorstop, it's the stone you once picked up on a beach in Devon.

Talk to the staff here, and this is what you'll find out. There are two principal types of paperweight: millefiori and lampwork.★ Lampwork is made from teasing molten glass into delicate natural forms like flowers and butterflies – a natural leap from the random swirls within a glass marble: PhD-level cake decorating, if you like. These are pleasant enough, but millefiori (the way they say 'a thousand flowers' in Firenze) is the real stunner. This technique, derived from the mosaic methods of the earliest glass craftsmen of ancient Alexandria, involves the production of tiny shaped and coloured glass canes that are cut into stubby lengths and arranged in patterns. The cane ends are clustered together into patterns or pictures, each cane presenting a cross-section like the lettering in a stick of rock, so that every cell of the image has further tinier patterns within. It takes

★ There is a third significant type – abstract – but because the glass is allowed to form whatever swirly shapes it fancies, it's basically cheating. It is to lampwork and millefiori what getting out of a comfy chair and yawning is to the 110m hurdles.

a really close gander to appreciate what's going on in there. Even then, it's like looking at a fractal picture: the closer you get, the more the detail reveals itself.

The Yelverton collection began in 1968 in Cornwall. The wife of Bernard Broughton, postmaster of St Tudy, was left a paperweight in a relative's will. Although it's unlikely Mrs Broughton had to fight off other relatives with a stick to get this bit of her inheritance, Bernard seems to have been rather taken with it, and soon accrued a collection of a few hundred more weights, which he opened to the public. The display got bigger and bigger until it overflowed from his post office and, in 1978, Broughton moved to Yelverton, where he continued to showcase his hobby and do deals with other enthusiasts until his death in 1984. The current owners carry on his work, dealing and displaying examples from the Broughton collection alongside beautiful paperweights of all prices and levels of collectability.

Bernard Broughton didn't have a passport and never left Britain. However, the wider world wasn't entirely closed to him because he spent his evenings twiddling dials as an enthusiastic radio ham. It may have been over the airwaves that he first made contact with King Farouk I (although the story, like the radio reception, is a little fuzzy). The Egyptian monarch

loved trinkets and, when he was eventually exiled by Nasser, his paperweights, some of which are likely to have been sourced by Broughton, were among the possessions auctioned off by the new regime. His other effects were said to include one of Churchill's watches and a ceremonial sword belonging to the Shah of Iran, neither of which he was supposed to have in his possession. Whether or not Farouk was a light-fingered monarch (and, say some sources, accomplished pickpocket) is mostly rumour, but it would take royal balls like a pair of paperweights to get away

with nicking a statesman's time-piece or a shah's antique. This hobby is clearly not just one of skilled glassblowing and fractal cane appreciation, but international diplomacy and scurrilous gossip as well.

Treat yourself to the short video showing at the Yelverton Paperweight Centre and the mad intensity of the cane-making process becomes as clear as glass. Each of the canes inside a millefiori paperweight may include dozens of different-coloured glass rods. These tiny rods are grouped into a pattern – called the gather – which is pressed into a mould and allowed to cool. When cooled, it is reheated and rolled in another layer of glass. Then, or after several repeats of all the above, the cane is stretched and sometimes twisted until it is about twenty or thirty feet long and has a diameter of less than a quarter of an inch. Of this, about three feet will be considered suitable for use, and the rest melted down. (This level of waste is a mark of the perfectionism of the weight-makers.) Those three good feet of cane are then cut into tiny pieces about an eighth of an inch long. After all that gathering and firing and moulding and stretching, all that's left is a scattering of pieces of glass smaller than cigarette filters.

Armed with tweezers, the weightmaker arranges a hundred or so of these tiny bits of glass into the design for the interior of the paperweight. This then has to be turned into a flat-bottomed glass ball – another discipline as lengthy and complicated to explain as cane-making. Suffice to say that the amount of attention to detail crammed into every paperweight is almost absurd. No two are alike – because they're hand-made things made from lots of hand-made things made from lots of hand-made things. Despite all this eye-straining labour, a good glassworks will throw away four of every ten paperweights. Yelverton's informative video shows these 'seconds' (indistinguishable from their perfect cousins to any but the most expert eye) being slung back into a furnace, where molten glass is poured on them and

– like ice cubes meeting boiling water – they're gone. You almost want to scream, 'No! I'll take them!' to spare the makers' feelings.

Once you've witnessed this horrifying sacrifice, you're ready to look properly at paperweights. Suddenly what looked like a room full of mildly diverting snowglobes is racked with masterpieces of hypnotic precision and fascinating craft. Retrace your steps: had you noticed that the door handle was a paperweight? Had you really looked at those designs? Had you seen that each of those rods is a three-dimensional, hand-made pixel? Eek. There are street vendors in London and Paris who will carve your name on a grain of rice: impressive, certainly, but nothing compared to Lebanese master calligrapher Nassib Makarem, who could engrave the first chapter of the Qur'an or a map of the USA on one. Half an hour here and you'll decide, with an appreciative smile, that paperweights are towards the Nassib Makarem end of the spectrum.

Now your eye is attuned to the dizzying scrimshaw, it becomes a pleasure merely appreciating the exhausting amount of graft put into each of these glass pebbles, some of which sell for over £1,000. An 1850 Clichy millefiori basketweight went at Sotheby's in New York in 1990 for over a quarter of a million dollars. There's plenty of smart money in paperweights, yet each is not much bigger than a tennis ball, so Yelverton can fit hundreds of examples of stunning craftsmanship into a floor space the size of a modest village shop.

This is a collector's haven, and to get the most from it you need to be shown how to look by a true enthusiast. Which means you're going to have to initiate a conversation with a complete stranger who seems to be awfully busy with a duster. Don't worry because, as you'll find at many of the places featured in this book, it seems the British social taboo on bothering people you don't know is suspended when it comes to discussing hobbies, which we're more than happy to share. You could easily come away from Yelverton a complete convert. That's the thing about the quiet corners of life – you never know how infectious they're going to be. Even if you're sceptical when you arrive, you'll be amazed long before you leave. Just as long as you stand and stare.

Yelverton Paperweight Centre, Leg O'Mutton, Yelverton, Devon, PL20 6AD
01822 854250
www.paperweightcentre.co.uk

45

Beside the Seaside

Now I am in a holiday humour.

William Shakespeare, *As You Like It*

For the normally landlocked, a trip to the British seaside is a rare pleasure. The soul and shape of each town may vary, but all trips share that sweet theatrical moment when salt sea peeps out from under a band of cerulean sky, and you swing downhill between falling villas towards the last remaining unmetered sea-wall parking space. Whether glimpsed between a row

of rundown buildings or rippling over the crest of a sun-parched hill, those first waves crash right through us. To the young, it's a new world waiting to be explored and experienced, its watery edge hinting at loosened rules. For the old, it tugs at bypassed heartstrings, memories of visits past mingling with the aching symbolism of looking out at an unrestricted horizon. Small armies of pensioners, lured by its blue vastness, eventually retire coastwards to stare as far as they can across the water, wondering what will be on the other side.★ Standing in a wind-rippled mac on an average British seafront, the shiver of splendid isolation is so powerful that it's easy to forget that our coastlines once offered visitors more than an opportunity for quiet introspection over a polystyrene cup of chips. Once, they were so busy you couldn't hear yourself think.

Bridlington, like practically every other

★ *Angel of the North* sculptor Antony Gormley's *Another Place*, a hundred-strong army of six-feet-tall iron men, is, at the time of writing, staring out to sea on behalf of a busy nation at Crosby beach near Liverpool. If its future were secure, you would be reading a whole chapter about it.

British seaside town, is trying to discover its twenty-first-century identity within the defining shadow of its past. The flow of holidaymakers brought to the seafront and spa facilities by the steam railways has gradually ebbed away, easing the snobbery previously felt towards day-tripping hoi polloi by longer-term, idle-rich visitors. Suddenly all those kiss-me-quick hats seem quaint rather than common. The Lords Feoffees of the Manor of Bridlington (a charitable group of appointed individuals that has functioned as trustees for property around the town since the 1630s) are well aware of this and have commissioned Beside the Seaside – the Bridlington Experience – to help regenerate the place.

Even from the outside, Beside the Seaside looks classy. Eschewing the familiar peeling weatherboarding and blacked-out windows of the average seaside museum, it's tastefully decorated in nautical blue and cream, with a smart clock tower peeping from the roof. It could easily pass for Popeye's retirement pad. Inside, the cheery receptionists pop five brass Victorian pennies in your palm and hope you enjoy your visit.

Beside the Seaside is a guided tour of how we used to holiday. Britain was once crusted at the edges with stiff guesthouses named after royal residences like Sandringham or Balmoral. Local newspapers – *the Bridlington Quay Mercury* in this case – printed lists of everyone staying that week, encouraging folks to tick off who they met, in the manner of an I-Spy book. The closest you'll get to this today is by going to Greece for a fortnight and checking the *Faliraki Gazette & Herald* to see if anyone you've had a pint (or a fight) with has since been arrested or deported.

R&R at a B&B.

Beside the Seaside goes the extra mile to exceed expectations. Even the scourge of a thousand local museums, stiff dioramas of shop dummies in period dress, are here handled with panache, full of character and detail. Realistic hair (why don't other museum mannequins ever have decently fitting toupees?), believable expressions and even skin blemishes lift the waxwork models head-and-sunburned-shoulders above the usual plastic shop dummies and put many better-funded museums' shonky displays to shame. Although a timeline asking the visitor which era defined Bridlington's heyday could be seen as a eulogy or a threnody, attractions like Beside the Seaside provide an anchor for the resort's redevelopment, allowing it to understand its past in order to imagine a bright future. There is even a plan afoot to build a spanking-new

marina, although the plan appears to have been afoot for so long that its toenails need cutting.

Blackpool, that gritty pearl of our fun-packed coastline, wanted to snaffle the single supercasino licence, planning to become the Las Vegas of the north-west. (As if it needed any more Elvis impersonators …) Unostentatious Bridlington, whose visitors number thousands rather than millions, had no chance of landing that fish, or its thick-cut poker chips, but upstairs you do finally get a chance to offload those antique pennies that will, by now, have tarnished your sweaty palms to a natty green. The attraction's replica Victorian penny arcade has Punch and Judy booth décor and is full of slot machines which you feel can't be properly operated unless you own a black and white striped bathing suit, bald head and waxed moustache. The most fun comes courtesy of the machine least burdened with foofaraw: the basic bagatelle.* This prototype pinball game will probably eat most of your brass, and is almost as addictive as trying to win a can of weak lager with a twenty-pound note Sellotaped to it from a dodgy crane

---

* Why not buy a bagatelle game for a child's birthday? Yeah, they'll cry now, but when, decades later, at the back of the attic, they blow the cobwebs off the thing and finally give it a try, they'll be hooked, maybe passing it on to their son or daughter who'll also be convinced that someone is taking the piss. Obviously, don't try this with your own children because they'll hate you for it.

machine.* There are some seaside traditions, such as chucking all your loose change down the slots, that are compulsory. They're not called one-armed-bandits for nothing.

Please honour the heritage of the British seaside. At the edge of the sensible, solid land, surrounded on one side by playful waves, the British allow themselves to relax. Our seasides aren't places for wild abandon – nobody's scouring the internet for copies of *Bridlington XXX Uncovered Beach Babes Go Wet-n-Wild* – but the small, silly pleasures of burying yourself in the sand, kissing someone quick and getting your fortune told by a mysterious Romanian gypsy with a Romford accent are as much a part of our cultural heritage as *The Haywain*. So stick a knotted handkerchief on your noddle and head to Bridlington to find out what made our coastal resorts great – and help contribute to making them great again because, as a wise man once paraphrased Joni Mitchell so he didn't have to pay any copyright fees, you're not aware of what you have 'til it's disappeared.

Beside the Seaside, 34–35 Queen Street, Bridlington, East Riding of Yorkshire, YO15 2SP
01262 608890
www.bridlington.net/business/besidetheseaside

---

* We know it's a con but we'll never stop until we've won one. Or possibly four.

Hundred Acre Wood

And with thee fade away into the forest dim.

John Keats, 'Ode to a Nightingale'

Dorothy Parker only got as far as page five of *The House at Pooh Corner* before she 'fwowed up' (a sudden outburst of humming by the principals having proved too much) but plenty of readers with stronger stomachs, or perhaps just less acid in them, managed to read on. Millions now consider the adventures of Christopher Robin and Pooh as much a part of their own childhoods as chicken pox and telling lies about not having broken expensive ornaments. A. A. Milne's stories were amongst the first entertainments for children that bothered to include jokes for the parents too, helping a passion for Pooh pass effortlessly from one generation to the next, and setting a template for everything from *The Magic Roundabout* to *Toy Story*.

Since these warm, funny tales of a boy and his bear were first published in the 1920s, a lot has changed. Disney now owns Winnie's bear ass, and naturally their worldwide theme parks offer fans a ride through a simulated Hundred Acre Wood. Visiting these is going to cost you a fortune and, judging by videos posted on the internet, spending four minutes being hauled around Disney's vision of Pooh's Enchanted Place will be one of the single most terrifying experiences of your life: a deafening cheese dream about Day-Glo hayseed carnival heads. Thankfully, back where the stories actually began, British Pooh-lovers can visit the real homes of Piglet and Eeyore for the cost of a few gallons of petrol and a packed lunch, and the setting is peaceful, affecting and unspoilt.

The Milnes moved to Cotchford Farm near Ashdown Forest in 1925, and the stories were based on Christopher Robin Milne's bear-in-hand explorations of the nearby woods. The scenery is almost unchanged today, and anyone who has ever nurtured a fondness for Pooh is going to get a rush stepping into the car park. Unlike Dougal's magic garden or Alice's rabbit hole, Pooh's world is real and drawn from life.

The landscape is instantly recognisable. The undergrowth, the scattered pines, even the roll of the land itself, all come with nostalgic literary baggage. Every gorse bush you pass isn't just a gorse bush, but the kind of gorse bush a bear might carelessly tumble into while impersonating a cloud. The stories have a place, and you're standing in it. In his autobiography, which shows far more fondness for his boyhood's trees and rivers than for its celebrated toys and stories, Christopher Milne saves himself pages of scene-setting: 'Anyone who has read the stories knows the Forest and doesn't need me to describe it. Pooh's Forest and Ashdown Forest are identical.'

There is no doubt that 'Mr Shepard Helpd'. That modest credit is scrawled along the bottom of *Winnie-the-Pooh*'s endpaper map, a copy of which is mounted in a stone pediment in the Gill's Lap Car Park, at the recommended start point of the Pooh trail. For most visitors Pooh's world is as E. H. Shepard drew it. The illustrator was not simply commissioned by Milne, but offered an eighty-twenty partnership in the books.* This relationship – one of the greats, alongside Willans and Searle's *Molesworth* and Carroll and Tenniel's *Alice* – led to unforgettable dances of words and pictures, such as the Hundred Acre Wood map, and the signing of Eeyore's farewell poem ('POOH, WOL, PIGLET, EOR, RABBIT, KANGA, BLOT, SMUDGE').

Shepard spent long hours in Sussex sketching. His style may seem scratchy and loose, but his illustrations are full of draughtsmanlike observation. A trip round Ashdown Forest is like watching a slideshow of well-loved panoramas from the books. The ordered ranks of pines, the undulating yards of twiglet fencing, the huddles of pencil-thin trees exploding dozens of feet up into scribbles of foliage, every one is instantly recognisable, not from your own childhood, but someone else's, immortalised in print. Walking Ashdown Forest's puddled paths, the scenery as strangely familiar as the

---

* Shepard's other best-known work, *The Wind in the Willows*, had been out, illustrated by others, for a full twenty-three years before he was asked to have a go. Author Kenneth Grahame never lived to see this definitive version of Mole, Ratty and Co.

landscape of a recurring dream, you feel you are treading in ink.

Exploring the Hundred Acre Wood is best done with a map printed from the Ashdown Forest Rangers' website. You have to find your own way around; the unspoilt scenery would be spoilt by signs pointing to the unspoilt scenery. Use your imagination. Your inner child will come in handy here.

Put yourself in the sandals of a small boy or girl exploring the forest for the first time, and look for interesting landmarks; chances are, they'll be the same ones Christopher Robin picked. The tour is done backwards, beginning with the Enchanted Place where boy and bear go their separate ways at the very end of *The House at Pooh Corner*. Gill's Lap was rechristened Galleon's Lap for the book, but the soft grass and clustered, apparently innumerable trees are still there. From here, strike westwards towards where the map indicates the Lone Pine and a residual Heffalump Trap (unsignposted so as not to alert any potential victims), ascending to the commanding heights of the Weald.

Or, if you prefer, you can stomp around in big, aimless circles, turning the map over and over in your hand, and find yourself back at the innumerable trees. There's a lot of wandering about and getting lost in the Pooh books and it soon becomes clear why. Ashdown Forest is not a place for bustling purposefully to and fro, it's a place to amble around, blundering into stuff. One of the few things that is fairly easy to find is the monument stone to A. A. Milne and E. H. Shepard a little way above the Enchanted Place. The stone commemorates the men who 'captured the magic of Ashdown Forest and gave it to the world' and offers the sort of commanding view that could easily be mistaken for the top of the world by the Very Young.

To the east of the stone is the dip better known as the Sandy Pit Where Roo Plays. During the damp seasons this is more like the Boggy Pit Where Roo Drowns, but its familiar shape makes it one of the most satisfying discoveries on the walk. Roo was one of the latecomer toys, alongside Kanga and Tigger, given to Christopher by a father alert to their literary possibilities. The way Christopher played with them would be drawn upon to form the characters in the books. Only Rabbit and Owl, who the illustrations seem to indicate were based on real animals, were the elder

Milne's 'own unaided work'.[*] The process of collaboration between child's imagination and father's art was sometimes blurred: none of the Milnes could remember, for instance, which came first, the chapter or the game of Pooh Sticks, but the bridge from which it was first played still stands and is the area's most popular site of pilgrimage.

Visiting the bridge still involves a heartening amount of getting the locals to point and draw maps, but the best way is to start at the Pooh Car Park and forage for directions. It's in a little valley in Posingford Wood at the northernmost tip of the forest, at the end of one of those trademark taking-a-pen-for-a-walk fences. The structure is surprisingly free of corporate signage considering that one third of the restoration cost was raised by Pooh's current owners (in appreciation of a character who is second only in their earners list to Mickey Mouse). To its credit, Disney hasn't even asked for an acknowledgement, sensitive to local concerns about possible cultural pillage of the character they now market as 'Classic Pooh'.[†]

It's a good idea to bring your own sticks, as the area has been picked bare of loose twigs by visitors, making the Pooh Sticks Bridge one of the hardest woodland bridges in Britain

A tournament-standard Pooh Sticks Bridge.

Hundred Acre Wood

---

[*] These characters stand out amongst the cast as pompous, 'adult' voices. The critic Alison Lurie points out that scholarly pedant Owl is rather like Milne's description of his father, while fussy, appearance-obsessed Rabbit is a bit like his mother.

[†] Possibly to distinguish it from some future rebranding of Pooh as skateboarding bear from downtown Detroit who uses his human beatbox skills to teach Piglet about the true meaning of family.

to play Pooh Sticks from. It's suspiciously firmly bolted together with some additional stanchions supporting the instantly recognisable beams in a way that reeks of Health and Safety Risk Reports rather than wild walks in the woods with a bear but since young tourists falling in the river and becoming Pooh Sticks would be a Very Bad Idea, it would be disingenuous to carp. It's a solid modern facsimile of the original bridge that will likely stand for several more generations of fans.

Ironically, if you take a toy Pooh Bear down to the bridge to try and recreate a classic 1920s game, he'll be the least accurate part of your photos. The bear who really accompanied Christopher Robin was quite a different beast than the one we're used to, with a flatter, more teddy-ish face. The dumpy, snouted figure from the books was based on Shepard's son's bear, Growler. Both Growler and Piglet were eventually mauled by dogs (Growler fatally). Roo was lost somewhere in the orchard up the lane from Cotchford.

The surviving toys are on display in a case at the New York Public Library, much to the chagrin of British MP Gwyneth Dunwoody, who campaigns for their return with a fervour more usually seen in Greeks wanting their marbles back.

Everyone wants a piece of Pooh. It drove Christopher Milne potty, feeling his own childhood had been hijacked by strangers. The Milnes were shy, and the boy Christopher Robin loved Ashdown Forest for the same reason it's such a pleasant day out today: it's a long way away from the crowd. The area around the Pooh Sticks Bridge is the only clue as to the forest's fame; the crowd has come, and they've pinched all the sticks.

Ashdown Forest has survived a great deal of human interference. Its seemingly natural landscape is made of what was left behind when a park fenced in for deer hunting had been given a good going over by iron smelting, common land grazing and estover (firewood) gathering. This patch of countryside seems able to withstand whatever is thrown at it, even tourism for a global megabrand like Pooh. Ashdown attracts over a million visitors a year, yet the woodland remains refreshingly undamaged. There isn't a Tigger tea room or a Rabbit & Co. Fruitarian Smoothie Bar. It hasn't been rebranded as EuroPooh or expanded for the twenty-first century as the Billion Acre Wood. There aren't any signposts. There are over fifty car parks, and none of them spoils the view. Visiting on a crisp, snowy day, you could be the only person on earth.

A. A. Milne said that, as children, he and his brother wanted to 'wake up one morning and find that everybody else in the world was dead'. It's possible he expressed this desire through the fictional Christopher Robin, supreme monarch of a kingdom of toys and animals, the closest thing to a grown-up in a land without grown-ups. In the interwar years, these woods were for walking. Few people had cars, and visiting isolated woodlands was done on foot or not at all, so a local child like Christopher Robin could have the place to himself. He later said that 'Pooh could never have stumped a forest that was littered with picnic parties playing their transistor radios'. Alone amongst the pines, Ashdown Forest could become Christopher's own, a magical world built over the top of the real one.

Even small children can need to escape from everyday bother. The Hundred Acre Wood is a sanctuary away from the spit-covered hanky and the relentless don't-do-that-dear. The urban fuss of the first Christopher Robin book, *When We Were Very Young* – all proper mealtimes and trips to Buckingham Palace with starchy nannies* – has vanished completely in the second, *Winnie-the-Pooh*. Between the two, the Milnes moved from London to Ashdown Forest, where things are simpler, more timeless. Retracing their steps for a day can be a powerful tonic. Sing Ho! For the life of a bear.

The Ashdown Forest Centre, Wych Cross, Forest Row, East Sussex, RH18 5JP
01342 823583
www.ashdownforest.org

---

* 'Christopher Robin went down with Olive' didn't rhyme with 'Buckingham Palace', which is why the Milnes's nanny was renamed Alice for the poem.

Valiant Soldier

'Good morning,' said I to the ancient man.
'Straight on,' he replied.
'Good morning,' I ventured again.
'About seven miles,' he retorted.
I felt that we were going to be great friends.
'Will you have a drink?' I asked.

H. V. Morton, *In Search of England*

Some time between 1747 and 1777, an inn opened in Fore Street, Buckfastleigh. In July 1965, it closed. And then the interesting part of the story began.

The Valiant Soldier is an extraordinary monument to the monumentally ordinary. It is full of contradictions: a pub that cannot serve alcohol; a hermitage open to the public; a tourist attraction on which hundreds of thousands of pounds have been spent to keep it looking austere and humble.

Mark and Alice Roberts took on the tenancy of the Valiant Soldier in January 1938. The pub, then one of more than a dozen in Buckfastleigh, had a public bar, a lounge (or 'snug') and living quarters. Landlord Mark worked part-time as a coach driver (he needed something to do since the Defence of the Realm Act had restricted pub opening to five and a half hours daily), while landlady Alice – the more visible of the couple – drew beer from wooden barrels kept behind the bar. Thanks to its proximity to the town's picture palace, the Valiant Soldier was a popular stop with cinemagoers and bright young things on their way to the local dance.

With the Second World War came a new wave of customers: American GIs. From 1941, the US 4th Infantry Division was barracked at two sites on the outskirts of Buckfastleigh (a place so quiet the newcomers called it Sleepy Valley). They wasted no time getting to know the town, sweeping the local girls off their feet (literally, by teaching them the jitterbug). Preliminary recces of the pubs revealed that the average GI Joe wasn't particularly fond of local Bulmer's cider, nicknaming the twopenny brew 'Invasion Juice'. (The land girls called it 'Loony Ale', implying that they

didn't rate its military effectiveness as highly as the Americans.)*

Buckfastleigh had built its reputation on wool.† In the mid-nineteenth century, there were four wool mills in the town (of which you can learn more in the exhibition at the end of the pub tour) but by the 1950s the industry was in decline. As was the Valiant Soldier. Norman & Pring, the brewery who owned it, became part of Starkey, Knight & Ford, which became part of Whitbread. And Whitbread saw their portfolio, and saw that it was good; and, lo, Whitbread decided they had too much competition in Buckfastleigh. In August 1964, Mark and Alice Roberts were served twelve months' notice of closure. The Valiant Soldier, said the brewery, was 'no longer a business proposition'.

The Robertses were understandably aggrieved. They stood to lose not only their business, but the home they'd occupied for over a quarter of a

Valiant Soldier

---

* Sadly, many of these infantrymen were among the 749 who perished in an exercise for the D-Day landings off Slapton Sands that was disastrously intercepted by German torpedo boats.

† It's also famous as the town with half the alphabet in its name, and the venue for the much missed annual Goose Shitting Contest, in which local boys, carrying their goslings to slaughter six weeks before Christmas, had to count how many times the birds shat on the route from Buckfastleigh to Deepy. Honesty was a prerequisite.

century. In July 1965, Whitbread withdrew the pub's alcohol licence, and the Valiant Soldier was forced to lay down its arms. The Robertses, however, were in no mood to wave the white flag, and continued arguing with Whitbread for two years (while cannily living above the pub, rent-free) until they negotiated to buy the property at a knock-down price of £1,800. As part of the deal, Whitbread slapped on a covenant permanently forbidding the sale or manufacture of alcoholic liquor on the premises. They must have thought they'd killed the Soldier. How wrong they were.

Mark Roberts died in 1967 at the age of 70. Alice steadfastly refused to move out of The Pub Which Was No Longer A Pub for a further twenty-eight years. What she and few others knew, however, was that downstairs from her modest living quarters, the pub lived on in suspended animation, exactly as it was on the night she had locked the door behind her last customer. Half-empty pint glasses sat on tables; an unfinished game of darts poked expectantly from the dartboard; hands of cribbage lay pegged on a table; the takings – fat old pennies and one stray American cent, a memento of the good old days – nestled undisturbed in the till.

Alice Roberts became a recluse. She was a familiar figure around town, neatly dressed in her homemade hats and dresses, usually to be spotted pulling a wicker shopping trolley full of scavenged kindling behind her. Occasionally, she would venture along the A38 to Ashburton, returning with a large branch, which her kindly neighbour would chop into logs for her. However, she allowed nobody into her home. As time went by, her utility supplies were cut off due to non-payment. Alice simply stole water from a neighbour's tap in the alley behind the pub, and put out bowls during rainstorms. More than once, the Valiant Soldier suffered a chimney fire, and Alice reluctantly allowed the fire brigade access to the property. Stubbornly, she supervised their entrance and exit, refusing them access to the attic or any other room to check for structural damage.

Clearly, Alice was suffering from some sort of nervous distress. She was a religious woman, and punters at the Valiant Soldier (in its pub days) would occasionally hear her thumping out *Onward Christian Soldiers* on her piano in the parlour above the buzz and chuckle of the public bar. 'Soured your beer,' recalled one regular. Occasionally, officialdom would come knocking at her door – presumably asking for unpaid bills to be settled. When the suits were met with no reply, the more persistent would knock next door.

'We're looking for Mrs Roberts,' they'd ask. 'She's in,' the neighbour would say. 'Well, she's not answering,' they'd continue. 'No,' the neighbour would reply, 'and she won't.' 'Fair enough,' the officials would say, 'we'll wait.' 'Good luck,' the neighbour would say. 'Have you brought a tent?'

Her health failing, Alice Roberts moved into a nursing home in Torquay in 1996, and the Valiant Soldier came on the market. Some bright spark alerted Teignbridge District Council to the perfectly preserved pub's extraordinary potential as a heritage project and, with commendable foresight and imagination, the council sprang into action. A trust was established and, the following year, the Valiant Soldier was bought for £63,000. Volunteers moved in to start cataloguing the artefacts, and must have been flabbergasted at what they saw. Not only was the pub (closed in 1965, but not modernised since the 1940s) a time capsule, but so were Alice's living quarters. A gas-operated fridge and a meat safe stood in her scullery. Her kitchen contained an enamel table and a Caddymatic wall-mounted tea dispenser. Linoleum half a century old floored her parlour. The yellowing labels of Pulmo Bailly, Fuller's Earth and Mucilaginous Laxative peeled on the shelves of her medicine cabinet.

Time stands still, gentlemen, please.

An inventory was taken of *absolutely everything* found on the property – down to the spoons, spare radio valves and discarded counterfoils. £45,000 worth of structural repairs were undertaken to make the property safe and free from damp. The building next door (previously a sixteenth-century-themed restaurant – the mind boggles) was bought and converted to a ticket office. Finally, in July 2000, the Valiant Soldier opened as a tourist attraction.

And what a remarkable place it is. All the fixtures and objects are original – with the exception of the spirits,

Valiant Soldier

sweets and pickled onions behind the bar (thankfully) and one lamp standard that needed to be sourced. The walls (covered with heavy-duty Lincrusta wallpaper – either you remember it or you don't, but it's like rhino-hide Anaglypta) are painted two-tone chocolate and cream.* The remains of the Robbialac gloss are in a tin on the landing. A heavy 78rpm disc of Gandino and His Salon Orchestra is ready to play 'Valse Triste' on the phonograph. A Coronation plate stands in the cupboard next to the kitchen.

The effect – the curators' clever idea – is that, wherever you stand, somebody has just left the room. Thus, downstairs, with the Woodbines ashtray and the coin-operated Ronsonol lighter-fluid dispenser and the made-do-and-mended cap hanging on the coat hook, voices can be heard coming from the next bar – locals reminiscing about those cold winters when they'd pull the poker from the grate and plunge it into their cider for a couple of minutes to take the edge off the brew. You can still, faintly, smell the beer and cigarettes in the public bar. Alice's slippers sit next to her easy chair in the upstairs parlour. Her chamber pot sits under her bed. The effect is eerie, yet homely, simple and warm.

One room, on the other hand, has undergone a spectacular refit. The second of the two bedrooms has been turned into an attic – a change from most home conversions which are performed in the opposite direction – to showcase the stunning variety of bric-a-brac the volunteers recovered from the original attic (which was a real place and therefore had to be closed for not being Health And Sodding Safety compliant). Here is a very humbling reminder of the assortimentia the British accumulate in their lifetimes – that teetering Kilimanjaro of junk that is your disappointing footprint in the sand of time. You peer at the Valiant Soldier's dusty clutter in the dark with a torch (as you would in a real attic), and can't help but think of all that guff weighing down the rafters of your own home.† Here are three stone cider bottles, an iron bedstead, a Union Flag, a brace of stuffed badgers, a box of Blakey's cricket spikes, a gas mask, a model Lancaster bomber, a copy of *Blighty* magazine, a chemistry set, a top hat, a Morse code transmitter, a pair of Bakelite headphones and numerous biblical samplers. This is the

---

* The pub-friendly, nicotine shade of cream that *Roger's Profanisaurus* terms 'fagnolia'.

† Amongst other things, the authors have in their attics a pornographic Rubik's Cube, a cardboard cut-out of John Ratzenberger, a copy of ex-*Blue Peter* presenter Simon Groom's single 'I Can't Help Falling in Love with You', an Austin Maestro launch catalogue, a *Clangers* script, someone's sister's didgeridoo, a Hurricane Higgins LED snooker game, a trio of bumble bees in three spice jars, a signed Biro portrait of Willie Rushton, a blue teddy bear called Parsnips, a four-hour video of Michael Fish weather forecasts and an 'I've Been to Dungeness Lighthouse' badge whose owner hasn't.

random rubbish of living memory, but the Valiant Soldier might as well be Anne Hathaway's Cottage (or a sixteenth-century-themed restaurant for that matter) to anyone below the age of about thirty.

The irony – and it won't have escaped you – is that you're peering into the furthest and most trivial corners of a life that could never have anticipated such posthumous examination. This wasn't the home of a Churchill or Keats, the sort of person who might make plans to leave their cutlery drawer to the Ashmolean Museum for the good of the nation. This was the shuttered bolt-hole of someone very private, a building in which no one was allowed for nigh on thirty years, and here you are in the attic. Alice Roberts, a first-order recluse, left her laxative and her footwear for you to peer at.

We're all prone to deferring to the mighty in one way or another, whether it's genuflecting at their statue or oohing and aahing at their writing desk. What we don't often find ourselves doing – except when a regional sales manager makes the headlines by saving a child from drowning in a pond – is praising the ordinary. At the Valiant Soldier, you're invited to have a thorough sniff around the life of a very ordinary woman with a husband, two sons and a steady job, sixty years in the same home, of whom you've never heard, about whom you can't know very much because her life was so firmly closed – the sort of person you pass by every day without even noticing. And you're only able to do this because someone's stubborn eccentricity in never clearing up has accidentally singled out this one tiny stitch from life's rich pattern. This is as close to social history as you can come. The Valiant Soldier promotes itself as 'the pub where time was never called'. You might think it more accurately 'the pub that lived up to its name'. This is a genuine public house.

The Valiant Soldier, 79 Fore Street, Buckfastleigh, Devon, TQ11 0BS
01364 644522
www.valiantsoldier.org.uk

Clowns' Gallery

It is a curious thought, but it is only when you see people looking ridiculous that you realise how much you love them.

Agatha Christie

It has become an irksome cliché, boys and girls, to claim that you're scared of clowns. That's not to say it's impossible to suffer from coulrophobia,* but the number of phantom cases vastly outnumbers the genuine. It's probably the fault of Stephen King and friends, but it's the most glorified phobia of our time, despite the presence of other strong candidates. What's wrong with kathisophobia (the fear of sitting down), arachibutyrophobia (the fear of peanut butter sticking to the roof of the mouth) or hellenologophobia (the fear of Greek words)? Perhaps one of the other phobias will one day step up to the plate and end the unnecessary vilification of the poor old clown. Honestly, he's only trying to get you to smile . . .

For one afternoon a month you are exuberantly invited to roll up, roll up to the Clowns' Gallery in Hackney, a museum and archive of the history of the craft. Originally, the Gallery was a display of clown paintings, founded in 1960 by the world's first clown organisation, Clowns International (honorary life president: Ron Moody). The organisation publishes its own magazine and holds an annual service in the Clowns' Church, attended by its members in full clowning regalia. The church, aka the Holy Trinity, has a stained glass window dedicated to Joseph Grimaldi, the clown daddy, and can be found a half a dozen custard-pie throws from the Gallery.

The borough of Hackney was recently voted the worst place to live in Britain by sneering television types. They rated Winchester, Horsham and Orkney as the best, but were obviously not taking number of Clowns' Galleries into consideration; where the posh cousins muster a disappointing grand total of nought. Yes, Hackney's Clowns' Gallery looks like an inner-city community centre from the outside, but inside it's bursting with tip-top big-top fun. The Gallery only has enough room for twenty visitors at a time and it would be a rare occasion for that many to walk in off the

Clowns' Gallery

---

* From the Greek: *Kolobathristes*, a stilt-walker, and *phobia*, meaning 'I don't like it'.

street and sample its magic, which is a damned shame. Mind you, the small number of visitors means that you'll almost certainly be offered a mug of tea the moment you set foot through the door, so there are benefits.* You're likely to also get the full, one-on-one attention of a master pratfaller, talking you through their honourable craft: something which, like their squirty flowers, is not to be sniffed at. The guides are all practising clowns – as you may have guessed – but you wouldn't know it to look at them, dressed in mufti. They've removed their make-up and driven to work in cars with round wheels, straight axles and doors that don't fall off. Their clowns, minute flashes aside, have pretty much gone to sleep.

If you find it exhausting watching a clown, imagine performing as one. Matthew Faint, in his role as curator and one of the directors of the Clowns' Gallery, speaks of his alter ego Mattie in the third person. Mattie is nearly

forty, Faint is a little older (a gentleman never asks a gentleman his age). He is relaxed off duty and so are you, reassured that you aren't about to get a bucket of water in the face. Mattie is not just a clown clown, he is also a clown doctor at Great Ormond Street Hospital. He doesn't stand in operating theatres pulling out yard after yard of a patient's intestine like silk handkerchiefs from a sleeve; rather, Mattie is a trained laughter therapist – a job that he plainly finds very rewarding.† Apparently clown doctoring works most effectively with children aged seven or under. Once

they get past that age, blind cynicism starts kicking in and the magic stops working. This 'clowns aren't funny' mindset is accepted without question for the rest of our lives: if a clown looks like a traditional clown, then he's old hat; if a clown acts in the same way but looks like Rowan Atkinson or

---

* We were given a KitKat as well. Stand-up opera librettist Stewart Lee was there on the same afternoon recording a programme on clowns for Radio 4 so they may have been especially purchased for his visit. Their website definitely promises that you'll be given tea, but it's probably best not to bank on the KitKat.

† He even manages to put forward a convincing argument for watching *Patch Adams*, the Robin Williams film based on the life of pioneering American laughter therapist Hunter Adams.

Stan Laurel, then we permit ourselves to laugh. Sometimes the best camouflage for a clown to wear is no make-up.

Clowns come in several flavours, and these archetypes are used by comedians whether they're in greasepaint or not. The Whiteface is a clown authority figure, a bit of a pompous know-all, ready for a pie in the face. This look, used by Grimaldi, became so popular it buried the old commedia dell'arte Harlequin completely (which is why you don't expect Harlequins to be funny any more, you expect them to sing 'Ashes to Ashes'). Auguste clowns are clumsier and sillier, the fool character who causes all sorts of terrible mix-ups. Then there's the Character clown, very often a tramp type with a melancholic, put-upon disposition and heavy black make-up that looks like their razor is the worst a man can get. Suddenly the cast of

characters in *Father Ted* seems awfully familiar.

These strict roles are vital for clowns who work together, typically at circuses. The Gallery's staff clowns are solo acts, a very different skill to team clowning. Their big-booted stamping ground is children's and adults' parties, parades, shopping-centre promotions and fêtes. Mattie the Clown was once asked to attend a wedding in character, Gingernutt sometimes moonlights as a magician and puppeteer and Bubbles is a balloon-modelling expert who once left Rowan Williams speechless by presenting him with a balloon Archbishop of Canterbury.

Every British member of Clowns International can register his or her own unique clown-face make-up with the organisation by painting it on an egg, plenty of which are on display at the Gallery. This egghead catalogue was started in 1947, as a hobby, by the organisation's founder, Stan Bult. The blown hens' eggs were occasionally loaned out for reference or display. Some turned up later at a Warwickshire museum, others got destroyed after a long-term loan to a now-defunct restaurant. Clown omelette, anyone? Amazingly, given that when eggs and clowns are brought together disaster is usually never far behind, a few of Bult's original painted eggs can still be viewed at the Gallery.

The eggs, with their clown slap faces and matching costume eggcups, are now carefully watched. As many of the originals as possible have been recreated, and newly registered faces are today painted onto sturdier 'pot eggs' (the artificial eggs farmers use to encourage recalcitrant birds to lay).*

---

* We think that these are laid by clay pigeons but we haven't checked.

The range of faces is outstanding, showing the variety not only in paint and costume, but also in clown names. Step forward Cuddley Custard, Tom Fun, Conk and Gary the Musical Clown among many others guaranteed to produce messy nose laughs through your complimentary tea.

To a clown, there is no such thing as a generic clown; it's the uneducated who think they all look the same. Gingernutt (Ian Thom according to his birth certificate) is the clown (man) to talk to about the importance of the face-paint registration scheme. As Gingernutt's look is particular to himself, his comedy brand if you like, it is understandable that Thom was somewhat aggrieved to discover his unique clown face being used as a stock image on both Saturday morning telly and a Gambian stamp without recompense or mention of the character's name. The outside world is unaware of the fraternity's code of honour.

If the Gambians have Gingernutt as their face of clowning, where is ours? Once we had Grimaldi, whose memoirs were edited by Dickens and who didn't live to see sixty thanks to the ravages of years of performing. Charlie Cairoli, whose dazzling sequinned costume was donated to the collection in 1975, was huge. Coco, known to a generation of schoolchildren as the road-safety clown, received the MBE for his work, and his miniature Belisha beacon (a painted pole topped with an orange toilet ballcock) is at the museum along with a recording of him discussing road safety. Where are their like today? The only clowns regularly seen and widely known in Britain today are American: Krusty or Ronald, the McClown. We're not lovin' it.

You don't have to be zany to work here but it helps. The Clowns' Gallery is a smashing attraction, fervently run by practitioners of the art who have rightly earned their face on an egg. The frames of the display cabinets, lovingly painted by a canal-boat artist, bear images, props and artefacts suggestive of a more innocent age. A guided tour of this unusual attraction has all the mystery and magic of being inducted into a secret society, a master craftsman whispering some of the tricks of the trade in your ear. There is the suspicion of something ancient and honourable in clowning as it's depicted here, as if it were the last of the mediæval guilds. It's all down to the enthusiasm and evangelism of people like Mattie that this exclusive clown clique still exists, but as it gets trickier to find outlets for clowning, it gets harder to attract new blood. It's a sign of the times that children's entertainers in our less-than-brave new world have found it increasingly useful to advertise themselves as CRB-checked.

Old age is a concept that never bothers clowns in character. If a clown gets out of their depth while entertaining the kids, Mattie says their best move is always to 'fetch a grown-up'. As clown performers themselves grow older their make-up changes to work with the new creases in their faces, but the clowning profession faces a tougher struggle to cover up its own creases. It's not trendy – in fact, it's often seen as old-fashioned. But funny is funny. Team clowning is the basis of many much-loved sitcom relationships, and the solo clown, with his licence to misbehave, is still doing business disguised as whichever TV prankster (from Emu to Ali G) is attacking the great and good this week. Clowns suffer terrible cultural snobbery, but there's no point sticking your nose in the air, unless it's a big red one. Come on, girls and boys, isn't it time for us to become coulrophiles?

Eggshelves.

The Clowns' Gallery, All Saints Centre, Haggerston Road, London, E8 4HT
08701 284336
www.clownsinternational.com

Beaumaris Castle

'Begin at the beginning,' the King said, gravely, 'and go on till you come to the end: then stop.'

Lewis Carroll, *Alice's Adventures in Wonderland*

Being a castle used to have a real sense of purpose: keeping people out, keeping people in, marking territory, showing off your owner's wealth, scaring the uppity locals. The job description has narrowed in the twenty-first century, and an advert in the Fortresses and Strongholds Wanted section of your local paper would most likely stress the need for good people skills and an ability to look attractive in jigsaws.

The castles built by Edward 'Longshanks' the First★ as an iron ring to stamp his authority on thirteenth-century Wales are enviable jigsaw subjects. They must rank amongst the prettiest military installations ever erected in Britain: Caernarfon's nests of polygonal turrets, teetering like piles of oddly shaped foreign coins; the soaring walls and arches of Conwy; the way Harlech Castle looks as if it has been not so much built as whittled delicately from the top of the cliff. These are proper knights-in-armour castles with all the trimmings. You can keep your French chateaux and Bavarian follies. If a seaside bucket is described as 'castle shaped', it looks like one of these.

The chap Edward got to design his supercastles was ace mason Master James of St George, a Savoyard craftsman at the peak of his powers. Every time Edward commissioned a stronghold to put the willies up the Welsh, the castle he got from James was more defensively cunning, more imposing and (importantly) more symmetrical and beautiful. Beaumaris was going to be James's masterpiece.

Driving through the town today, you might easily miss it. Beaumaris doesn't proudly dominate the skyline with arrogant Edwardian fistfuls of flags and towers. It crouches at gutter height at the end of the high street, not much taller than its own gift shop. The castle is beautifully

---

★ What happened to regal nicknames? How much better would the nation feel owing forelock-tugging fealty to Elizabeth 'Nice Hat' The Second?

proportioned in every direction but one: upwards. Beaumaris is not a ruin – in fact, it's beautifully preserved. What you see today is pretty much how it looked in its prime. It's a bungalow castle. The masons got to the first floor, downed tools and stopped.

An artist's impression in the thoroughly splendid guidebook shows what Master James had planned: a skyscraping chivalric dream-castle, with thumping great bastilles and colossal elephant-foot gatehouses. The stubby towers that stand incomplete today round the outer wall were meant to be overlooked by elegant turrets at least four times as high. Instead, they are overlooked by a low hill where people go to walk their dogs.

Plans for a stronghold on the site had been drawn up in 1283 but, thanks to the success of Edward's policy of building terrifying castles at them, the Welsh had gone unusually quiet, so work was never started. However, when Madog ap Llewelyn kicked off an unexpected rebellion in 1295, building another big, frightening castle suddenly seemed like a good idea.

Llanfaes, the prosperous Welsh town that had been happily going about its business nearby, was closed down. The inhabitants were cleared out by royal decree and rehoused in a new Anglesey settlement called Newborough – a name that shines across the centuries as a tribute to the pale, cardboard imagination of the town planner. Edward's attempts to subdue the Welsh often had the mimsy tang of the parish-council planning committee. Following the death in 1284 of the rebellious Llywelyn ap Gruffydd (the first, last and only native-born Prince of Wales), Edward wasted no time in having romantic, rugged, unmanageable-sounding regions like Gwynedd, Powys, Buellt, Deheubarth, Gwent and Morgannwg wiped from the gazetteer. His administrators replaced them with polite English counties with well-behaved names like Flint, Anglesey and Cardiganshire. If you want an area to keep itself to itself and send its tax return in on time, you can't do much more than name it after some knitwear.*

Work on Beaumaris started briskly, thousands of labourers swarming over the site. This was to be a royal castle, big enough to house the whole court, and possibly the household of his son, the new Prince of Wales, as well. Edward visited personally, and was so keen to get the monarch-in-residence feeling going that he had a temporary thatched cottage run up in the courtyard, and got everyone round for a harp recital.

Here's where the storey ends.

But the enthusiasm didn't last long. In 1296 spending on Beaumaris was slashed by two thirds and, by May of that year, the wages for the workmen had run out. In the summer of 1295, the exchequer had splashed out a whopping £6,000 for work on the castle; in all of 1300 it coughed up a single measly payment of £100. Wales was old news. Edward had found a whole new bunch of intransigent Celts to wave his sword at, and was now busy in Scotland, having a spot of bother with William Wallace and friends, like in that film where Mel Gibson has a blue face.

In 1306, frightened that the Scots might get into Wales from the sea via Beaumaris, a report was commissioned into the castle's defensive problems. There were quite a few. The outer walls were barely eight feet high, and the southern approach could have been stormed

---

* The Welsh got their own back when they were left to tidy up the mess following the Wars of the Roses and their man ended up on the English throne. Henry Tudor, grandson of a Welsh squire, sired the dynasty that singlehandedly invented standing with your legs apart, waving a chicken leg and bellowing 'Off with her head!' – a cornerstone of the English national myth so precious that its depiction on screen was entrusted to Sid James.

quite comfortably by a man of average height, providing he had remembered to bring a wooden box. A wise Scots tactician might have attempted a pincer movement – men standing on wooden boxes to the south, old ladies and children strolling in from the north where there were no walls whatsoever. Beaumaris needed finishing.

The castle you visit today is almost exactly as it was left in 1330 when the final gaps in the walls and gatehouse had been plugged. Romantic tourists of the past seeking fairytale castles to visit or paint often passed Beaumaris by, considering it underwhelming.★ But its understated silhouette is what makes it unique. It was meant to be Edward's supreme statement of arrogant state control, to dominate the horizon, and it has been charmingly neutered – literally cut down to size.

Because it's not set in acres of grounds or thrust dramatically onto a rocky outcrop, fitting instead neatly into a corner just down the road from the chip shop, you might expect the castle to be pretty compact. However, as you pass through the gatehouse, an ambitious fortress spreads out before you, vast and regal. Half-finished, Beaumaris wasn't worth attacking (it was only pressed into emergency service a couple of times, once during the Owain Glyn Dwr revolt, and once in the Civil War) so it's not been knocked about much, and that means there's a lot more of it still standing than there is of some of Edward's completed castles.

The parts that did get finished are in spine-tingling nick, and you certainly don't feel short-changed for opportunities to explore. The long passages carving through the inner walls are undamaged, shadowy and satisfying, stripes of glaring sunlight splashing across the stonework. Doorways lead off to dozens of tiny rooms, each containing nothing more than an arrow slit and a space for a bench. At first you pity the poor soldiers stationed at such cramped defensive positions, but these weren't guard posts. These ventilated back-to-back cubicles run along the sides of the castle, taking advantage of the moat and sea-level location to keep themselves flushed; the garrison at Beaumaris would enjoy the most extensive lavatory facilities of any Welsh castle.

Wandering around this coastal fort on a quiet morning, you feel pleasantly cocooned by the unbroken stonework. Step into one of the abandoned towers and startled pigeons clatter from their casements, swirling up to

---

★ A 1742 engraving of the castle by Samuel and Nathaniel Buck has elongated it skywards to make it look a bit more like a proper castle ruin. Turner did have a go, but only from memory. Beaumaris's low-rise outline lurks in his painting as a turquoise smudge on the shoreline behind his usual paddling yokels and carts.

perch on an arched crossbeam that never saw the upper floor it was meant to support. Staring up at the sky, you can't help but wonder whether people's eyes used to be better at dealing with extremes of light and dark before everything was flattened out by the electric bulb. Imagine running around this castle trying to defend it. You'd be constantly blinking. Every time you glanced in from your arrow slit, you'd have serious trouble finding your quiver.

Your eyes may also boggle at the ivory starkness of the immaculately preserved royal chapel. Regular castle-goers will know that the chapel is usually an undistinguished rectangle of low rubble, which you can only identify with the help of the guidebook. Beaumaris's beautiful, vaulted chamber needs no such labelling. Mediæval fashion would have opted for colourful, even garish, décor, but the Shakerish simplicity of this room can be quite affecting, stripped of all set-dressing bar a wooden crucifix. From the observation chambers, you can peer down towards the altar just as King Edward would have done whenever he fancied catching the highlights of a particularly end-to-end Mass.

The imposing North Gatehouse, with its rigorous symmetry and just-try-it-sunshine solidity, gives some clue as to how the completed castle might have looked. It presents an impenetrable defensive facade, even though it's missing an entire storey and yards of crenellated turret. Instead the neat slice through the building offers an uninterrupted walk round the top of the inner walls. Health and Safety flim-flam occasionally closes bits of the wall walk, but the potential for a thoroughly good promenade is there. Because it's an unfinished building rather than a toppling ruin, adapting Beaumaris so nobody falls off it has been done with an admirably light touch: safe but not unattractive.[*]

It's estimated that, had the walls been completed to battlement level, the outer curtain wall alone would have offered 300 firing positions. As

---

[*] Ideally, we'd always rather have a sign saying 'for goodness' sake be careful', but Beaumaris's unfussy handrails are fine.

confident as a castle may seem, it is a fortified dwelling, and a fortified dwelling is a sign that you're frightened; the modern equivalent is the house bristling to the rafters with CCTV and alarms. The castle fits so snugly into the town, it's easy to forget that this cosy set-up was imposed by force. The town was designed from scratch on the bastide model, the castle and town harnessed together for protection and trade. Beaumaris and Edward's other bastide towns were English-only gated communities, the Welsh not allowed in outside daylight hours, unarmed and forbidden from trading. A siege mentality prevailed; all of Edward's castles could be supplied with food by sea, to avoid land blockades by the furious Welsh, and state-of-the-art defences were essential. Caernarfon's castle walls had ingenious arrow slits that three men could fire out of at once, creating a kind of archery machine-gun. It was almost expected that the locals were going to attack. Build an impregnable fortress, and you still have to sleep with one eye open.

Any vain or cowardly mediæval nobleman interested in turning his home into such a fortress would apply to the monarch for a Licence to Crenellate: that is, permission to add battlements to his manor-house walls. (Not that this necessarily stopped anyone; in 1150, there were over a thousand unlicensed castles in Britain.) But what made a castle, by royal assent, were the little up bits (merlons) and down bits (crenels) at the top. In which case, it's sweet to realise as you stroll round the stumpy walls of this cut-down stronghold that, by the king's own definition, Beaumaris was never really a castle.

Children's books often show an artist's impression of a building cut in half so you can see people going about their business within. That's what Beaumaris looks like for real, as if its upper half had been sheared off by somebody driving it under a low bridge. It was supposed to be the most impressive castle in the country, and it never quite made it. Homes throughout Britain are full of half-finished projects – leftover wood, bits of DIY wreathed in back-of-the-garage cobwebs, things that were going to be great, but somebody ran out of money, or time, or plain lost interest. If our homes are our castles, it's nice to find a castle that's a bit like our homes.

Beaumaris Castle, Beaumaris, Anglesey, North Wales
01248 810361
www.beaumaris.com

Fan Museum

O lang, lang may the ladies sit,
Wi' their fans into their hand.

Anonymous, 'The Ballad of Sir Patrick Spens'

Consider the following: you're caught out in the wilderness, evening is drawing in and it's getting cold. Luckily, a minimum of equipment – two flints, some dried leaves, a Ray Mears – and you've got an instant source of heat. When things get a bit parky, there's nothing better to warm the extremities than a cheeky drop of the old dancing orange stuff. That's cold sorted, but what did our ancestors do when they got too hot?

In two adjacent Georgian townhouses opposite Greenwich Park is a museum commemorating the history of that socially acceptable way of producing man-made wind, the fan. Though the museum isn't historically or symbolically tied to its elegant Regency setting (Greenwich isn't famous for fan making, and neither of the townhouses is an air-conditioning retailer) it feels right that these fans should be living somewhere suitably sybaritic and posh.

The Fan Museum, which opened in 1991, is the only registered fan museum in the world – a fact of which the staff is justifiably proud.[*] The largest part of the collection belongs to director and curator Hélène Alexander, a widely acknowledged expert on the subject and all-round fan fan.[†] She admits she would definitely have used a fan in a previous life, which is interesting, because it implies that even the biggest fan aficionado would think twice before using one casually today. For an item that was once so commonplace, the fan seems to have fallen out of favour.

The museum has two galleries. Downstairs, a fixed display charts the evolution of the fan, while upstairs is a permanently changing exhibition. This themed overspill is necessary since, iceberg-like, only part of Hélène

[*] Although there's a hand fan museum in the Hotel Healdsburg in California and the Musée de l'Eventail in Paris, neither is officially registered and the Parisian one is apparently 'in a bit of a state' according to one of the Greenwich staff.

[†] Sorry. We promise we won't do 'fan club'.

A landscaped fan.

Alexander's expansive collection is ever visible at one time, lest the building capsize into the Thames in a tidal wave of fans. There's a shop downstairs selling fan mugs, teabag tidies and, obviously, fans. The building has fan-shaped windows, an orangery with hedges cut into the shape of fans and a toilet with fan-shaped soap, fan tiles and an extractor fan.

Looking at the size of early fans, you can see why they began life as a luxury lifestyle accessory for our rich ancestors. Without a full staff of fan-waving skivvies, you'd have broken into a dreadful sweat flapping all that metal and ostrich feather. This is the conundrum of the self-manned fan: is the body heat generated by using it less than the cooling effect it produces, or is it more energy efficient to rest your arms and take shade under a tree? The most common fan in the museum is the decorative folding fan. This ingenious semicircle originated in Japan around the twelfth century, where it was known as a *hiogi*. Europe caught up during the Renaissance and suddenly the whole world went fan crazy. Back in Blighty, Elizabeth I made the fan into a status symbol and, obviously, the more it resembled a portable peacock, the better.

Fans became so elaborate and expensive that they would often be plundered for their goodies. Louis XIV, who was used to getting his own way ('if I were not King, I should lose my temper'), used to prise any valuable jewels he fancied off fans and sell them as spoils of war. And it wasn't only the jewellery that was worth a pretty penny: the delicately painted leaves were rare and special works of art too. The fan was so popular that artists (particularly the Impressionists) used to squeeze extreme panoramic landscapes onto its semicircular shape, as if viewing the scene through a fish-eye lens. The museum's framed Gaugin leaf looks like a nineteenth-century experiment in CinemaScope.

Removed and flattened, these painted leaves would either be mounted in expensive fan-shaped frames, or pasted into ordinary rectangular ones and an artist hired to fill in the rest of the design (to give the impression of a full landscape painting). Nothing went to waste when salvaging fans; the ribs and handle could probably have been boiled down to make a decent stock. Japan, ever at the pinnacle of fan technology, busied itself producing pornographic fans, where opening the decorative leaf one way would display an innocent scene, whilst opening another would display a hundred per cent prime Japanese filth. With a flick of the wrist it was the perfect way to alternately shock and revive your lady guests at functions.

Equally horny are the two elephant tusks on display 'by courtesy of HM Customs and Excise, Heathrow'. In the unenlightened pre-Bakelite years, ivory and tortoiseshell were commonly used in the manufacture of fan handles: a grisly practice which, after seeing the Russian fan on display made from vegetable ivory, begs the question: why did people hunt elephants for their tusks when carrots and aubergines are so much easier to catch?

Before ownership of a Costa Del Boy lobster tan became a way of proving you had enough money to fly abroad (or at least get a bus to the tanning salon), a ruddy face on a lady might be misconstrued as a sign that she had swept into the ballroom fresh from a hard day working in the fields ('you look like an Irish labourer!' was the unkind turn of phrase). So, the Fire Fan was introduced. When placed between the face and the fireplace, the

Fire Fan would shield delicate feminine features from the heat, preserving a young lady's fashionable just-sneezed-in-a-bucket-of-flour appearance.

There's no denying that fans were *the* must-have fashion accessory for women during the eighteenth century. Those in the know even developed a fan language where, with subtle movements, they could convey all manner of silent communications across a noisy room. Some useful phrases include:

Touching tip of fan with finger − I wish to speak to you
Fanning oneself slowly − I am married
Placing fan on left ear − Go away
Drawing fan through the hand − Piss off

Young ladies were taught the intricacies of this sanctioned flirtation by a dance instructor who made sure their fan etiquette was up to scratch. As a blossoming soubrette, your fan handling was a measure of your refinement.

Possibly the most intriguing exhibit in the museum is a fan with the names of its (lady) owner's dance partners etched on its back. Like a Little Black Book, or FiloFan, it's the 200-year-old equivalent of hurriedly swapping mobile numbers in the dying moments of a party. Handily incorporated into its design is a tiny stylus for inscribing, like the miniature pencil in a Day-to-Day Diary. Elsewhere, there's a fan incorporating its own repair kit, in case your wafting became so hectic that it caused material damage; and one with a built-in ear trumpet − ideal should you become so overheated that you go deaf.

A well-earned place in the museum's timeline of fans is taken by that stalwart of the package holiday, the Pifco electric hand-fan. For years, men saw fans as they do moisturiser: something mystical and delicate and exclusively the domain of women. Pifcos, however, are probably the ultimate unisex fan. Sales would rocket if David Beckham were photographed using one. Men and fans tend to make odd bedfellows. However, stick an engine to a fan and it's a different story. Suddenly it becomes a Man Fan. Replacing

an Austin's fan belt with a silk stocking used to be a standard 'manecdote' – the perfect yarn for the alpha male: a combination of problem solving, saucy underwear and a raised car bonnet.

These days, big manly fans cool V8s and CPUs. Turn a motorised fan back to front and it becomes a Hoover or a 747. One of the master partners of the Worshipful Company of Fanmakers, formed in London in 1709, was Mr Royce. (Yes, Mr Rolls's mate.) However, if you want a *real* man's fan, look no further than the ball-breaking Welsh slate job on display here, produced in 1999 by J. W. Greaves and Sons Ltd of Blaenau Ffestiniog. Just seeing it makes your arms ache. This is a remarkable bit of stone engineering. A fan this sturdy might well enhance its cooling effect by removing neat slivers of warm flesh from your face.

It's hard to believe that Greaves's sculpted millwheel of a fan could share a museum with the dainty social props in the other cabinets but it's one of the unexpected revelations here. You can't necessarily calm your blushes with a computer cooling unit or coquettishly peer out at your intended over the top of a jet engine, but they are fans all the same. The Fan Museum, pretty, fascinating and delicately presented, collects examples of an object that, even as it seemed to be disappearing from our culture, was being quietly assimilated into the technological revolution.

Fan Museum, 10–12 Crooms Hill, London, SE10 8ER
02083 051441
www.fan-museum.org

Port Logan Fish Pond

An ye'll get a fishie
On a little dishie
Ye'll get a fishie
Whan the boat comes hame

Anonymous, 'Dance Tae Yer Daddy'

We Brits have the same peculiar attitude to eating that we do to certain other messy and unavoidable bodily urges: we do it sadly, in a hurry, often

standing up or while thinking about something else. And, if we're eating something that was recently alive, we'd rather not know, thank you. Carrots must have the mud washed off them; chicken must be served in anonymously shaped little lumps from a popcorn bucket; and, most importantly of all, fish must be tailed, gutted, filleted and under no circumstances ever look us in the eye. You've probably eaten more fish and chip suppers

than you care to remember but, unless you work on a trawler, it's unlikely that you've ever actually seen a cod face to face.* With this in mind, a trip to the Port Logan Fish Pond is long overdue. It's time to meet your dinner.

The sky over Port Logan is simply enormous, with incongruous shapes cut from it by the prehistoric fronds of cabbage palms and tree ferns (courtesy of the mild Gulf-Stream climate). Peaceful and unspoilt, the Mull of Galloway is quietly, unfussily beautiful. This southernmost point of Scotland, with its pale cottages and crunchy beaches, is the closest you can get to being on a remote Hebridean island without actually having to go all the way to a remote Hebridean island.[†]

At the end of an unmetalled coastal road is the entrance to Port Logan's nineteenth-century fish pond: a miniature, whitewashed cottage, discreetly garnished with battlements, towers and arrow slits. Appropriately enough, it looks like one of those toy castles you put in the bottom of a goldfish bowl to relieve the boredom (yours or the fish's, it doesn't matter). A couple of very satisfied cats prowl lazily past the lobster pots to greet you as you walk in. They've every reason to look happy. This must be the best posting a cat can get.

Make your way through the little castle (once the fish keeper's cottage, now the gift shop), and a stairway takes you down into a concealed hollow, about thirty feet across, twenty feet deep, and open to the elements. Lollopy curtains of vegetation froth at the sides, softening the rocks rising twenty feet all around you. After the crashing surf outside, it's eerily calm, the walls deadening the sound of the tides that originally carved this hollow. At the bottom is an unruffled pond and, if you stand at the edge and hold out some fish food (you can get a bag of pellets from the gift shop in

Port Logan Fish Pond

---

* EU quotas permitting. At the time of writing, fishermen were still allowed to catch fish.
[†] A fact not lost on budget-conscious filmmakers. Not only were scenes for *The Wicker Man* filmed nearby (see the chapter on his legs), but the BBC shot three series of the Michelle-Collins-on-a-Scottish-island drama *Two Thousand Acres of Sky* in Port Logan. Michelle liked her pretend island so much, she came back in 2001 to open their real fête, which was nice of her.

And mushy peas and a pickled egg, please.

exchange for a donation to the RNLI), the fish will come to say hello.

Almost all of the fish in the pond are brown, and most of those fish that aren't brown are grey. The fish that aren't brown or grey are invisible. Outside of a conference suite, you will never have seen so many sensible, muted colours, and the fish haven't even livened up their outfits with a cartoon tie. We're used to captive fish being sunshiny koi carp, or glam-rock tropicals; the fifty-or-so specimens at Port Logan, on the other hand, are all proudly domestic varieties. They're the fish we normally see covered in batter or white sauce: cod, pollack, plaice, turbot, trout, grey mullet, eel or, if you're in the mood for shellfish, lobsters and crabs. These fish haven't been brought halfway round the globe from some distant ocean, they're from a few feet away in the Irish Sea, just the other side of the surge-proof valve (all except for the trout, who are normally freshwater fish, betrayed by their tell-tale accents and countryside ways). It's as close as you can get to our islands' native fish without hiring a wetsuit.

Your guide helps things along by throwing in some chopped mackerel. Once they know there's food, the fish bustle at the surface. The plaice lap their smeared boxers' faces over the edge of the pond. The dark blue, cloudy eye of a coley lumbers up from the depths, looking for scraps. Baby cod poke their whiskers into the air. A patch of piebald colour in the pond suddenly moves; it's not a rock, it's a gigantic turbot the size of a dustbin lid. The flatfish are always a surprise, their cubist eyes and mouths serving as a natural camouflage to any predator looking for recognisable faces in the water.* It's an aquarium

---

* Flatfish like turbot are born swimming upright with eyes either side of their head, until they reach maturity, when one eye moves entirely round to the opposite side, so both their eyes are on one side of their head. If a similar thing happened to humans, it would make it much harder for teenagers to get served alcohol under age.

without glass, an interactive, mud-coloured screensaver – and it's rather hypnotic.

The fish pond was built between 1788 and 1800 by Andrew McDouall, the Laird of Logan, to supply food for his table. The owners say that it's the only surviving example of a Victorian fish larder left in Britain. No one's sure exactly how it worked, but it seems that saltwater fish (they'd either swim in or be caught) could be stored safely here in their natural habitat, ready to be plucked out for a starring role in dinner at Logan House. The pond was adapted from a natural blowhole, and it's such an organic part of the landscape that it's hard to see where the rocks end and the buildings begin (though McDouall has helpfully signed his bit with a big 'AMD').

The advent of refrigeration rendered McDouall's fish pond an unnecessary luxury. Victorian excess didn't last well into the new century. Logan House itself was once covered in outrageous additional turrets and battlements courtesy of influential Victorian architect David Bryce. They were stripped off when austerity bit hard, and the house reduced to the single manageable Queen Anne wing underneath, yet another casualty of more reasonable times.★

The larder has been a tourist attraction for over a century. George VI visited in 1935, and Princess Juliana of the Netherlands dropped by later that same year. Plenty of elderly visitors who fed the fish as children are delighted to discover it's still in business when they come back for a visit. In the little bathing hut that sprouts from the crags near the cottage entrance, there is a display of historic photographs of the pond – people of all eras doing just what you've been doing: monochrome 1950s girls with flick hairdos, sepia flappers with boyfriends in *Great Race* motorcycle helmets, all pictured perched on the feeding stone, offering scraps to the fish and trying to pull their fingers clear before they get nipped. The fish are unfazed by humans, like squirrels in a city park, and normally learn to eat from the hand in a couple of months. Port Logan has had cod so domesticated they would eat from silver spoons, and for a time was run by a woman who would take the fish out of the water briefly and cuddle them.

The pond's architecture deliberately puts as little as possible between you and the fish. A gladdeningly sane notice on the wall reads, 'To keep the pond's natural look there is no rail around the fish pond, so please keep

★ Bryce was keen on suffocating perfectly good buildings with horrendously ostentatious other ones. One of his other Scottish baronial monsters, Panmure House, was completely demolished in 1952 when no one could find a use for a building that looked like a pile of Towers of London with no electricity, no heating, 130 rooms and only two bathrooms.

children supervised. Thank you.' You definitely have to restrain the temptation to jump in. If you've ever watched a bird in your garden so closely that, when it took to the skies, you felt a momentary sadness that you weren't able to leap into the air and join it, you'll get a similar sensation watching these fish; they're so close, so friendly, yet so alien. It's a small taste of that buzz people report after swimming with dolphins. That urge to interact with another world leads directly to the aeroplane, the bathyscaphe and David Attenborough whispering in a gorilla's lap. Either that or you'll just get hungry. The place is like a chip-shop poster come to life.

At the side opposite the feeding stone is the fissure that formed the pond, carved into great curving ribs by the action of the waves, striped and mottled in red, olive and black. Walking into this small, dim cave is like being swallowed by the whale from *Pinocchio*. Inside are tanks with baby plaice, mermaid's purse egg sacs, starfish and other favourites from the days when a trip to the beach meant gazing into rock pools, not staring at your tan. If you've ever wondered what the white spot is on top of a starfish, the handy information boards will tell you. It's the starfish's arse. Which makes sense, otherwise it would spend all day sitting in its own effluent, and starfish have more class than that. The silence of the fish, the splash of water and the gentle trickling of the filters is blissfully soothing: a winning mixture of fish food and soul food. Port Logan Fish Pond is a pensive place, not in a melancholy way, but pleasantly lonely and thoughtful.

It's a suitable place to consider our strange relationship with fish. All around the world, people are tucking into fish delicacies that come from the British Isles, everywhere except Britain, where we prefer our fish in finger form. We eat sardines (check the tin in your cupboard, they're usually imported from Portugal, often in their natural habitat of thick tomato sauce), but we ignore the pilchard. Cornish pilchards, or *Salacche Inglesi,* have been exported to Italy since 1555. There they are a staple of any grocer's shelves, but no one in Britain will touch them. What's the difference between sardines and pilchards? Nothing. Pilchards are the same fish, but older and with the heads, tails and guts still in place (so they look like fish). Britons steadfastly ignore the fish on their doorstep that other nations go potty about. These include the spider crab (huge in Italy and Spain), the razor fish (a mollusc which goes down a storm in Europe and the Far East), the megrim (a trout-like fish that, again, is loved by the Italians and Spaniards), the internationally renowned Colchester oyster and, of course, the langoustine.

The langoustine (or Norwegian Lobster or Dublin Bay Prawn) may be the saviour of our fishing industry, since export prices are excitingly high, and we aren't especially interested in them. Britain's coast is chock-full of langoustines, but they're normally cooked live, which makes us go a bit peculiar. We're only prepared to eat them if the giveaway fish-shaped body is thrown back in the sea, the tail broken off, dipped in breadcrumbs, frozen and sold in bags in supermarket freezer aisles as scampi. This squeamishness about food may be a hangover from the super-hygienic, factory-fresh, zing-o-riffic astronaut-tablet future we and the United States were promised in the 1950s, but, wherever it came from, it is surely unforgivably prissy and weird to have eaten countless cod steaks in batter but to have never seen a cod.

Port Logan is a salutary reminder that it's time to reconnect with the natural world, face your fish and consider your supper. It's a one-of-a-kind historic monument, a truly interactive attraction and a peaceful way to while away an afternoon. There really is no better place to meet plaice.

Port Logan Fish Pond, Port Logan, Nr. Stranraer, Dumfries & Galloway, Scotland, DG9 9NF
01776 860300
www.loganfishpond.co.uk

Bakelite Museum

He abhorred plastics, Picasso, sunbathing and jazz – everything in fact that had happened in his own lifetime.

Evelyn Waugh, *The Ordeal of Gilbert Pinfold*

There are some happy accidents of scientific tinkering without which life would be much the poorer: penicillin, for instance, polythene or Play-Doh. Even the lightweight glue strip on the back of a Post-It Note was a failed attempt to develop an adhesive about twice as powerful as superglue (itself the result of a research accident). Bakelite, the first synthetic plastic, is another such laboratory luck-out. Invented by Belgian-American chemist Leo Baekeland in 1907, it's the chunky ancestor of all the plastic that now surrounds us, the sturdy material that made the proud, sculpted curves of vintage radios as slick and stylish as a BBC announcer's Brylcreemed hair. Bakelite is waterproof, terrifyingly resilient, doesn't melt and is a great electrical insulator. It could probably destroy Superman if held close enough. If not, you could certainly knock him unconscious with it, because it weighs a ton.

The Bakelite Museum in Somerset is barely contained by its home, the picturesque Orchard Mill. Sprawled over three wonderfully rickety floors linked by steeply inclined steps, it's an immense collection. There's so much on display that you'd easily get your money's worth even if you never made it past the ground floor. The museum is the work of artist Patrick Cook, a contemporary of Peter Blake at Goldsmiths College. Cook's hip sixties eye and wit inform every aspect of the layout and design of the museum.★
From floor to ceiling, there's obvious joy taken from surreal juxtapositions: multicoloured plastic eggcups are laid out with the precision of a terracotta

---

★ While we're in 1960s hip artist territory, it would be neglectful not to mention that Andy Warhol was an enthusiastic collector of all things Bakelite.

army; 1950s fridges open to reveal plastic dinosaurs and Dali-esque lobsters; an audience of colourful sock darners basks before a phalanx of vintage bar heaters. From the evidence on display, Cook is cut from the same cloth used to run up grand British eccentrics like Vivian Stanshall.

Everything about the museum conjures up a redolent past. The mellow whiff of this much Bakelite gets deep into your nostrils. You can easily imagine that this is how the first half of the twentieth century smelled (if you weren't around to sniff it). The gentle lighting, whilst providing sufficient illumination to see the darker pieces of Bakelite – and a lot of it is very, very, *very* brown – is just right. You could be in the mahoganied atmosphere of a pre-war parlour with its warm valve radio and charmingly lethal light sockets.

It's not all brown at the Bakelite Museum, thankfully. The addition of urea to Bakelite's formula in the mid-twenties produced a lighter-hued

variation of the plastic that lent itself very nicely to the addition of dyes. Other companies and rival brands sprang up to take advantage of the new exciting coloured plastics. The precursors to the pastel glory of Tupperware – products like Bandalasta – still look fresh, in rows of gaily co-ordinated eggcups, cruet sets, bowls, teacups and Thermos flasks. The rainbow parade of lemon squeezers is mouth watering, their sherbet shells lined up like a psychedelic citrus circus.

The true stars of the museum, though, are those first-generation Bakelite items in brown or very brown. A selection of vintage radios displayed on an old mill wheel look like science fiction fungi, sprung from the wooden workings of the building. Compared to the uniformity of modern plastics, the lightly marbled grain of true Bakelite feels organic: not something you'd expect from a substance whose real name is polyoxybenzylmethylenglycolanhydride. (Dr Baekeland, you might have guessed, named his remarkable brown substance after himself – more out of expediency than egotism, it would seem.)

Plastic fantastic.

The breadth of the exhibits, linked by nothing but the materials from which they're made, sets this museum apart from other collections of ephemera. There are razors, televisions, dice, toys, picnic sets, a selection of Corby tie presses, plugs, hairdryers, some clarinets – and even funeral caskets. Try and spot the two (count 'em) Bakelite coffins here (one's easy, the other's the pedestal for the Bakelite false teeth display). These dignified boxes were made by the Ultralite Casket Company of Manchester, whose sales brochure is on hand. Do have a nose at it, because it contains some of the most blithely archaic faith in a wipe-clean future you'll ever read. 'New and revolutionary … hygienic … leak and vermin proof … the result of seven years' scientific research …' and so on. Available models included The Halo, The Valley, The Presence, The Harmonious and The Noble (which came fitted with a window in case the deceased changed his mind). Since it was suited neither to cremation (being non-flammable) nor to burial (being acid- and waterproof), time all too predictably buried the concept of the Bakelite coffin.

Back in the land of the living, things are just as bizarre. Propped up in one corner is the Visible Woman Assembly Kit ('The wonders of the human body revealed! Assemble, remove, replace all organs!'). This transparent plastic model of a woman gave children of the past the chance to jigsaw together their own anatomically correct woman with a smooth crotch and no internal reproductive system.★ And for the grown-ups, there's the 1950s Television Drinking Set, six glasses each adorned with a celebrity's likeness and autograph of the calibre of *Six-Five Special* presenter Josephine Douglas or, less disappointingly, the calibre of Terry-Thomas.†

'Drink with the Stars!' urges the lavish presentation box. Presumably the glasses are made of some Bakelite imitator that mastered transparency: the museum does include a fair showing of other historically forgotten plastics such as Lucite, Catalin and Linga Longa Ware.

Most of the objects aren't locked away in cases and can be picked up (carefully) and examined if you wish. It's nice to be trusted to behave like an adult, even if it's hard to resist abusing the privilege by prancing about in the collection of populuxe sunglasses, pretending to be Tippi Hedren. The same trust is implicit in the presence of an honesty box in place of an entrance fee – a commendable move, especially as the museum is non-profit making. To keep the place going, Cook tops up the voluntary donations with sales of his Pod mini caravans (which have enough space for two to sleep side by side and look like scaled-up models of Bakelite radios on wheels). He also sells marvellous cream teas in the garden, and a face full of clotted cream in the drowsy sunshine makes for a perfect post-Bakelite-bonanza H. E. Bates moment.

Bakelite's story was brief. Inevitably, newer, more sophisticated plastics

---

★ The box gingerly warns that 'understanding female biology requires observation of those parts relating to gestation. Included therefore is a separate group of components representing this phenomenon ... the model can be completed without incorporating these elements.' Quite right too. You can sell plastic guns to my kids, but don't you dare go telling them about the creation of life.

† By coincidence, Terry-Thomas's personal archive used to be displayed in the museum.

eventually won the day; even so, Bakelite is the classy, elegant forefather of a material now synonymous with everything naff, shoddy and false. Although Bakelite seems eminently more suitable for product design than metal (which rusts and conducts electricity), wood (which rots and catches fire) or china (which smashes into pointy smithereens), it was a victim of its own success. Competitors and imitators were two-a-penny and Baekeland sold out early, in 1939, having successfully sued and swallowed up enough rivals like Condensite and Damard (geddit?) to form the Bakelite Corporation. Despite this, advancing technology meant the writing was already on the wall for the prototype plastic; the Material Of A Thousand Uses never became The Material Of A Million Uses.

Bakelite is now highly sought after. You're even advised to make sure it's the real thing (not what collectors call Fakelite) before you buy it. And the ripples generated by Bakelite can still be felt, plastic being the material of choice for any designer wanting their innovative product to look modern: you can't imagine a brushed steel Dyson or a wooden iPod, can you? But a Bakelite Dyson would be great, and don't pretend you don't already want a Bakelite iPod. The museum is such an affectionate tribute to this revolutionary phenol that you're bound to think it deserves a little renaissance, as a heritage plastic or a specialist finish. Technology moves on, but a classic style will never go out of date. It's not always what's inside that counts.

Bakelite Museum, Orchard Mill, Williton, Somerset, TA4 4NS
01984 632133
www.bakelitemuseum.co.uk

Bakelite Museum

Cartoon Museum

The wisest and best of men ... may be rendered ridiculous by a person whose first object in life is a joke.

Jane Austen, *Pride and Prejudice*

Bloomsbury's civilised enclave of lantern-windowed bookshops and fusty collectors' outlets is a delightful firebreak of leatherbound calm amongst the paperback-packed chainstores of central London. The area seems to be hunkered down in a commercial rain shadow, protected from inclement financial weather by the cultural mountain of the British Museum, and basking in the warm, timeless currents emanating from James Smith & Sons' New Oxford Street umbrella emporium.*

Even though many of Bloomsbury's small businesses are probably struggling to find two 1875-minted collectable pennies to rub together, to walk these charming streets is to lose yourself in a Hollywood set dresser's fantasy London: neatly ordered squares filled with absent-minded professors, twill-clad booksellers, apoplectic colonels and nannies wheeling Silver Cross prams. Tourists who have alighted halfway up Tottenham Court Road (amid the pile-'em-high electrical outlets) and wondered where the hell Mary Poppins's London has gone are advised to take a brisk stroll east.

The Cartoon Museum couldn't be more perfectly placed to commemorate and undermine some of those stereotypes. While the British Museum

Cartoon Museum

---

* A spectacularly frontaged Victorian boutique so stubbornly and delightfully unchanging that it closes at 5.25pm, conjuring up mental pictures of Old Mr Smith who did so like his cup of tea at half past, and insisted it was steeped for at least four minutes ...

places the clutter of the great and good on pedestals, this one thumbs its nose at them from a side street; even its logo shows a naughty, grinning goon looming out from behind the grand museum's portico. The Cartoon Museum, which opened in February 2006, is Bloomsbury's court jester, preserving centuries of iconic irreverence. If a keynote of the British character is our inability to take anything totally seriously, it's incredible that we've waited so long to build a celebration of it.

Arch social satirist H. M. Bateman proposed a national gallery of cartoon art in 1949, to little response (though he may have been relieved that at least nobody went up on the tips of their toes, threw their arms

in the air and popped their eyes as happened in his drawings). Unlike the French, Americans and Japanese, we tend not to regard our cartoons as a vital part of our idiosyncratic national identity. While theatre in Britain has managed to shake off its bawdy, disrespectful, one-step-up-from-the-brothel origins to become Royal and National and terribly highbrow, comic strips are for lining rabbit hutches.

Cartoons have never courted the affection of the establishment; in fact, the term 'cartoon' itself began as a satirical barb. In 1843, Prince Albert, finding himself with a new Houses of Parliament in need of some nice frescoes, invited competitors to submit 'cartoons' or rough preparatory sketches, which he then exhibited to the public. The young *Punch* magazine snapped savagely back with an illustration by John Leech showing starving paupers bowing their heads in front of a wall of elaborately framed portraits of Albert, accompanied by the words, 'The poor ask for bread, and the philanthropy of the State accords – an exhibition.' At the top of the picture was the exciting caption 'Cartoon No.1'. The name stuck.*

The museum attempts to afford this cheeky artistic underdog some belated respect. The collection rotates regularly, but the first display cabinets are regularly stuffed with lovingly curated loft-fillers: Giles annuals and anthologies of Thelwell, rescued from the sides of bunk beds and toilet cisterns, a jumble sale behind glass. To either side are familiar-looking sketches recontextualised in gallery frames; dozens of original hand-drawn pocket cartoons in the *Private Eye* mode. This artwork was intended for cheap high-contrast reproduction on low-grade paper, but here's a chance to see the pencil marks, whiteout, slips of the compass, pen spatters. Most cartoons are drawn at least half as big again as they'll be printed, and it's rewarding to get up close, to consider the process that has gone into something you might normally absorb in a matter of seconds.

And they're funny. To allay worries that taking cartoons seriously might be missing the point, the museum wisely starts with a batch of cracking one-liners. Though the building is compact, split over two floors (single-frame cartoons downstairs, strips upstairs), you can comfortably lose a couple of hours here. The early exhibits, tinted etchings from the hands of Gillray, Cruikshank and Hogarth, are full of absorbing detail, each one crafted to be purchased and pored over; relics of an age when visual images weren't a fast-food fix, but a nourishing meal with enough leftovers for a sandwich. There is a half-hour sitcom's worth of detail in every busy frame.

Modernity arrives at the turn of the wall; suddenly the pictures are freer, drawn with looser strokes. Advances in printing liberated the art from the constraints of engraving, and these are more recognisably cartoonish to our modern eyes. Particularly eye-catching are Will Dyson's astonishing depiction of a slum landlord, bloated like a barrage balloon, leering in through the window to suck the milk from a baby's bottle, and Bruce Bairnsfather's dry-as-a-bone Great War cartoon of two foot soldiers gone to ground in a

---

* Leech's other contribution to British culture was the development of our image of John Bull, replete in Union Flag waistcoat, bulldog at heel, which is credited to him and fellow *Punch* cartoonist John Tenniel (of *Alice* fame).

tiny crater beneath an oppressive shell-filled sky. Bairnsfather's image was so striking that its caption, 'Well if you knows of a better 'ole, go to it,' became a frontline catchphrase.

In difficult times, the stiff upper lip can be easier to maintain if it's smiling. One war later, David Low was buoying the nation's spirits by reducing the enemy to comic fools. Low noticed that countries like Denmark, whose cartoonists depicted the Axis leaders as irresistible, rapacious monsters, would buckle under the jackboot pretty sharpish. He adopted our usual national response of refusing to take anything seriously, drawing the baddies as outrageous idiots: the kind of enemy we could easily beat. (It probably helped that dictators seem driven to grow facial hair that enables them to be easily reduced to a couple of pen strokes.)

Equally persuasive is the notion that all British technological advances are made in sheds by men with four pairs of spectacles on their heads. For that we probably have to thank William Heath Robinson, the gentle lampooner of scientific progress who thrived on the improbabilities of the machine age. His ramshackle design, on display here, for a string-and-pulley device to blow out the fuses on Zeppelin bombs now looks no more ludicrous than the airship it's up against. The idea of alchemising technical gold from the base metal of knotted string was so fondly embraced by

wartime code breakers at Bletchley Park that they named their prototype computer Heath Robinson.

Rowland Emmett went one stage further than Heath Robinson by realising his own rococo doodles in brass. Emmett, whose curlicued follies were the hit of the 1951 Festival of Britain, was practically the mad inventor laureate, and his legacy can be seen in the work of modern mavericks like Tim Hunkin.[*] His wonderful Self-Golfing Machine ticks away in its own display cabinet like a perpetual-motion engine on its day off. According to a plaque, the machine is 'on loan from Town Centre Securities plc', so all hail the Cartoon Museum for saving Emmett's piece of whimsical public art from languishing in some anonymous corporate foyer.

On the first floor, you can see the vigorous original artwork for such British cultural icons as proto-punk Dennis the Menace, cheery knitwear model Rupert, slinky forces' pulse-quickener Jane, working-class hero Andy Capp and leather-clad authoritarian pisstake Judge Dredd. Our strip-cartoon heroes come from a land of slower, simpler plea-sures than their wham-bang cousins overseas. Flash Gordon never had a pipe, for instance, but Pilot of the Future Dan Dare wouldn't be the same without his sturdy briar. The prototype Dan was headed for an even more respectable career as dog-collared dullard *Dan Dare, Space Chaplain*, until the Sunday-school tendencies of creator the Revd Marcus Morris were overcome by the *Boy's Own* tastes of illustrator Frank Hampson. That the issue was even up for debate is somehow very British indeed.

One of the pleasures is putting artists' names to the boggle-eyed faces. Contributors to children's weeklies would often have their signatures painted out to create the illusion of a Mr Beano Artist (occasionally represented by a brush-holding hand poking in through the fourth wall), but here they are given long-overdue credit. Hero of the hour is undoubt-edly Leo Baxendale, the Milliganesque mind behind *The Bash Street Kids* and *Little Plum*. Much of what we find titterworthy as youngsters can seem hackneyed when we're adults, but, like *The Goon Show*, Baxendale's stuff is still laugh-out-loud funny.

From Gillray's *The Plumb Pudding in Danger* (two lip-licking generals slicing the globe) to Fougasse's immortal *Careless Talk Costs Lives* posters,

---

[*] See the chapter on the Under the Pier Show for more on Hunkin.

the museum is full of images that have entered our cultural vocabulary. Nicholas Lezard, discussing Ronald Searle's *St Trinian's* drawings, referred to the 'deep furrows [Searle] has made in the national consciousness'. The St Trinian's girls are not alone. Look around and you spot reactionary imperial throwback Colonel Blimp, Carl Giles's irrepressible proto-Royle family, Donald McGill's lecherous but henpecked seaside postcard husbands, Churchill as a bulldog and Mrs Thatcher as a wild-eyed harpy. These simplified characters, whether based on a famous individual or a recognisable type, are a persuasive shorthand, changing the way we see ourselves and others.

The Cartoon Museum is a monument to the often unsung artists who have done so much to reflect and define our national character with their thumbnail sketches. Is there really that much difference between this unassuming museum of social history and its big brother over the road with the impressive columns? The pointy-eared hieroglyphs on a pharaoh's sarcophagus are surely the distant ancestors of Korky the Cat, and the British Museum's hugely popular Lewis Chessmen have only won the public's hearts thanks to their lively characters and instantly appealing cartoon eyes.* Why not dash between the two museums and compare and contrast? If you're lucky, you might trip over a burglar in a striped sweater rushing out of one of the rare-coin shops and get a big pound note as a reward. Then, what better way to end your day out than a slap-up meal at the Hotel De Posh with fistfuls of sausages erupting from a steaming volcano of mash? You deserve it. Eh, readers?

The Cartoon Museum, 35 Little Russell Street, London, WC1A 2HH
02075 808155
www.cartooncentre.com

---

* The Lewis Chessmen provided the inspiration for the characters in Oliver Postgate and Peter Firmin's *Noggin the Nog*.

Clarks Shoe Museum

Here are the gumboots you ordered, madam.
David Nobbs, *The Fall and Rise of Reginald Perrin*

The worship of the brand is something every decent Briton finds rightly embarrassing. We snort when transatlantic advertising tells us our choice of fizzy drink says something about us. What kind of cultural midget could shackle their identity to the logo printed on a can of pop or stitched to the side of a pair of sports shoes? We don't need Coke and Nike, for goodness' sake; we've got Shakespeare and Milton and Morecambe and Wise. But there is one British label that makes us come over so unnecessary that it really deserves a whole museum dedicated to it. Luckily it's got one.

Clarks didn't start off as shoemakers. Nineteenth-century Quaker Cyrus Clark was trading as a rug-maker when his teenage brother James came up with a neat use for the sheepskin offcuts otherwise going to waste. The Clark brothers' 'Brown Peter' slippers were a hit, and before long the family was supplying footwear to the Empire. Worker relations were cordial – the company avoided the unionised unrest that followed mechanisation in other shoe centres such as Nottingham – and the business boomed. Like other forward-thinking industrialists, the Clarks built a pleasant town almost from scratch for their workers. Street now had a library, a reading room and a pub at the factory entrance, though to reflect their temperance beliefs the Bear Inn was dry. (The boozer finally got its alcohol licence in 1980, welcome news when you stagger gasping from the engrossing museum, tongue like a brogue.)

The Clarks Museum is part of the company's headquarters, a vital stitch in the leather upper of its brand, so it's free to get in. Visitors of a certain generation come here for one of two things. Firstly, they're looking for that big metal measurer thing that gripped their childhood foot, grading its width from A to E, or, secondly, they want to catch a glimpse of the fantastic badge that came free with a pair of Clarks Commandos.* The museum wisely gets the foot gauges out of the way in the first display, to avoid hordes of measurer-hungry visitors tearing the place apart in a frenzy. The block-lettered 1973 Commando badge is at the other end; between the two, there's a wealth of history, education and nostalgia.

The story of the firm is told through documents, posters, display boards, equipment and shoes, with breaks for appealing novelties such as the largest leather boot in the world, made for Queen Victoria's Jubilee in 1887. Because Clarks is such a household name, and makes such everyday objects, this corporate history is unusually lively and engaging. The detritus of the Clarks manufacturing past is the stuff of high-street memories, the showcased clutter all warmly familiar.

The museum cabinets are stacked with historic shoes from all centuries; the upper floor looks like someone put Imelda Marcos's stair cupboard under glass. There are delicately decorated slippers and ornate high heels for the ladies, golem-footed Russian army snow boots and clumping great platform shoes called 'Steve' for the gents. This gender differentiation, it turns out, goes all the way back to Roman times. Men's sandals were nailed in no-nonsense straight rows, the women's in fancier S-shapes or with diamond patterns, an otherwise unisex item of clothing ornamented to make it his-and-hers, like the transposed buttons on gents' and ladies' shirts.

In successive cabinets you can relish the Spanish espadrille, the Moroccan goatskin babouche, the Irish pampootie, the North American moccasin, and the gorgeous Greek military slipper with its lovely pompom. Surprisingly few armies have adopted slippers as footwear (mainly because they're hard to polish until you can see your face in them, a cornerstone of military discipline) but the Greeks are so proud of theirs they show them off by marching about like John Cleese, pompoms high as you like.

Clarks shoes may never have been as uncool as the Greek army slipper, but they've come close. Nathan Clark's immortal desert boot has saved them from terminal unfashionability twice thanks to its adoption by stars of the Beat and Britpop eras. Based on the work boots bought by British soldiers in Egyptian bazaars, the boot is awarded a plinth of honour in the museum, complete with a stirring tale of one pair's uninterrupted service from 1957 to 1992. If Clarks want to find another surefire banker, they

---

* Naming their iconic school shoe 'The Commando' shows true Quaker forgiveness, considering that the Clarks factory was attacked for no good reason in 1942 by a rogue squad of British commandos who had to be fended off by the staff using broom handles.

could do worse than start making the 1979 Levi's Dude trainer again, which is voted the most wanted shoe by our visiting party. If you must pay lip service to the American training shoe, do it as confidently as these rangy, CB-era beauties, trucking down the highway with the wind in their laces.

Peppered through the museum are pedestals of fanciful footwear by eminent contemporary artists and designers such as Tracey Emin and Red or Dead. Again and again, the creators' accompanying notes pay homage to that iconic and magnificent foot gauge. That simple machine has a place in the nation's heart, and may be the best idea the company ever had. As post-war couples were reunited after six years apart and got straight down to baby-booming, cleverclogs Clarks started concentrating on their children's shoes, and key to this was their revolutionary foot gauge and its width-fitting system. The company recognised that there was vast variation in foot shape and size amongst its smallest customers, and the field was wide open for anyone who could meet the demand for almost bespoke footwear.★ You'll never lose money by telling parents their little angels deserve better. If the local branch of Peter Lord (Clarks didn't trade under their own logo in the high street until 1980) was the only shop measuring your kids' feet properly, that's where you'd go. Generations of children have had their toes pressed against that sliding metal toecap, either measured manually with straps and tape, or subjected to the talk-of-the-schoolyard robot version, which menacingly closed in on your imperilled foot like the trash compactor in *Star Wars*.

Innovation runs in the family. In 1845, John Clark invented the Eureka

---

★ In the fourteenth century, Edward I decreed one inch was equal to three dried barleycorns, and the measurement is preserved in one place: shoe sizes. A size thirteen British child's shoe is thirteen barleycorns long.

machine, an early computer that promised to rid us all of the workaday drudgery of composing Latin hexameter verses. The museum really misses a trick in leaving this gadget in storage rather than displaying it in its full glory. Otherwise, the exhibition makes clear that, deep in rural Somerset, away from the usual industrial centres, technology was constantly moving on to make our lives more comfortable. The fitted shoes we have all taken for granted since childhood thanks to the likes of Clarks are a fairly recent innovation. Two centuries ago, shoes for left and right feet were unishoes, both exactly the same shape; within living memory, if you wanted wearable footwear it was sensible to get a cobbler to whittle you a personal wooden last from which to mould a lifetime's shoes. Ever since they came up with

the Victorian slogan 'hygienic and anatomical', Clarks has mass-produced shoes that fit the ordinary man's foot like a glove.

There's something about Clarks that makes what is effectively a corporate promotional tour feel human and sweet. Perhaps it's the logo (dating from the 1930s and based on Bancroft Clark's own signature). Handwritten logos are always trustworthy: think of Wall's and their reliable promise of fine ice cream and extremely pink sausages. Or maybe it's that the company has remained true to itself; no matter how fusty or unfashionable it's become, they've weathered the storm. Clarks is the largest non-sports shoemaker in the world, and it takes some determination to resist the creeping popularity of the trainer and stick with the sensible brown shoe.

The tide may well and truly have turned on polishable leisure footwear, but the British should never surrender the idea of shoes you can't play basketball in. When everyone is in soft running pumps, something great will have been lost. One of the joys of adulthood is rediscovering the sensible, shiny, brown shoe, shorn of its associations of schoolboy smartness and playground teasing ('new shoooes … new shoo-oooes!' sung to the same tune as 'haircu-ut … hair cu-u-ut!'). When you feel that it's time to get some proper grown-up shoes, it's good to know there's a high-street shoe shop with some wall space that isn't covered in size-eight spaceships that will be in and out of fashion faster than you can tie the laces.

Clarks remains a family-owned business, producing one core recognisable product. The top job in the company was held by a Clark right up until 1986 and, despite enormous pressure, the shareholders, eighty per cent of whom are family members, have resolutely refused to play the silly expand-and-devour games of the stock market. If you're sick of finding out your gas is being supplied by some

Belgian confectionery multinational, you should applaud this rare example of a company sticking to its guns and doing one thing rather well.

Bigfoot strikes again.

The whole of Street is woven into the Clarks shoe empire: the museum is part of the town and the town is part of the museum. The old factory buildings have been transformed into one of the most pleasant shopping developments in the country, open to the sky, the sandy stone walls strewn with forget-me-nots, the only piped music coming from a carousel organ. Unlike the dreadful nowhereness of a typical shopping complex, the Clarks retail village is an organic part of its town. Springing naturally from its surroundings, paying proud tribute to its local heritage, a celebration of an uncommonly British family-run success story, the museum fits perfectly. We'll take it.

The Shoe Museum, 40 High Street, Street, Somerset, BA16 0YA
01458 842169

Dunwich

RICHARD: I mean, what is there east of Ipswich?
MR BURRILL: Only some of the most unspoilt and beautiful coastal
scenery in the country.
RICHARD: I want to go somewhere spoilt.

Michael Palin, *East of Ipswich*

Everybody loves ghost stories. Even people who don't believe in ghosts love ghost stories. Ghosts are so thrilling precisely because they're not there.

They're flutterings of the imagination, induced by memory, fear, suggestion and a chiliad other provocations, that mount an assault on our rationality. The biggest shocks are the ones that slap you round the face with the news that the world isn't how you thought it was. Dunwich, a tiny village on the Suffolk coastline, is a ghost town.

East Anglia is a suitably spooky location for Dunwich. Borley Rectory, in north Essex, was reputed to be the most haunted house in England, before it burnt to the ground in February 1939.* Raynham Hall, in Norfolk, was the scene of the most famous ghost photo ever taken – that of the Brown Lady, an eyeless apparition of Lady Dorothy Walpole (the PM's sister) dressed in muddy brocade as she drifts down the staircase.† And there's Black Shuck, a sinister hound or 'the divel in such a likenesse', which has been spotted (often during storms) all over the region, from Cromer to Basildon.

Back in the early thirteenth century, Dunwich was the sixth largest town in England. It was a busy port, with a thriving market, a guildhall, storehouses, mills, schools, shops, workshops, fish smokeries and a prison

---

* Most of the nonsense about Borley originated with four young girls who lived there, and was disseminated by a journalist and amateur magician called Harry Price who saw a profitable motive in turning it into a string of newspaper articles and a book or three …

† The negative of which, conveniently, no longer exists to prove that the photo wasn't a double-exposure or superimposition, which it obviously is.

for those of its 5,000 population who found themselves pissed and/or wrong. There were eight churches, two hospitals and even a mint. Today, Dunwich has one pub, a fish and chip shop, a handful of houses, one church, no school and a population of around 130 – none of whom is a child. So what happened? War? Disease? An over-effective bypass? None of these. Dunwich simply fell into the sea.

Plenty of bits of the British Isles have fallen in the water. There is a sunken forest off the East Sussex coast at Pett Level, washed away by a huge flood in 1287. A whopping lump of Robin's Hood Bay, in North Yorkshire, was swallowed in the late eighteenth century. Hallsands, a fishing village in Devon, was washed into the English Channel on a stormy night in January 1917. The sea draws us towards it and into it, without mentioning that it can't be held responsible for its actions.

Dunwich is far from alone in its battle against the encroaching North Sea. The whole of the East Anglian coast is at risk. Beaches are constantly washed up-shore while the Environment Agency chases the tail of the erosion with enormously costly re-shingling and fortification schemes. Currently, Dunwich is disappearing at a rate of about a metre a year, which means you can walk inland from the shore, measuring, with your paces, how long the car park, the chippy and the Ship Inn have to survive. God only knows what buildings insurance costs if you live here, let alone how and to whom you might sell your house.

These days, Dunwich survives on tourism. Rightly too – because (a) it's on borrowed time, (b) it's not about to suggest it isn't on borrowed time, (c) the pub's great and (d) the fish and chip shop is reckoned to be one of the best in Britain. The busy museum is another gem. The first thing that greets you (along with a big grin from the staff) is a model depicting the town in its heyday – a lively mediæval conurbation doing a roaring trade in fish, wool, cheese and tree resin. A dotted line across the reconstruction shows you how much of the cake was eaten before you arrived at the party. At one end of the museum's ground floor is a gorgeous sixteenth-century painted sea-chest, left in the corner as a collection box (the museum doesn't charge an entry fee). The box is the sort of piratical antiquity that might be protected under glass in an average local museum. No such stuffiness here. Dunwich understands only too well that life's too short to make a fuss about worldly goods.

A few doors coastward of the museum (at the time of writing) is the Ship Inn, a drinker of some repute. On a good day, you can eat in the garden, in the shade of a fig tree that (along with the tables and pumps and kitchen) measurably only has a few decades left. The very thought is enough to sober you up. A little further along St James Street is the one remaining church – St James's, unsurprisingly – in whose graveyard are three notable peculiarities: the tomb of Francis Robinson, made entirely of fashionable iron at the time of his death in 1843, now made entirely of rust; the leprous remains of a Norman leper chapel, its casements bursting with wallflowers in summer; and a tall buttress, the last surviving piece of All Saints' Church, eaten away piecemeal as it stood on Dunwich cliffs (a process the museum depicts in an eerie series of photographs). The buttress was moved here in 1922 and it won't be long before All Saints' makeshift headstone has to be relocated again, together with St James's.

On the edge of the village is the ruin of Greyfriars, once one of the region's most important Franciscan priories. Founded in 1228, it was all but destroyed in the gigantic storm of 1287 and rebuilt further inland. The stone and flint wall that girt the priory remained relatively intact until the 1940s when the War Department, obviously bored of waiting for the sea to get round to eating the seaward wall, flattened it to accommodate an anti-aircraft battery. Nice touch. The surviving wall and gate hint at Greyfriars' former majesty (and are a great spot for a picnic).

Down on the beach, a wooden shed dangles over the edge of the crumbling cliff, the phone line attached to its roof seemingly the only thing holding it in place. Gorse, marram grass and bracken line the cliff edge – some of it strategically planted to bind the surface together and slow down the erosion. Sand martins nest in burrows and tunnels on the cliff face. A temporary fence on the beach bears warnings to the curious and keeps them a safe distance from any potential landslides (except where the fence has been overwhelmed by landslides, of course).

Up on the cliff top, there are some great walks to be had. If you keep your eyes peeled on Lovers' Lane, the coast path between St James Street and the remains of Middlegate Street, you might spot the two remaining gravestones from All Saints' churchyard. There was a third until 1990, when (while villagers were making plans to move it to St James's) a massive cliff fall sent it thundering to the beach, to be buried under a mound of debris. The last two headstones hang on, for the time being, squirrelled away in the bushes as if playing hide-and-seek with the advancing waves. All the other coffins, caskets, urns and masonry of All Saints' have become unwilling burials at sea. Bones are frequently washed up on local beaches.

Dunwich itself will one day be dead too, its memory left to haunt the coastline. Already, legend has it that the bells of All Saints can be heard ringing in the sea during stormy nights. The approach roads are littered with spectral fragments of Dunwich's bustling past – as you drive from Westleton, there's a gate standing in scrubland, quite alone, the last remnant of a fence that used to divide two long-forgotten fields. And although it's the size of a busy little village Dunwich doesn't feel like one. It feels like the dismembered limb of a great town, the outskirts of something long gone. If it hadn't been for the hungry tide, Dunwich might now be a busy port, like Harwich or Felixstowe; in reality, it's a town that became a village that will become a beach.

For now, at least, we can still go to Dunwich for a pint and a plaice. Like the butterfly on the branch of the sequoia tree, our lifespans are too brief

for us to appreciate that the thing we're standing on is alive and changing. But here's a place you can watch a town taking a final bow, as a salty curtain slowly lowers. The coastal erosion is so swift that if it takes you two days to read this book, another five-and-a-half millimetres of Dunwich will have been surrendered to the North Sea by the time you reach the last page. The town is disappearing more than thirty-eight times as fast as your fingernails are growing. For the record, the Environment Agency, with all its

A man on the edge.

shingle-dredging and redoubling of sea walls, has given up on Dunwich; an admission that here the sea has won.* The fat lady isn't singing yet, but she's certainly warming up. Pay your respects while you can – before it's just another ghost story.

Dunwich Museum, St James Street, Dunwich, Suffolk, IP17 3EA
01728 648796

---

* 'Managed retreat' is the Whitehall term for this inevitable surrender.

Stained Glass Museum

Light (God's eldest daughter) is a principal beauty in building.
Thomas Fuller, *The Holy State and the Profane State*

From Canterbury Cathedral's twelfth-century glazing to John Piper and Patrick Reyntiens's stunning postwar work on the Baptistry Window in Coventry Cathedral, Christianity has been stained glass's best customer. At first, religious buildings only used small panes of dark red and rich blue seeded amongst lots of white because the windows were small and daylight a priority. Advances in building techniques meant larger windows, and the panels became busier with red and blue bits. Fast forward to 1300 and someone discovers how to stain glass yellow. The church is delighted, as this cracks the important problem of how to do haloes. Gothic churches start to fill to the belfries with the stuff.

You can understand why. The colour and scale of these backlit Technicolor panels demand your attention and, whatever your faith (or lack of it), they inspire awe. It's hard not to be spiritually elevated by the ghostly puddles of primary colour that ripple across the floor of church buildings. For believers, this is God's house and it requires the most beautiful windows available, expressing the divine through pure light. For everyone else, stained glass provides artistic relief from the endless masonry and something to look at during the endless sermons.

It may seem unfair that windows so beautifully ornate should be placed so tantalisingly out of view. Granted, this stops people from smearing their greasy fingers up them, but it also prevents any detailed appreciation of the artists' work. The architect Gaudi, on being asked why he lavished so much effort on designing the ornate, multicoloured pineapples and grapes that top the towers of his gloopy Temple Expiatori de la Sagrada Família in Barcelona, replied, 'because the angels will see them'. It's an architect's pre-rogative. Like Le Corbusier, Gaudi was obsessed with placing God, rather than that other red guy, in the details.

Ely Cathedral's Stained Glass Museum gives the visitor a rare chance to look some of Britain's beautiful stained glass windows in the eye. Roundels and badges, normally hidden in the rafters, are pulled down for closer inspection. The museum's gallery, which forms a long corridor along the inside of the cathedral's south triforium, features ingenious display cases shaped like flying buttresses which shield each exhibit from direct sunlight.★ The cathedral's noseless, potato-faced gargoyles stare approvingly at these suitably gothic cabinets from the opposite wall, the arches between them affording some dizzying and commanding views of the cathedral. The appropriate soundtrack is provided by the echoes of whispered voices, the tick-tocking of footsteps over flagstones far below and the occasional trill from the cathedral organ.

Seeing so much backlit stained glass is like rediscovering a lost family collection of Kodachrome slides and checking them out on a handheld viewer. Unlike photographs whose colours fade and mislead (with the exception of snaps from the 1970s when things actually *were* that orange), illuminating an image from behind projects the colours rather than reflecting them. The stained glass here is more vivid and striking than conventional paint on canvas in the same way that digital photos on a computer monitor look better than your old snapshots. Mediæval imagery leaps from the walls like a tapestry on fire.

In a regular art gallery pictures can be shifted around without much bother, but displaying stained glass poses numerous problems. Individual display cases need to be custom shaped for every piece, each mounted with its own lightbox. Even two matching pieces from the same church will display slight variations in size, so once a window is fitted into its hole, that's it. You can understand why the museum's displays are changed relatively infrequently.

Remarkably for such an immovable art form, all the stained glass here has at some point gone for a walk. None of the exhibits would be in the museum unless they had been removed from their original home for one reason or another. 'Possibly from a Suffolk church' reads one label; these pieces can wander so far from the buildings for which they were made that even identifying the county

---

★ A bridge was constructed in 1996 to transport the collection over the nave from the museum's less easily evacuated (thanks, Health and Safety) and glaringly sunlight-riddled original home on the north triforium. It took a year's careful lifting to complete the move. Spare a thought next time you lose a glass to the kitchen floor.

of origin requires a little educated guesswork. Many are lent from dioceses around the country, a handful are from the Victoria and Albert Museum and a couple are from the charming-sounding Friends of Friendless Churches – a charitable organisation obviously dedicated to putting a reassuring arm round the forgotten churches of England and Wales and giving them a mug of hot soup.

Even HM the Queen gets in on the act, lending two pieces of glass, one from Buck House and one from Windsor. The first must be from a room far enough from Her Majesty's bedchamber not to cause a royal draught, the second is a spectacular James Pearson interpretation of the famous Joshua Reynolds portrait of George III. With Ely's backlighting now illuminating this ambitious work in its full glory, it's hard to believe that when displayed around the turn of the nineteenth century it was lit only by flickering candlelight in the King's Dining Room of the fire-prone castle. Perhaps the royal family was waiting until they'd collected a whole box of stained glass relatives and a projector that could be fetched from the loft when the in-laws visited.

Given the fragility of the medium, it's surprising how much stained glass has survived. The sad truth is that churches often don't provide the safest sanctuary for stained glass. When King Henry VIII and Co. started walloping their way through the sacred casements of England during the Reformation and Dissolution of the Monasteries, it was a reminder that these precious examples of the glassmaker's art might not be all that safe lined up in come-and-smash-me fashion across the side of public buildings. Like exhibiting Marcel Duchamp's Fountain on the street outside a gallery and trusting people not to piss in it, putting art a literal stone's throw away from devil-guided idle hands is frankly asking for trouble. And if the bricks don't get the windows, the brickies will. More and more churches are becoming highly-desirable-luxury-church-conversions, and no one

wants to watch daytime TV while being scrutinised by a six-foot depiction of the epiphany of St Paul. Still, it's the decent thing to do. In the same way that a bully removes his victim's glasses and puts them delicately to one side before kicking him in the nuts, removing stained glass windows before trashing a building at least preserves some of its dignity.

Stained glass is interesting as an art form because no matter how modern the subject matter, stained glass always looks, well, like stained glass. You can adjust certain elements, playing with the position of the calmes* and thickening the glass to avoid halation between panels, but you can't tweak the formula too far. Creating art from light, colour and shape ought to be as limitless as paint and canvas, but there is a continuity amongst the exhibits here that makes it seem as if time has stopped dead. As in folk dancing or James Bond films, the traditions are ingrained and innovation in stained glass happens slowly.

It probably didn't help that the Reformation was followed by a couple of hundred years when stained glass windows were about as popular as

---

* Lead strips between glass panels. The black bits.

dropsy, long enough for most of the skills learned in the glorious heyday of the trade to be forgotten. By the eighteenth century, the craft was in such a parlous state that there was a brief fashion for classically proportioned grid windows: sections of the image painted onto the glass rectangles of the lattice, like viewing an old master painting through the bottom of a milk crate. As if that weren't clueless enough, these windows were usually painted with coloured enamel on clear glass, missing the whole point not only of stained glass but also of windows. They're endearing in a useless sort of way, but no match for the dazzling crazy-paved light shows of the Middle Ages.

The barking-mad Pre-Raphaelites in their sparkling New Camelot got it right by playing at being mediæval artisans (while enjoying the riches of modern industrial Britain, naturally). How well they relearned the lost techniques can be seen at Ely in the stunning nineteenth-century restoration of the fourteenth-century window *The Visitation*. So close is John Hardman and Co.'s replacement glass to the original, it's almost impossible to tell them apart. There's a diagram on hand to help you spot the difference. One thing the Gothic revivalists did was to iron out the bubbles and wobbles in hand-made glass, exactly the imperfections that gave life to the light shining through it. Seeking to perfectly recreate these imperfections, Arts and Crafts craftsmen learned to deliberately introduce irregularities into their glass to reproduce this forgotten effect. They got so good at it, most of the mediæval windows you see in churches today are actually Victorian.

Because of stained glass's stuttering history, taking almost four centuries to find its way back on track, and its universal adoption by the clergy, the subject matter may appear peculiarly hamstrung compared with other art forms. At Ely, apart from the odd burst of heraldry and the occasional detour into myth (Reynard the Fox in the Middle Ages, good old King Arthur for any window commissioned by a man in a stovepipe hat), it's Bible stories all the way. Biblical windows were once used as instruction for illiterate churchgoers, which makes sense, but there aren't many media that have remained so tightly tied to their original purpose. Secular stained glass tends to just look pretty, revealing its relatively modern roots in the Arts Nouveau and Deco.

This is not to say that the more recent examples at Ely aren't as gorgeous and satisfying as the older pieces; *The Prodigal Son* by Moira Forsyth is a great piece of 1930s stained glass, showing a reworking of the parable as if it had starred characters from P. G. Wodehouse, while Brian Clarke's *Peel Cottage*

The light fantastic.

Window is a particularly striking early eighties abstract. But notably, as you leave these modern pieces and complete your loop of the gallery, you pass the earliest windows in the exhibition again. They are about 800 years old and feel as if they could fit at either end of stained glass's history. The English *Geometric Grisaille* wouldn't look out of place in a modernist cathedral, while the French *Bust of a King* looks almost Picasso-esque in its execution. For something so traditional, stained glass has always looked modern, using tricks of abstraction and stylisation that artists are only just trying again today. And that's why, when so many art galleries drably chase the latest fads, the Stained Glass Museum at Ely shines out like a timeless beacon.

Stained Glass Museum, The South Triforium, Ely Cathedral, Ely,
Cambridgeshire, CB7 4BL
01353 660347
www.stainedglassmuseum.com

Under the Pier Show

'(He) took out a tooth pick, a marmalade spoon and a pair of scissors, and soon had the machine wound up and adjusted ready to start.'
Norman Hunter, *The Incredible Adventures of Professor Branestawm*

The British seaside holiday has undergone a bit of a facelift over recent years. In an attempt to lure sun worshippers away from cheap flights abroad and back to expensive old Blighty, plenty of cash has been splashed around repairing and revitalising our sea- and poverty-ravaged coastal resorts. It's essential maintenance. Not only is the conservation effort helping combat the miles of coastline disappearing from our ever-shrinking island but it's an opportunity for the planners to redefine what makes the Great British Holiday so great. Anyway, if we keep insisting on warming the planet by flying to the Med for the week, soon the Mediterranean climate will come knocking on our doors like someone we met on holiday who took our offer of 'dinner someday' seriously. Our children might even live to see glorious all-year sunshine and the kind of packed beaches beloved of John Hinde postcards.★ Let's not get carried away, though. The winning formula for Britain's coastal resort of tomorrow will have to retain three key elements to deliver the true British seaside experience: pink peppermint rock, beaches strewn with dog droppings and amusement arcades.

Quite why amusement arcades are such an important part of the British seaside is anyone's guess. Dingy gambling dens filled with the aroma of ciggies and frying circuitry, illuminated by pulsating primary colours, conversation muffled by the screams of sirens, countless seven- and seventy-year-old hands

---

★ John Hinde was the postcard manufacturer who first gave us the luminous red London Bus and oversaturated reproductions of Butlins seaside resorts. They represent the holiday that we'd like our family and friends to think we're enjoying, far away from the grey reality of two weeks' continual rain and borderline malnutrition.

pumping recently loosened change into humming electronic thieves set to the lowest pay-out setting (even the change machine), the amusements are hardly

the place to top up your tan. Still, when you're young and have absolutely no taste whatsoever, in the same way that the best pubs are the formica-tabled seaside ones where you can get a glass bottle of Coke with a blue straw (for pushing up and down and making tiny bubbles), the most desirable resorts have a seafront heaving with sticky arcades.

Southwold, whose gaily coloured beach huts command prices up to £40,000, isn't the type of seaside town to cover its carefully restored Victorian pier with dodgems and doughnut cabins. The original Southwold Pier, like so many other examples, has led a turbulent life. Since its construction in 1900, it has spent a fair proportion of its time in battered pieces on the ocean floor, thanks to the actions of war and weather. Thankfully the millennium brought a restoration project, as millennia tend to do, with friends of the pier buying memorial plaques to fund the work. These little brass nameplates (over 3,000 of them) run the entire length of the pier's handrail and reading them is a charming way to punctuate your promenade, lost in other people's unfathomable memories:

'WE FLEW OUR KITE AND LOST IT HERE'; 'DAD FISHED I FROZE'; '4 FILLIES VISITED 1960 4 NAGS RETURNED 2001'; 'LLOYD HENRY PUSHKIN A FINE SUFFOLK FARM CAT'; 'THE FORTEYS CAN NOW PIER BEYOND THE GOBBLIES'; 'VENI VIDI EMI'; 'LUCY ALICE KAREN CHOCOLATE CIDER CRAB BAIT BOLOGNESE SCRABBLE AND SCREAMING'.

The often cryptic messages record decades of fondly remembered days at Southwold, every inscription a dedication to and from the people who wanted their pier back. A community who would build a pier out of memories is going to demand a similarly light, nostalgic touch from the amusements that cover it. Sure enough, a tasteful, family-friendly arcade at the pier's mouth leads to a brasserie (gasp), municipal clock★ (the very thought) and, the jewel in the crown, a truly singular collection of homemade slot machines (swoon).

Tim Hunkin's Under the Pier Show (conveniently located on top of the pier) could be the best amusement arcade you half-remember from childhood. It's the one with the machines that none of the other arcades had; the one that dictated where you wanted to go on holiday year after year; the one that you pestered your parents to take you back to every day for two weeks. Where else in the world could you go on a whistle-stop package holiday tour in an armchair, visit Robert Maxwell on the bottom of the North Sea and have a relaxing manicure, all for less than the price of a pint and a pie?

Hunkin, the man responsible for the wonderful Rudiments of Wisdom cartoons in the *Observer*† and the equally wonderful television series *The Secret Life of Machines*, is someone with the rare ability to make complicated things look incredibly straightforward. His illustrations, although often as intricate as a spider's web, have a deceptively childlike simplicity of line that lends itself well to explaining things, as if Haynes Manuals were drawn by Purple Ronnie. While his is not a name that resides on the tip of the nation's collective tongue, for his combination of dry humour and technical savvy, if you were looking to pick an Archbishop of Whimsical Engineering, Hunkin would get the cognoscenti's vote.

With his Under the Pier Show, Hunkin gets an opportunity to translate the workings of his scribbly brain into three skewed dimensions, creating an amusement arcade with machines so out-there that they make the latest Namco, Sega and Taito arcade monsters look like dull-witted dinosaurs. A small, tastefully painted weatherboarded hut marked by an ingenious crankshaft-driven sign, the Under the Pier Show is as unassuming yet welcoming as a Morris Minor, a blessed relief from the shouty Day-Glo muscle cars of regular seaside amusements. Although every machine here is expertly crafted, they're all made by hand, from salvaged bits and pieces. They look like everything and nothing

★ Partly created by the Under the Pier Show's creator, Tim Hunkin, with Will Jackson and Jack Trevellian, Southwold's elegant sheet-metal clock features a couple of bathing gentlemen who squirt water at each other while two boys beneath them cross urine swords over a toilet.

† A series of cartoons explaining everything from photocopiers to cannibalism. They are collected in a now sadly out-of-print book entitled *Almost Everything There is to Know*, which it really is.

Under the Pier Show

The future of dog-walking.

else you've ever seen before. If you've ever had to scour the local library for guides on how to construct a Zimmer-frame simulator or fit an antimacassar-laden armchair to the frame of an old *Space Harrier* machine, you'll appreciate the problems that face Hunkin on a daily basis in his quest to push the boundaries of slot-machine design.

Hunkin's machines are the oversized cousins of those countertop boxes where a two-dimensional wooden dog nods at your ten-pence piece as it trundles down a slide towards the NSPCC, so it comes as no surprise that he manufactures elaborate charity collection boxes for hospitals and museums too. Ever since the early days of automata, people have happily parted with their money to see a mechanical show.

Hunkin's approach to arcade-game manufacture is much more inventive than the screen-and-joystick identikit-cabinet approach of most game-makers. By developing prototype machines, refining them and then moving on to the next project, usually completely different in mechanics, size and game-play, his unique arcade shines with an abundance of fresh ideas. Far from attempting to emulate the slick Las Vegasisms of most arcades, Hunkin revels in the homegrown look of his attraction. From the use of Edward Johnston's London Underground typeface in its droll signage, to the occasional nods to UK culture and minor celebrities, the Under the Pier Show is as unashamedly British as Mum's apple crumble.

We've long since tired of electronically chasing a ghost around a maze using a hungry disembodied head (how will we explain that to our grandchildren?). Hunkin has realised that it's much more fun (and in keeping with British seaside humour) to take a life-sized model dog for a television walk.* What's more, it's entertaining for onlookers who, by the end of your game, will be modelling the gleeful gurning expressions previously only seen on the family from the

---

* Rent-A-Dog, the dog-walking simulator, finishes with an on-screen credit for panting. Step forward, Colin Uttley, and take a bow-wow.

front of a box of Twister (The Game That Ties You Up In Knots). A visit to Hunkin's arcade is a social experience, the games so bizarre that the ice cracks on normal British reserve and people you've never met before come up and chat about your experiences with the machines.[★]

Though the Under the Pier Show's entertainments are often built around the bones of modern coin-operated machines, they are more closely related to the mechanical amusements of Victorian and Edwardian penny arcades. Think laughing Jolly Jack Tars, gypsy fortune-tellers and mechanical horse-racing machines and you'll have a decent idea of what to expect. For the generation raised on a diet of high-score tables and state-of-the-art graphics, Hunkin's machines could confuse and terrify. There's no real element of interaction with mass-marketed kick-fests such as Street Fighter 23, or 3D Combat Chimps; no sense of the machine being able to bite back or toe-cap you in the shins if you lose a life. Submitting yourself to one of Hunkin's beasts is akin to strapping yourself into a wooden roller coaster built by a good friend. You trust him, but you've got no idea what to expect from the ride. Moving your foot from the safety of your shoe into the slot at the bottom of 'The Chiropodist', or placing your hand blindly into the dark space under the 'Test Your Nerve' machine's salivating, red-eyed dog is not an experience for the faint-hearted or easily offended. You'll be groped, shaken and shocked by his contraptions and, unlike other amusement arcades, you'll actually come away amused.

The unstoppable march of PlayStations and Xboxes has dealt a severe blow to the arcade-game manufacturing industry. The technology available to the hordes of entertainment-satiated, daylight-dodging home gamers is almost identical to that running the latest video games in the arcades, so why waste time and money pouring fifty-pence pieces down an endless chute to replicate the same experience you can have at home for free? The trinity of comfy sofa, video football and beer may have brought the arcade industry to its electronic knees, but there's still nothing available over the counter that can quite replicate the mind-blowing experience Under the Pier.

Under the Pier Show, Southwold Pier, Southwold, Suffolk, IP18 6BN
01502 7221055
www.underthepier.com

[★] A short while after we'd left the arcade, a young couple we'd never met before ran up the pier after us waving the photo foursome they'd just received from Hunkin's 'Expressive Photobooth'. The first three photos showed the pair in various poses, labelled with appropriate captions, while the last showed the authors (who'd been in the photobooth twenty minutes earlier) with the caption, 'Reincarnated'. Only Hunkin would send you home with a souvenir of someone else's visit.

Rochdale Pioneers Museum

Keep thy shop and thy shop will keep thee.

George Chapman, *Eastward Ho*

With all the squillions of pounds made by big super-markets over the past few years, it's a wonder that the Chancellor of the Exchequer hasn't solved the country's fiscal difficulties by opening a smart grocery chain of his own called, perhaps, *Price X-Checka*. The government could copy the private sector and merrily steam-roller over any planning objections, building stores wherever they damn well liked – even in the middle of other supermarkets. The mark-up on Prime Minister's Smooth Blend™ coffee granules and HM Government Value Beans could be spent easing prison overcrowd-

Back to basics.

ing and filling the NHS with four-poster beds. Reward cards would be a thing of the past. You'd just swipe your biometric passport at the till instead. All those loyalty-card computers recording your consumption habits could be replaced by a single state-owned alternative (with a chummy name like B.E.R.T.I.E.) which, if you left

the country for a trip abroad, would instruct the National Shop stock-control system not to order quite so many packets of cheese and onion crisps in your absence. This might sound like Communism, but we could try it without the moustaches and far less marching. It could be brilliant: the British government as the biggest shopkeeper in a nation of shopkeepers.

In their own Victorian way, the twenty-eight whiskery Lancastrian craftsmen who made up the Rochdale Equitable Pioneers Society also wanted to establish a shop that would serve the community rather than take its money and run. A shop selling fair products at fair prices. And one that had its own reward system for paying its members back. Eventually the shop would get a nice logo that said 'Co-op'. And the logo would be the same colour as blue-sky thinking.

At the corner of Rochdale's Toad Lane is number thirty-one. Roughly 5,000 visitors a year come to visit what's left of the Lane (now a picturesque conservation area) and pay their respects at this modest shop (now the Rochdale Pioneers Museum). 31 Toad Lane wasn't the first co-op store, nor was it the first co-op in Rochdale. It wasn't even the first co-op in Toad Lane, yet so iconic is this shop that in 1991 Japanese co-operators built a double-sized replica of it in their home city of Kobe. The basic principles established here in 1844 remain the ground rules for the global co-operativist movement. The Co-op may be best known in the UK for their friendly-looking family of shops, banks, travel agents, funeral arrangers and insurance providers,* but their practices were revolutionary and represent a powerful way of sneaking socially responsible thinking into the marketplace

---

* Not to mention the co-operative movement's very own version of the Scouts, the Woodcraft Folk, which has quietly garnered thousands of young members, actively encouraging them to get involved in peace campaigns such as the Stop the War Coalition, something that would have horrified Baden-Powell's knee-length socks right off.

without making an absolute hippy fist of it. To look not terribly far overseas, co-operative dairies in Denmark ganged up against cheap imitations to jointly market their own butter in 1900. In 1957 their very Danish butter was rebranded, stupidly successfully, as Lurpak.

The Rochdale Pioneers Museum is as unfussy and honest as the goods it originally sold. The admission fee is so nominal that on entry you may feel humbled enough to cast away your clothes and don a hessian sack. The museum's Spartan interior is as wholesome, unpretentious and uncomplicated as a slice of brown bread. If you were hoping for the chance to strap

the kids into a gravity-defying Victorian Idealism Simulator, you're in the wrong place. What you do get for your almost-no-money is a faithful recreation of the original shop with its gigantic weighing scales and a table laden with the staple comestibles stocked on opening: sugar, butter, flour and oatmeal. From a photograph on the wall, thirteen of the twenty-eight original Pioneer shopkeepers look sternly down on these four elementary goods as if challenging you to bake anything other than a nourishing co-operative flapjack with them.

The original Pioneers weren't wealthy. They were flannel weavers and wool staplers – trades that sound quaint and charming to modern ears but would probably break the wrists of the average Human Resource Manager in minutes. What the Pioneers wanted to offer was an alternative to the exploitative 'truck shops', the factory-affiliated stores that exchanged overpriced, adulterated grocery supplies for tokens the workers were given in lieu of proper wages. Unable to afford to give up their day jobs, the Pioneers initially traded on Saturday and Monday evenings only. Within a month the frugal co-operativists had made enough money to treat themselves to a pair of curtains and some aprons. Within three months they were opening four evenings a week and all day Saturday. The Rochdale Co-op was run by and for the workers, opening when the mills and factories closed (so the shop could catch workers on the way home) and allowing the Co-op staff to fit shopwork around their own industrial dayshifts. It was a full seven years before they cracked normal opening hours.

The old storeroom forms the main body of the museum. If you found the photo of the Pioneers on the wall of the shop mildly intimidating, brace yourself for the larger-than-life blow-up of the same shot on the storeroom wall. Dressed in black suits with neckties, the frowns outweigh the smiles eleven-to-two. The Pioneers really look as if they mean business (or at least mean to start one based on sound principles). Visiting the museum is as much about experiencing the building and environment as it is about hearing the story, so it's good that the decor of the original storeroom with its black timbered ceiling and grey flagstone floor isn't swamped by the displays.

The stock that would have filled this room was paid for using weekly subscriptions collected from the twenty-eight founders. Punters were enticed to shop by the promise of dividend payouts: after any absolutely necessary deductions, members were entitled to a share of the society's profits based directly on how much they had spent there during the year. Their name and address were not added to a mass-marketed mail-out list, nor did they receive vouchers entitling them to a limited range of half-price products that had cost half as much the week before. This was a real reward for loyalty, not a strong-handed sales gimmick.

And so the 'divi' was born, with Co-op members recouping sometimes fifteen per cent of their total spend. The divi's fair distribution of wealth was revolutionary enough to win the approval of sometime Manchester resident Friedrich Engels, who signed the Rochdale Co-op's visitors' book when he popped by. The book has been on the go since 1862 and though celebrated ex-Co-op milkman Sean Connery hasn't found time to add his name yet (typical – some people become James Bond and you never hear from them again), it does bear the signatures of the Queen and the Duke of Edinburgh – so posh that they get a page each. Engels probably wouldn't have approved quite so much of that.

In time, the dividend was mostly replaced with the simpler savings-based stamp book, until this too was phased out in the early 1980s. After decades of honourable service in the nation's handbags and kitchen drawers, it seems only right that examples of this well-thumbed favourite get a display of their own in the museum (in what used to be a library and reading room for local members).* Following the demise of their iconic stamp book, the Co-op freewheeled downhill without the universal

* Who, if the fancy took them, could borrow not only books but also a microscope, zoetrope, telescope or cosmoscope.

profit-share system that had been its making, eventually losing custom to the key supermarket players and their copycat reward schemes. But in 2006 a new dividend card saw the return of at least some of the Rochdale Pioneers' revolutionary notions (though the we're-all-in-this-together 'members' had become, like everyone else in the country, merely 'customers').

Not many retailers earn their own song, but the Co-op scored a modest hit, revealing the esteem in which it was held by the country at large, when Rochdale native Gracie Fields recorded *Stop and Shop at the Co-op Shop* in 1930. Spurred on in song, the following year the Rochdale organisation made the felicitous purchase of 31 Toad Lane, which they'd outgrown (rather like Gracie's aspidistra) seventy years earlier. However, the move to greater things hadn't diminished the attachment that the clan Co-op felt for Toad Lane, the brick and mortar catalyst for such immense social upheaval, and they reopened the building as the museum later the same year.

Apart from a temporary closure for repairs in the 1970s, Toad Lane has stood fast ever since. Do stop and chat to one of the supremely enlightened wardens, Dorothy Greaves and Malcolm Price, who have taken care of the museum for thirty-five years between them. One has a dedicated Rochdale tourist information background, the other worked for the Co-op for a quarter of a century and is the British Lions rugby union team's seventeenth-highest points scorer of all time. We'll leave you to work out which is which.

The Rochdale Pioneers Museum is a small tribute to an extremely big idea. The original Pioneers' desire to take an ethical stance in a business world more accustomed to rapacious opportunists still resonates today and continues to pay its own dividends for the companies that continue their work. At a time when shoppers and suppliers alike are feeling the numbing, enervating, destructive effects of indiscriminate, inconsiderate retail expansion, the Co-op story should serve as a plucky reminder that there might be another way of doing things. When it comes to the weekly shop, don't believe the hypermarkets.

Rochdale Pioneers Museum, 31 Toad Lane, Rochdale, Lancashire, OL12 0NU
01706 524920
museum.co-op.ac.uk

Centre of Britain

Worth seeing, yes; but not worth going to see.

Samuel Johnson

Haltwhistle, in Northumberland, is a proud little town. Slipped between the Pennines and Hadrian's Wall, with the Newcastle to Carlisle railway running through it, it has lived several lives: as a centre of paint manufacture, before which it was a coal-mining town, before which it was a Norman fortification and possibly a Roman settlement. On Main Street is a converted fifteenth-century Border Reivers' pele tower, now a very fine hotel called the Centre of Britain. Here's why.

Haltwhistle sports banners advertising it as the town slap bang in Britain's heart. It came to this conclusion by finding the mid-point on the median running north to south between the Orkney Islands and Portland Bill and placing it equidistant from the east and west coasts. So far, so good. However, there's a problem with this: Haltwhistle seems to have overlooked the Shetland Islands. Factor those in and you get a different answer.

Every civilisation reaches a stage where they've built so many parthenons and bridges that the only thing left to do is pointlessly work out where their middle is. The Egyptians, the Greeks, the Vikings and the Romans all had a go, usually allowing a bit of latitude so they could proclaim the centre of their country somewhere picturesque, preferably with a commanding view. The English had a fair crack at it too, with mixed results. The village of Meriden, in Solihull, is known as the Centre of England, with a 500-year-old sandstone monument on the village green to prove it. Eleven miles south of Meriden stands the Midland Oak, a tree with an accompanying plaque commemorating its ancestor's ancestor, which was said to be at the Centre of England. George III regarded Weedon Bec, in Northamptonshire, as the Centre of England. (Mind you, this was a man who thought London was an underwater city and called his pillow Prince Octavius, so perhaps his assessment should not be regarded as definitive.)

The trouble is, calculating the centre of a country is awfully tricky. For instance, if you stand on the beach looking at the sea at low tide, the coast you're on is bigger than it is at high tide. Britain is losing East Anglia to the

sea* (having had a decent stab at recovering it). We won't even get started on plate tectonics or the polar ice caps melting. There's only so far you can go with an argument. Britain changes shape. With that in mind, how can you accurately pinpoint its centre? For that matter, what are we calling 'Britain'? Is it the mainland? Is it the mainland and its associated islands? How about British overseas territories? Add the Falklands, Montserrat or the South Sandwich Isles to the mix, and you'd probably end up in the middle of an ocean. Add all the British embassies around the world (which are treated as British territory) and you're getting close to the earth's core. The Centre of Britain is a nebulous concept. It isn't the same place twice.

Still, why let that get in the way of a good barney? Let's go with the Ordnance Survey for now. They, after all, know more about mapping than hoteliers, stonemasons or porphyric monarchs. In 2002, they were asked to calculate the exact centre point of Blighty, so they fed a gutful of information into their computer and asked it where, if Britain were a cardboard cut-out, the country would balance on a pinhead. The computer coughed up an answer. And a very muddy one, at that.

Dunsop Bridge, in the Forest of Bowland, is a pretty village, set about a well-kept green. There you'll find a post office, a babbling brook and a scattering of other postcard clichés. Step inside the phone box – the one

---

* See the chapter on Dunwich.

on the green, BT's 100,000th (installed in 1992, unveiled by Sir Ranulph Fiennes and completely unnecessary, since there's another one round the corner and has been for yonks) and you come face to face with a placard insisting you're in the nearest village to the Centre of Britain.

Hurrah. But hang on. 'Nearest village to …'? That's not the Centre of Britain, is it? It's as near as you're going to get to it and still be able to buy a bunch of flowers or be attacked by a duck, but it's not the actual, bona fide,

won't-take-no-for-an-answer Centre of Britain. That, says the OS's computer, is some four-and-a-half miles away, near the Whitendale Hanging Stones. Their very name reeks of misty antiquity – as do so many other local landmarks like Middle Knoll, Hard Hill and Wolfhole Crag. The Forest of Bowland is a place of strange happenings.

In 1652, shoemaker George Fox stitched himself into a leather suit and, packing his

lunch of dried locusts and wild honey, mounted Pendle Hill and had a vision that inspired him to found the Quaker movement. The Pendle Witches (Alice Nutter and friends – no, really), the area's most infamous locals, were hanged in 1612 for, amongst other perversities, laming a pedlar, allowing a black dog to suckle from a woman's breast and, most incriminatingly, turning milk into butter. King of the nerds J. R. R. Tolkien was smitten by the Forest of Bowland and used it as the inspiration for the aptly named Middle Earth.* The stuff of myth. And yet, the Centre of Britain proper is a clump of grass. In a peat bog. On a farm.

If you've got the legs and the boots for it, you can walk to the Centre of Britain. Local maps show you the way. Nothing marks the

---

* None or all of these exhibitions of eldritch behaviour may have something to do with the profusion of hallucinogenic Liberty Cap mushrooms that grow on Pendle Hill. The authors tried Liberty Caps once (before the things were outlawed), during a holiday in Norfolk. The evening started well, with wild muppets swinging from tree to tree and a boathouse breaking into a broad grin, but ended less fortuitously when one member of the party couldn't bring himself to finish the bowl of pasta that had started talking to him.

Britain's 100,000th phone box - why not visit them all in order?

spot (how very British) but, if you take some sort of GPS gizmo with you, you'll find it at 54°0'13.176"N, 2°32'52.278"W (grid reference SD 64188.3 56541.43, for those of you with nothing more sophisticated than a map). It's on Brennand Farm, where farmer Geoff Walker breeds award-winning Belgian Blue cows. At the time the OS made their announcement, he said he didn't anticipate the site becoming a tourist attraction because there was nothing there. He was right. This is a spot strictly for the dedicated yomping enthusiast – it's a seven-mile round trip through creeky, lavender-dotted bogland. For the truly hardcore walker, there's a forty-six-mile hike called the Journey Through the Centre of the Kingdom. But no road leads to the Centre of Britain.

When the people of Haltwhistle heard about the OS's conclusions, they were furious. In David Taylor's case, you can see why: he owns the Centre of Britain Hotel, the Centre of Britain Gallery and the Centre of Britain Laundrette (and styles himself an 'amateur centrographer' in case you've missed the point so far). He told one journalist that he found the Dunsop Bridge business 'irritating' and branded the OS's methods 'inappropriate' and 'incomprehensible'. Clearly, he's in no mood to become the proprietor of the Seventy-One Miles From the Centre of Britain Hotel, Gallery and Laundrette, no matter how many virtual cardboard models the Ordnance Survey wave at him. So, as well as being a near-inaccessible bog, the Centre of Britain is a bit of a sore point.

In September 2005, well-known corner shop Harrods bought a year's lease of the square metre of land at the Centre of Britain and gave it away as a prize in their 'Truly British' promotion.* Sadly, the lucky winner – an American lady who lives near Harrods – couldn't find the time to pay the spot a visit during her year-long stewardship of it. However, in a piece of poetic justice almost too symmetrical to believe, at the time of writing, the Centre of Britain Hotel is up for sale, and David Taylor has given first refusal to Mohamed al Fayed.

You might not think yourself hardy enough to go tabbing through difficult terrain to find yourself in what might just as well be called the Middle of Nowhere. Nonetheless, the Forest of Bowland and the surrounding Ribble Valley is thoroughly gorgeous, and well worth a sniff on that basis alone. In fact, the area comes with the highest possible recommendation: the Queen has talked about retiring here. Now, that would really piss Haltwhistle off.

---

* Which also included offers like one free Krispy Kreme doughnut when you bought a dozen – what was wrong with pork pies or bath olivers? – and the opportunity to buy a pair of Choccywoccydoodah high-heeled chocolate shoes.

Bovington Tank Museum

Walter had never seen a tank before and laughed when he did. It was like an elephant in an idiot's dream.

Bruce Robinson, *The Peculiar Memories of Thomas Penman*

The most surprising thing about the world's largest collection of tanks is that nobody planned it. It's the lazy curator's dream: objects of interest gathering together naturally in one place, an empty field of junk turning slowly into a collection in the same way a chemical solution evaporates into crystals. In 1916, the Machine Gun Corps used this unpromising patch of Dorset scrubland to try out some new trench-busting vehicles. Three years later, the vehicles were returned to the place whence they had been despatched, and left there, rusting ingloriously in a field, awaiting the scrap man. A fence was thrown round some of the more interesting models, so future designers could pick up some tips. In 1923, a visiting Rudyard Kipling suggested that these might form the basis of a tank museum, and in 1947 his dream came true.

The museum's hedge-hemmed approach road is painted either side with incongruously urban double yellow lines; Bovington is still used for army training and the implication seems to be, 'Don't park here or we'll park on you.' From the outside the Tank Museum looks rather homely, its neoclassical greenhouse portico protruding from an undistinguished aluminium shed. If it weren't for the two gun turrets making a ceremonial arch at the mouth of the car park, the museum could be mistaken for an out-of-town garden centre. The feel of Sunday afternoon pottering is helped by the pushchairs and young families trundling into the museum in the shadow of 120mm cannons, as if these armoured behemoths were nothing more than unusual lawn ornaments.

The tank has been ignored before. It took an unusually long time for the military to decide it might be handy to have a huge gun that could drive over anything and was almost impossible to stop. The godfather of the tank was probably Irish eccentric Richard Edgeworth, who in 1770 sketched plans for a 'Portable Railway and Carriage', the first set of wheels with their own road attached, effectively the ancestor of the caterpillar track.* The

Nice weather for – duck!

idea was refined by Sir George Cayley, aviation pioneer and inventor of the seat belt, who patented his own 'endless railway' in 1826. A few decades later, armoured steam tractors were deployed in the Crimean War, and in 1907 the army lashed a gun to a caterpillar-tracked farm vehicle, ran it round the block on some exercises and never ordered another. The idea of an armoured gun on caterpillar tracks was proposed, and summarily rejected, again and again: in Britain in 1899, in France in 1903, in Britain again in 1908, in Austro-Hungary in 1911, in Germany that same year and back in Britain yet again in 1912. Nobody could find a use for one.

By 1916, though, the Great War had got firmly stuck. Using artillery against an entrenched enemy churned up the ground so badly that, once you'd stopped firing, it was impossible to advance the guns over the broken terrain. The Russians toyed with giving their guns simply enormous wheels, like armoured penny-farthings, but this turned them into shooting-gallery targets; all an attacker needed to do was score a bullseye at the hub of the wheel and the vehicle fell over. The solution was to

---

* Despite being a father of twenty-two children, Edgeworth found time to try to invent the telegraph (to cheat at the races) and design a water pump that dispensed halfpennies automatically to the beggars that operated it. Typically, he stumbled upon his caterpillar-track idea while working on plans for a wall-climbing, eight-legged wooden horse.

have another look at the military equivalent of the kid picked last for football, the caterpillar-tracked tank.

The army had rejected the idea of the tank so often by now that only the navy would give it the time of day. First Lord of the Admiralty Winston Churchill set up a tank think tank, which he called the Landships Commission; to the navy, this was merely an extension of operations onto mud.* That may explain why if you climb inside one of the early tanks at Bovington, it's got a hint of the submarine about it. The name 'landships' failed to catch on, and the codename 'tank' (as in 'entirely innocent water container, nothing to see here') was the one that lasted.

Tanks are a by-product of the trench, so Bovington starts by sending you down one. You begin your tour at the makeshift table of a village hall recruiting station, where you are invited to lie about your age if you're a small visitor, and enlist for King and Country. The next door drops you straight into a shadowy maze of ditches with looped machine-gun fire crackling overhead and speakers in the benches sending mortar explosions through your underpants; only the dry, pleasant smell of a modern museum ruins the illusion. If you're a member of the X-Box First Person Shooter generation, you'll be familiar with the sensation of scurrying around a simulated trench, but don't get complacent.

Out of nowhere, the dingy safety of the dugouts is rudely smashed by a tank, its riveted trapezoid sides teetering on the crumbling lip of the battlefield above you. After the closeness of the trenches, it's just about the biggest thing you could possibly imagine: a voracious steel beast bearing down on you and the panicking German mannequins like something from Goya. The Tank Museum's trench exit may be one of the most impressive museum displays in the country, beautifully paced and full of dramatic craft. It pulls off the neat trick of making an educational point by simply shouting 'boo!' very loudly.

Maybe only the introduction of the war elephant or the siege engine would have put the wind up the average infantry soldier in the same way. Throw tanks into a conflict and the scale of the battle becomes inhuman and terrifying, dwarfing the combatants. These early tanks have the slow, inexorable, unstoppable qualities of the most enduring monsters. Think of George Romero's zombies, or Governor Schwarzenegger's Terminator

---

* Churchill cautioned, 'We must beware of needless innovations,' something he may have overlooked later in the excitement of the Second World War when he commissioned an aircraft carrier made of ice and sawdust.

lumbering out of the flames with half his face hanging off. These invulnerable slabs of relentless purpose move with the horrifying, unhurried pace of whatever it is that chases you in your nightmares. You can run, you can throw stuff at them, but they keep on coming.

It was because tanks could move forward that they became so suddenly essential. Where wheeled carriages struggled, the tank advanced. The caterpillar track spreads the tank's bulk so efficiently that the pressure exerted on soft ground by a seventy-seven-ton tank is roughly half that of a car. Tanks could bulldoze through barbed wire, roll over trenches and carry as much equipment as a whole platoon of foot soldiers. Soon, trench warfare started to seem like a really stupid idea again.

There are loads of these literally groundbreaking early tanks on display (the British alone were coming up with a new design every seven weeks), divided into 'male' and 'female' as if they've been brought in for breeding purposes. It turns out female tanks have ladylike light machine-guns, while male tanks (you guessed it) have a massive cannon. In the Great War, the boy tanks were greatly outnumbered by the girls. The Germans never really bothered trying to build a tank fleet of their own, and infantry are better engaged with machine-gun fire, so there was nobody for the boys to wave their big Freudian weapons at anyway.

All the tanks are accompanied by schoolboy-friendly Top Trumps fact boards, giving weight, armament and so on (modern tanks still in service have 'TOP SECRET' emblazoned over the top in a way guaranteed to make a certain kind of man wet himself), but reminders are everywhere of the human cost of war. Ominous bullet holes pepper the sides of the Mk II Flying Scotsman, audio reminiscences talk of tank crews poisoned by car-

bon monoxide from their own vehicles and the centre of the first hall is reserved for a Remembrance Day poppy stand.

Leaving the War To End All Wars and entering the seemingly unending hangar containing the pockmarked hulks of the next one, you may feel that same weary shrug that's audible in Neville Chamberlain's famous 1939 announcement ('consequently this country is at war with Germany'), as if he were tempted to make a slight pause at the end, sigh, and add the word 'again'. All that terrifying hardware of 1916–18 was only the beginning, the product of a mere two years of conflict; there's almost a century more to come. The size of the place is astonishing; the land belongs to the army, so the two things they've got loads of are space and tanks.

The shapes change now, skulking lower, as if ducking and hiding from each other. From now on, tanks fight tanks. The Germans planned to win this time by superior, crushing technology, and that meant ditching the pointy helmets and getting the biggest tanks the twentieth century could offer. One of only six surviving Tiger tanks in the world is on display at Bovington (so few made it through the war because their crews would destroy the cutting-edge vehicle rather than let it fall into enemy hands). The Tiger was the biggest, most powerful tank ever built. Sure, its engine caught fire and its fiddly suspension was hopeless in mud (not great, that, for a tank), but when one appeared round a corner, it scared the living daylights out of people. The Germans loved this idea and began commissioning bigger and bigger tanks just for the hell of it. In 1942, they even drew up plans for the Maus, a vain and idiotic 200-ton supertank, which would have collapsed bridges, sunk in water and crawled across the battlefield like a huge snail with 'shoot me' painted on its shell. Utterly impractical, the plans were most likely leaked just to give Allied soldiers the unnerving idea that, somewhere out there, Hitler might be pootling about in a tank the size of a house.

Tanks are meant to be scary. Even the Tiger would blanch to its stripes at the armour and armament of some of the examples in the later halls, with their garish warpaint and gung-ho custom paint jobs (the Yanks are the worst offenders, calling theirs reassuringly adult things like 'Trigger Happy' and 'Hothead'). It is pleasantly bizarre to watch smiling family groups sauntering about. Almost 300 tanks are arrayed in safe lines, neutered and tamed like tyrannosaur skeletons, killers reinvented as museum exhibits. Children dash to and fro, mums and dads wheel baby buggies between the armoured flanks, spending an afternoon in a hall of broken Daleks. Normally you'd run from a tank, but the gift shop has toy Shermans for little boys of all ages (incongruously racked next to soft King Charles Spaniels for the girls) and for £3 a person you can take tank rides through the Bovington dust all through August.

The museum commemorates industrial ingenuity, technical expertise and the bravery of countless tank crews with a truly impressive collection of vintage and modern hardware. What's more it provides some genuine food for thought. The journey a visitor makes from the simulated dirt of the trench to the crisp technology of the present day is a sobering reminder that the invention of the tank was part of the mutation of warfare from something done at the point of a bayonet to something done at the end of a remote missile guidance camera. These developments protect and insulate troops from one another, rolling over less technologically advanced soldiers (and whoever else is in the way). In this sense, the tank can be seen as one British idea that destroyed another. Created out of necessity, it set off down a road that would lead to the dehumanisation of combat, blasting a huge hole in the precious British idea of the lone gentleman soldier.

Just outside Bovington camp is Clouds Hill, the cottage home of T. E. Lawrence. Lawrence served here briefly in the 1920s, adopting a false name and lowly rank as a way of escaping the annoying burden of being a British icon.* The mythical Lawrence of Arabia persona that so got on his nerves is one of those lantern-jawed types – Richard Hannay, say, or James Bond – that we love to think represents us at our best. These are chaps who can solve the world's crises single-handed, face to face, with fist, swagger and pistol. They very rarely feel the need to roll up in a tank. Yet the bigger the machinery gets, the harder it is to look your enemy in the eye and give him a dizzying sock to the jaw. Come to Bovington and see the machines that killed off Biggles.

The Tank Museum, Bovington, Dorset, BH20 6JG
01929 405096
www.tankmuseum.co.uk

---

* He had been ejected from the RAF when they rumbled 'Aircraftman Ross'; he hid at Bovington as 'T. E. Shaw' of the Tank Corps. When Lawrence later returned to the RAF as '338171 Aircraftman Shaw', Noel Coward teased him by sending him a letter beginning, 'Dear 338171 (May I call you 338?)'.

Bramah Museum of Tea and Coffee

Look here, Steward, if this is coffee, I want tea; but if this is tea, then I wish for coffee.

Punch, vol.123 (1904)

Right, first things first. Let's have a nice cup of tea. And let's make it properly. A teabag in a filthy mug won't do. A proper cup of tea, says Edward Bramah – the horse's mouth of the cup of tea world and eponymous proprietor of the Museum of Tea and Coffee – is made thus:

Ingredients

Freshly drawn water
A kettle
A correctly sized teapot (with a grille at the base of the spout)
A teaspoon
Good-quality orthodox tea (one teaspoonful per person plus one for the pot)
A tea cosy
A tea timer
A tea strainer
Room-temperature whole milk
A slop bowl

Method

Bring a kettle of freshly drawn water to the boil. (Not water that's been sitting in the kettle since yesterday, and not water that's already been boiled.) When the water is near the boil, tip some of it into the teapot, swirl it around and empty it away. Put the correct number of teaspoons of orthodox tea into the pot (and not CTC tea – of which more later

– which is what you'll get if you buy most branded teas*). As soon as the kettle is boiled, pour the water onto the tea leaves. Stir gently for a few moments, put the lid on, cover with a tea cosy and allow to infuse for five minutes. (This is where your tea timer comes into play.) Pour the room-temperature whole milk (about one and a half tablespoons per cup) first. (Not milk from the fridge, nor skimmed or semi-skimmed milk, because there isn't enough butterfat in either to bring out the flavour of the tea.) After infusion, pour the tea into each cup via a mesh tea strainer. After the first pouring, add more boiled water to the teapot to draw further flavour from the leaves for the second round. Always discard any dregs from cups into a slop bowl before pouring a fresh cup.*

Tea, you see, is a serious business. And for those of us who blearily dunk our shrivelled bags in boiling water every morning, there's plenty to learn at the Bramah Museum. Edward Bramah had the idea for the project in 1952 and, in keeping with a man who knows that it takes time to do certain things (like brew a pot of tea) properly, opened the museum a mere forty years later. He'd been smitten with all things tea and coffee since his days working on a Nyasaland tea plantation (where he trained as a tea taster) and later, in Kenya, as a coffee broker. The Tea and Coffee Museum is the product of decades of experience, knowledge and enthusiasm. The public face of the museum, a saucer's throw from London Bridge,

---

* Typhoo, for instance, or PG Tips. Typhoo (from the Chinese, 'dai-fu', meaning 'doctor') was the brainchild of William Sumner, author of *A Popular Treatise on Tea*. PG Tips was branded as Brooke Bond Digestive Tea until it became illegal to link tea-drinking with good digestion. Digestive (as it was colloquially known) therefore became the ungainly Pre-Gest-Tee (cannily implying that drinking it was good for digestion, without explicitly linking the two) before Brooke Bond came to their senses and adopted the abbreviation their salesmen used: PG. The word 'tea' also originated in China, as 'tu', 'she' and 'jia' (depending on dialect), of which 'tu' became 'tea' and 'jia' became 'cha'.

is a gentle salmon-pink tearoom. A pianist noodles away in the corner. It's enormously civilised and very British.

Tea originated in China over 1,000 years ago. Legend has it that the plants sprouted from the spot where Dharuma, a monk who kept nodding off during prayers, punished himself by cutting off his eyelids and dropping them to the ground – more bother to get a cup of tea than even Edward Bramah would be prepared to consider. The drink gained popularity in Britain during the mid-seventeenth century thanks to London's Leisure Gardens – open spaces where mothers and children could walk, play and

generally avoid the sludge and debris of the rebuilding work following the Great Fire. London's recently plague-ravaged population lapped up both the gardens' healthy atmosphere and the medicinal Chinese drink made from boiled (and therefore plague-free) water that was sold there.

In no time at all, tea became a Great British Institution, infiltrating all strata of society and giving its name to tea dances, tea towels, tea rooms, tea roses, tea ladies, tea courts and tea gowns; it even marked out the day, like an alternative clock, with its tea breaks, afternoon tea and high tea. This drink has made such a huge impact on our little island, yet one can still be startled by the range of teas available. You enter the museum along a corridor of open tea crates full of fragrant tea leaves: Jasmine, Gunpowder, Green, Oolong, Earl Grey. If you've ever felt the need to make a really big pot of tea, this is the place. And you could do exactly that since, just round the corner, amongst displays of Victorian teacups complete with glorious moustache protectors, is the world's biggest teapot. Commissioned by Bramah from Master Potter Alan Caiger-Smith, its 240-pint capacity is enough to brew 800 cups of tea (i.e. 801 teaspoons of tea: remember – one for the pot), but pouring the first cup would probably break your arms.

You'll also discover the hideous truth about the abomination that is the teabag.★ Orthodox tea (see recipe above) is the real thing and features the tips, or bud and top two leaves of the tea plant, picked, dried and rolled

---

★ Tony Benn's aunt sent him a pair of scissors so he could open his teabags.

in a circular drum. Teabags, on the other hand, contain coarse lower-grade leaves that have been through a large mangle, crushing, tearing and curling them – the so-called CTC process. A teabag can do its botched job in hot water in thirty to fifty seconds; orthodox leaves, with their subtleties of flavour, need around five minutes' infusion. Bramah admits that teabags aren't his cup of tea and, after sampling a proper cuppa in the tearoom, you'll agree. Teabags are the ready-meals of the hot-beverage world.

But tea, bagged or straight up, is only half the story at Bramah's marvellous museum. Midway, its shelves swap leaves for beans, china cups for espresso mugs and teapots for coffee-makers to reveal the owner's second great passion: coffee. Perhaps surprisingly, coffee's arrival in Britain predates that of tea, with London's first coffee house, Pasqua Rosee's Head, opening in London's financial district in 1652 and starting a trend that percolated across the City. Brokers and traders began to gather in coffee houses to discuss deals away from the bustle of the Royal Exchange. Eventually work would catch up with them; Edward Lloyd's Coffee House, a popular haunt of sailors, merchants and ship owners, became Lloyd's of London, and Jonathan's Coffee House, in Change Alley, became the London Stock Exchange. Others did less well: William Hogarth's father opened a Latin-speaking coffee house, a roaring failure (or *ingens deficio*) which landed him in debtors' prison.

But the Great British Cuppa stole a march on coffee, and reigned supreme until the Second World War, when the Blitz stopped the London tea auctions and the nation's drink of choice was rationed. Then, in 1952, just as the auctions resumed, the first espresso bar opened in Soho. The sleek chromium curves of the coffee machine (there are plenty in the museum – some designed by Bramah himself) stood for all that was new and shiny and exciting.★ In the age of the atom-ball clock, fibreglass furniture and the Skylon, coffee acquired a modern, continental cachet that made the familiar pot of tea look decidedly long in the spout.

★ Making a decent espresso is even more technical than making a decent pot of tea. Two tablespoons of 89° high-mineral-content water must be forced through 7g of finely ground coffee at a pressure of 9 bars for exactly 25 seconds. Probably easier to pop into a coffee shop then.

Mr Tea.

When commercial television arrived in Britain in 1955, the advertisement breaks seemed like a good opportunity to make tea – except that they weren't quite long enough. The makers of instant coffee plunged into the gap in the market. Until then, there had been no fashion for instant coffee at all (a) because it was as impossible a space-age notion as deodorant, margarine or fish fingers and (b) because it was crap.* Still, Britain fell for it, hook, line and Gareth Hunt, and sales of tea fell into the decline in which they remain to this day. The last tea auction in London took place in 1998. Naturally, Edward Bramah was there, marking the end of 319 years' history.

Bramah is the guardian of the traditions of our traditional drinks. Without the common-sense advice you can pick up at his museum, you might be fooled into thinking the most important thing about tea or coffee isn't where it comes from or how it tastes but that you can get it made before the adverts finish and the programme comes back on. Or would you rather take your tea-making tips from the government, whose homely advice comes in the form of BS 6008/ISO 3103, 'Method for Preparation of a Liquor of Tea for Use in Sensory Tests'? Complete with a helpful diagram of a teapot, this cracking read includes such memorable titbits as 'Weigh, to an accuracy of ± 2%, a mass of tea corresponding to 2g of tea per 100ml of liquor (i.e. 5.6 ± 0.1g of tea for the large pot or 2.8 ± 0.05g for the small pot described in the Annex) and transfer it to the pot (fig 5.1).' What's more, it suggests adding the milk after the tea. The very idea. Tsk.

We must remain vigilant. It's important. Coffee is the second most traded commodity in the world, after oil. Tea is still the planet's second most consumed beverage

---

* This opinion isn't universal: in some parts of South America, it's seen as a mark of sophistication. Even the most expensive hotels will proudly present your table with a jug of hot water and a jar of labelled instant coffee.

(after water, and not C★★★-C★★★, you'll be relieved to learn) although it's not the Brits who are the largest per capita consumers of tea, but the Irish. And while the British have all but abandoned the pleasant ritual of afternoon tea, wealthy Americans have picked up the idea and made it a fashionable institution. Sad, then, that we haven't reacquainted ourselves with decent tea, because it's far superior to the shagged-and-bagged type. The V&A used to style itself 'an ace caff with a nice museum attached'. The Bramah Museum of Tea and Coffee could happily borrow their slogan.

The Bramah Museum of Tea and Coffee, 40 Southwark Street, London, SE1 1UN
02074 035650
www.bramahmuseum.co.uk

Bramah Museum of Tea and Coffee

National Gas Museum

My Lord, I had forgot the fart.

Queen Elizabeth I

Put your hand over the word 'gas'* in the title of this chapter and, without peeking, see if you can answer this question. What do the following everyday household items have in common: trouser press, photo enlarger, waffle-maker, magic lantern and samovar? That's right. All of them can be powered by gas. In fact, gas is so integral to modern life that, like a clean water supply, it's hard to imagine life without it. But how many of us know our Town Gas from our Natural Gas from our Classical Gas? Gas probably barely crosses your mind until it pops out of your cooker to heat a pie or blows the house on the end of your street 300 feet into the air. So, carefully remove all cigarettes, extinguish any polyester undergarments and take a journey of gaseous discovery to the National Gas Museum in Leicester.

The Gas Museum's extensive collection lives in the gatehouse to Leicester's old Aylestone Road gas works. It's an impressive building with a *Trumpton* town-hall clock rising high above it, telling the correct time for Leicester (thanks to a successful restoration campaign spearheaded by the museum's curator, Maurice Martin). When the works behind the gatehouse closed, the Leicester branch of British Gas moved in and expanded to fill the available space, converting it into their regional headquarters.

The privatisation of the gas industry in the mid-1980s spelled the end of the British Gas Corporation and the twelve regional gas boards that served the nation. A few of these had museums attached to their headquarters

---

* The word 'gas' was coined in the seventeenth century by physicist Jan Baptist Van Helmont, who was trying to say the Greek word 'chaos' (meaning 'formless void') but found his Dutchness got in the way.

that, probably because they couldn't be sold abroad at a profit, were shut down. Leicester's Gas Museum escaped the cull and received the cream of their exhibits as the other museums closed. This is the reason the shop sells merchandise branded for long-defunct institutions from all over the country. Why not pick up an East London Gas Museum tea towel, mug and oven glove set featuring the nifty Mr Therm?* Your kitchen will thank you. When a Monopolies and Mergers inquiry into British Gas in the early 1990s concluded that the company's regulatory structure was 'rather complex', they had no idea how much worse it was about to get. British Gas has since split and split again, sprouting new companies, shedding old ones and generally making a bit of a mess, as is usually the case with gas explosions. If it makes it any clearer (which it won't) the three companies responsible for your gas supply are: BG Group (who were previously named BG plc, although that was before they split into BG Group and Lattice

(now part of National Grid plc (previously known as TransCo plc))); National Grid Gas plc (previously TransCo plc (you know, that Lattice lot formed from the BG split – see the bit on BG Group a few brackets back)); and finally Centrica plc (who sometimes trade under the identity British Gas (seeing as the name was up for grabs in Britain, although they can't use it abroad – BG Group have the overseas rights to the trade name British Gas)). Oh, and Scottish Gas in Scotland. Got that? The upshot is that now, when the gasman cometh, it's hard to work out from where.

Thankfully, the Gas Museum is much better laid out than its sprawling parent companies, and gas history turns out to be rich with cultural and social titbits. Domestic cooking, heating and lighting were the gifts of gas

---

* Mr Therm was the chirpy flame-headed character created in the 1930s for the Gas, Light and Coke Company by the talented British illustrator Eric Fraser.

long before electricity got a look in.* When curator Martin demonstrates some early gas lamps, you can't help but recoil slightly; it's a naked flame, spouting straight from the wall: the equivalent of lighting your home by leaving the gas hob on. Of course, in the days before central heating, the heat from a gas jet lamp would be quite welcome in a breezy sitting room. A conventional light bulb, by the way, uses ninety per cent of its energy making itself nice and toasty, and no one sits around enjoying that, so all the heat goes completely to waste. Who's the energy weirdo now?

Gas lighting allowed people to enjoy the night fully for the first time, either sitting at home reading, or walking the streets without being set upon every fifty yards by shadowy brigands. A century of gas lighting

National Gas Museum

ended with the arrival of the upstart new spiky-haired kid in town: electricity. Gas responded by moving into other areas such as heating and cooking. Domestic ovens had previously burned wood, so encouraging people to take up the strange new method required some tricksy thinking. The Carlton New World Series 2 Range, for example, combined the old and the new ovens: a gas outlet right next to the flames of a solid-fuel stove. The museum doesn't say how many New World users made it as far as dinner without losing their eyebrows.

---

* William Murdoch is the man credited with inventing gas lighting. He walked from Scotland to Birmingham in 1777 to seek employment with the engineers Boulton and Watt. It is said that Boulton, fascinated by Murdoch's hand-lathed oval wooden hat, offered him a job on the spot.

The museum is full of similarly odd but homely equipment. When fresh new Natural Gas from the North Sea replaced smoky old coal-derived Town Gas (which took twice as much energy to cook the same sausage), a startlingly thorough ten-year amnesty saw Gas Board engineers visiting every house in the UK to offer their occupants appliances that worked with the new supply. The Hobson's Choice changeover was so vital (do you want gas or not?) that eventually the boards were giving away gas-powered cookers, fires and hair tongs for next to nothing. The vanloads of redundant appliances the gas men took in exchange formed the basis of the nation's gas museum collections, a lot of which ended up here in Leicester.★ The museum's row of round-cornered cream and avocado gas cookers is the stuff of Doris Day-dreams, while the wood-framed Flavel Debonair, the legendary gas fire that warmed the extremities of post-war Britain and became the ornamented focal point of a million granny flats, adds a domestic rosy glow to its display.

A smashing Meccano model of one of the British landscape's trademark gas holders preserves an everyday sight that will soon vanish from our skylines now that excess gas is kept in coiled rural underground pipes. If you've ever wondered how a telescopic tin is able to store something as slippery as gas, the answer is annoyingly obvious (cherished childhood theories crumble; it's not down to a big balloon inside after all, but a clever water seal between the sections of the cylinder). It's a pity that these metal monsters are gradually being phased out, as there was something rather comforting about the slow rise and fall of the gas holder. Compared to wind farms (slightly menacing), electricity pylons (menacing) and nuclear power stations (terrifying), these tubby giants seem positively charming; like an elegant network of Victorian pistons that once powered Great Britain.

Downstairs, displays concentrate on the gas basics: history, manufacture and supply, plus the applications we know and love (lighting, cooking and heating). Upstairs, the gas memorabilia gets wonkier, a joyous assortment of technological dead-ends, most rendered redundant when electricity took over as the utility of choice for running household gadgets. It's here you'll

---

★ The stuff that wouldn't fit ended up as part of the Science Museum's overspill in huge aircraft hangars in Wroughton, near Swindon.

find gas-powered radios, ACME gas mangles and gas-driven washing machines. There's also a small selection of gas irons and a copy of the iron collector's magazine *Pressing Matters* for you to flick through (just don't curl the corners).

Also here are two push buttons. Though the interactive button is almost never a good idea, this pair is perfectly justifiable. The first button summons up a short 1975 British Gas film featuring the debut of Nicholas Spargo and Kenneth Williams's much-loved Willo the Wisp character, originally designed to pimp North Sea Gas. The second is arguably the most important button in Britain (after the one that launches Trident). It bears the simple label, 'TOUCH HERE to hear the "Ascot Water Heater Song" '.* Bring your dancing shoes.

The Gas Museum is a fascinating tour around a power source whose popularity will eventually lead to its extinction. Although the discovery of North Sea Gas on Britain's doorstep in the 1960s looked to herald an exciting era of self-sufficiency, the trade of these same gas reserves on the open market left Britain's supplies shockingly low. It's estimated that by the year 2020 Britain will be forced to import ninety per cent of its gas from overseas. And since natural gas is a fossil fuel, even these supplies will be gone before we know it, vanishing as fast as Britain's gas museums.

There was a futuristic coal board TV advert in the early 1980s that showed a Not-Quite-Darth-Vader character who, after a hard day exploring space and dodging George Lucas's copyright lawyers, returned home to a roaring coal fire. The advert proclaimed coal to be 'the fuel of today that won't run out tomorrow' with enough in the ground to last another 300 years. They didn't point out that when UnDarth had emptied the last lump from his coal bunker, it'd take another few hundred million years of geological process before the next supply was ready.

National Gas Museum, 195 Aylestone Road, Leicester, LE2 7QH
01162 503190
www.gasmuseum.co.uk

---

* Seriously, you really do need to hear this at least five or sixty times. Performed by Henry Hall and his Orchestra (of "Teddy Bears' Picnic" fame) it features the unforgettable opening lines, 'Happy in the morning / 'cause the water's hot / he can bath an army / the Ascot does the lot.' We only stopped pushing the button when the museum closed for the night.

National Gas Museum

Partick Thistle Stadium Tour

ERIC: Now, may the best team win.
ALBION CAPTAIN: Why?

Jack Rosenthal, *Another Sunday and Sweet FA*

If James I had any say in the matter then this attraction would be a car park. James – several kings of Scotland before Idi Amin claimed the title as his own – ruined the exciting 1423/4 football season by deciding that, 'Na man play at the futeball under the pain of fiftie schillings.' James I – Football 0. To be fair to the auld killjoy, the fifteenth-century version of the game was little more than a couple of neighbouring villages using a few inflated animal bladders as an excuse for punching the hell out of each other, but it gradually dawned on football that in order to survive the next 600 years, it would have to play the long game. Fortunately, it eventually learned to behave itself so well that current Scottish king HM the Queen even watches the occasional match (listing amongst her hobbies presenting World Cup trophies to that nice Bobby Moore).★

In Maryhill, north-west of Glasgow, there nestles a modest ground, quietly hosting a descendant of that unruly village game, just a few miles away from the Ibrox and Celtic Park stadia where the city's top teams, Rangers and Celtic, stare furiously at each other. While Glasgow's battling behemoths have faced a long struggle to quell sectarian enmity between some of their supporters, this Maryhill club has never been seen as either Protestant or Catholic. Firhill Stadium, guided tours of which are available by

---

★ Forthcoming Scottish king the current Prince of Wales appears to favour polo over football, although he has so far not proposed a ban on the latter. Forthcoming heir apparent Prince William is President of the English Football Association, so we can safely assume that, when he eventually ascends the throne, he won't be declaring the beautiful game illegal either (despite being an Aston Villa fan).

arrangement, is home to Partick Thistle, a team in the somewhat unglamorous second tier of the Scottish League system at the time of writing.

A Glasgow district a little way from Maryhill, Partick was the birthplace of Thistle, a club that has survived to a grand age where its immediate predecessor Partick FC couldn't, and where the fragrant Partick Violet FC just faded away. Formed in 1876, Thistle's earliest games were played on the site of what is now the city's Kelvingrove Art Gallery and Museum. After that, they drifted around the area for a few precarious years, their longest-standing home (a prime spot on the bonnie banks of the Clyde) becoming unsuitable for football when a dirty great shipyard was built all over it.

In 1909, Maryhill welcomed Partick Thistle with open arms (and an open rent book, since the club was unable to afford the price of the stadium outright). It was rumoured that the club was to be renamed Maryhill Thistle but the name stayed, preserving the Partick locals' claim on their estranged team. The first game pencilled in for the new ground was to be against Scotland's pre-eminent team of the era, Queen's Park, but an

inspector sent by the Master of Works wouldn't let anyone near a ball with the terracing still unfinished – an impeccable example of Edwardian Health and Safety.* The first game played at the Firhill ground (v Dumbarton Harp) eventually took place a week later.

Robert Reid, honorary club vice-president, PTFC historian and your genial Firhill tour guide, isn't old enough to have seen that first match but he has witnessed many of the ups, the downs and the frequent standing stills of the Jags, as Thistle are affectionately known to their fans. Imaginative nick-

---

* Once Glasgow's first team, now its fourth, Queen's Park flutters around the lowest divisions and is the nation's sole remaining wholly amateur league side, pulling in a crowd of 400 to 1,000. Their home is Hampden Park, Scotland's national stadium, which is capable of holding up to 52,000 people. That must be quite some echo.

names always make a side decidedly more appealing. 'Come on, you Reds!' (well done, Man United) or 'Come on, the Blues!' (what a clever Chelsea you are) are blandly uninspiring battle cries in comparison with 'Come away, the Jags!'. All the money in the world can't buy you imagination.

The Partick Thistle tour can be booked via the club's refreshingly straightforward website, free from strobing pop-up ads for subscription-only club news broadband TV channels, which appears to have hermetically sealed itself from the vulgarities of the modern game (particularly the web-design company single-handedly responsible for homogenising almost every other British football club website).★ And it's one of less than a handful of clubs thoughtful enough to mention that tours of the ground are available at all. Plus you've got to admire their kit – hoops are always cool, especially red and yellow hoops.

Reid will cheerfully tell you how those colours came about, explain why there's a ballet shoe in the boardroom display cabinet and reel off the side that beat Rangers to lift the Scottish Cup of 1921 with the rhythm of an accomplished poet. Thistle have only won Scotland's top cup competition on that single occasion. A brief but successful campaign in 1928's maverick one-off Glasgow Dental Cup (held to commemorate the opening of the local tooth hospital) had to suffice until their next and only other major triumph when, exactly half a century later, they defeated other local juggernaut Celtic to take the Scottish League Cup against all expectations.

Soon-to-be Thistle defender Alan Hansen was just too wee to play in that 1971 cup-winning side, although

Football booty.

★ The authors visited far too many football club websites in search of the ideal stadium to tour and they aren't even that bothered about football. They number one Fulham supporter who hasn't seen them play for several years and three half-arsed England fans who get a bit fizzy biennially. Their favourite footballing moment occurred during a wintry trip to Whitley Bay FC when it was so blustery that a goal kick arced straight back over the keeper's head, thus gifting a corner to the opposition. Result.

his elder brother wasn't. Hansen minor went on to demonstrate his later infamous *Match of the Day* soundbite that one doesn't win anything with kids by not winning anything with Thistle as a kid, then winning everything with Liverpool as an adult. One of Hansen's predecessors at the club was also Anfield-bound – the legendary Bill Shankly, who started his career with the exquisitely christened Glenbuck Cherrypickers. The future Liverpool manager was stationed at nearby RAF Bishopbriggs, turning out for Thistle as a guest player – a common practice during the war years for footballing servicemen posted too far away from their own clubs.

Although only a handful of household names have played for Thistle, there have been plenty of memorable characters, especially between the wars. Peter McKennan, a fearsome player known to his teammates as Ma Ba (after his constant in-game shout which translates from the original Glaswegian as 'my ball'), tried to put opposing sides off their game by telling them that they'd got the football upside-down. And keeper Johnnie Jackson once got so bored when Partick were winning by a five-goal margin that he was seen to sit down in his own goalmouth and start eating the grass.

The Partick Thistle Stadium tour sweeps you comprehensively around the boardroom, treatment and dressing rooms, match official areas, even the laundry. There is, however, nothing to quite match the moment when you finally get to walk out of the players' tunnel and onto the pitch. Whether you're interested in football or not, your pulse will bop a little faster, the exhilaration only slightly tempered by a twinge of disappointment that nobody managed to arrange a full house to cheer and applaud your very presence. Regardless of the size of pitch you're hovering on, it's always thrilling to close your eyes and imagine that you're about to wow a record crowd with your not-very-silky passing skills and some impressive two-left-foot-work. When you open your eyes again, your audience is likely to number no more than a couple of groundstaff and any students peering down from the windows of the flats built smack behind Firhill's north end, but it's a magnificent moment of indulgence.

Sadly you can't do the stadium tour and a match on the same day (unless you're shelling out for one of the hospitality packages) but watching a team like Partick Thistle play is an uncommonly British day out in itself.[*] The hopeful hoofing of lower-league games can induce more stress than fun, but the simple pleasures of attending a match can be found in the peripherals. A meat and potato pie with a squeaky white cup of Bovril is a non-negotiable essential and the Thistle programme is an elegant add-on, its tasteful deco design inspired by the work of local-boy-done-very-good Charles Rennie Mackintosh.

A mere decade ago Thistle were on the verge of having their ball kicked away permanently, only to be saved by many safe pairs of hands in the shape of the seriously impressive fundraising supporters' group Save the Jags. With short-term survival assured, Save the Jags blossomed into the Jags Trust, a body that now represents the fans' interest and, unusually for the sport, has gained them a seat and a voice on the Thistle board. With the salivating ghoul of financial disaster nowadays lurking on the heels of all but the very richest British clubs, Thistle can take solace in that they have always bounced back from their unfair share of money woes. Football is football wherever it's played, but the consequences of failure could be far more dire for the fans at Firhill than for those parking their spoilt arses at posh grounds like Stamford Bridge. When a club like Partick Thistle needs your support it's a case of never mind the quality, feel the passion.

Partick Thistle FC, Firhill Stadium, 80 Firhill Road, Glasgow, G20 7AL
01415 791971
ptfc.co.uk

---

[*] The authors were in Glasgow long enough to see Thistle get mashed 6–0 by Gretna on a bright September afternoon. (Attendance 2,395, plus four.)

Whipsnade Tree Cathedral

My soul into the boughs doth glide.

Andrew Marvell, *The Garden*

Whipsnade Tree Cathedral, an open-air church made out of countryside and fresh air, is awe-inspiring. It has everything in the right place, the nave, transepts, chancel, cloisters and chapels sketched in with borders of bushes and trees. Whispering is still de rigueur within its viri-descent walls, but don't expect the typical church echo; your muttering will ascend straight to Heaven. And with all respect to Michelangelo, that fussy old Giacomo of all trades, Whipsnade does have the best church ceiling in Creation.

The architect of this sacred grove was Edmund Blyth, a veteran of the First World War. His close pals Arthur Bailey and John Bennett failed to return from the conflict, but infantryman Blyth survived with his haunted soldier's memory intact. The death of another friend, Francis Holland, in a car crash in Canada twelve years later was the final piece of the inspirational jigsaw; Blyth became a kind of Father Nature, creating a man-made memorial to his three fallen comrades on the land of his Chapel Farm.

Churches are alive with the murmur of death. Stained glass martyrs gaze down on ancient tombstones, decorated with tortured crosses. We mark our remembrance with gardens and floral tributes, strewing wreaths and poppies on graves and monuments, planting saplings in memory. A tree church is therefore an elegant and fitting way to commemorate the departed. What's more, it grows its own flowers, so the decorative assistance of the ladies of the Flower Guild is not required.

Blyth was first overcome by the urge to grow his own cathedral in 1930. He and his wife had taken a rest break by the side of the road while return-

ing from a trip to see the construction of Giles Gilbert Scott's Liverpool Cathedral.* Watching the sun setting through the Cotswold trees, an idea took hold and, as soon as he got home, Blyth set to work. (Good job they didn't stop at a motorway service station or this could all have become rather ugly.) His tree cathedral was almost completed by the outbreak of the Second World War and, having avoided a Coventry-style flattening while Blyth was off making his second foray into Europe, work on the overgrowth resumed immediately on his return.

The tree cathedral is a beautifully contemplative and tranquil place. There is no suggestion that the hubbub of Whipsnade Wild Animal Park is less than a mile away, the roaring of hippos and the sweet song of the zebras muffled by the cathedral's planted walls. The natural architecture of the cathedral tips a respectful mitre to ancient ideas of the cyclical year, and the experience will vary according to when you visit.† Sun-baked grass crunches underfoot; fresh morning dew is kicked up; angry clouds scud

---

* It's a pity that Scott's other designs have failed to inspire similar interpretations, depriving us of a tree Tate Modern, fir phone boxes and a bush Battersea Power Station.

† We visited early on a weekday morning and the only other people there were a couple walking their dog. A simple wordless hello was nodded and even the dog kept its yap shut.

overhead; a drybrushed sky yawns coolly down. This is a cathedral for all seasons.

In fact, at the suggestion of Blyth's wife Whipsnade Tree Cathedral has a chapel dedicated to each one. Autumn's harvest festival could happily be held in the Lady Chapel, whose evergreen cedar leaves remain as others grow bare. Winter is celebrated by the Christmas Chapel, and spring by the Easter Chapel. The tree cathedral provides a Summer Chapel just in case, but the Christian church doesn't make much fuss about midsummer any more, usually marking the solstice with a coconut shy and a guess-the-weight-of-the-cake competition (if left to celebrate the summer solstice by building a henge, the C of E would have made it from trestle tables).

Walking down the aisle.

Standards of religious architecture have fallen sharply; building cathedrals just seems to take too damn long for our attention spans. There's no appreciation of eternity any more. Nature will never fail to be impressive, however, and a tree cathedral can come together in less time than a brick or stone cathedral takes to design, construct and get retrospective planning approval for. The Cathedral Church of St John the Divine in New York, one of the few Gothic cathedrals anyone's tried to erect in recent years, was started in 1892 and still hasn't finished putting up its gargoyles, and Scott's Liverpool Cathedral was finally finished eighteen years too late for its creator. But Blyth lived long enough to witness the completion of his own cathedral. It would outlast him, and will outlast generations of his offspring, thanks to the innovative use of renewable building materials.

Naturally the cathedral is stuffed to bursting with

trees; any more and it wouldn't be a cathedral, it'd be a forest. Limes line the nave, ashes mark out the path of the cloisters, and the transepts are fringed with horse chestnuts that drop God's wonderful conkers. Trees of all creeds are welcome to worship here. Birds keep their song in reverent check, butterflies swig down communion nectar and squirrels gambol up and down the nave like fluffy choirboys late for practice.[*] This is a wild but holy space. The normally satisfying scrunch of a pine cone underfoot brings with it an overpowering sense of guilt, as if you've torn a hymnbook in half at Westminster Abbey.

Since the mid-1980s nearby Milton Keynes has been growing a tree cathedral of its own, going to extraordinary lengths to keep up with the arboreal Joneses. This means there are two tree cathedrals in the Home Counties, and none anywhere else in the rest of the country. Perhaps other areas of Britain might pull their green fingers out and start growing tree cathedrals before the open land they require disappears under dinky starter homes. Tree churches or chapels would do, there's no need to be showing off.

Since 1952, Whipsnade has periodically hosted interdenominational services that have the congregation kneeling on tussocks rather than hassocks. The worship of god in nature has a long history. The Norse myths had Ygdrasil, a tree that linked their versions of hell, earth and heaven with its roots, trunk and branches. Finding faith in the wonderful natural world makes a lot of gut-level sense. For example, it's a mystery how anyone managed to persuade people to stop worshipping the sun and switch to deities you can't see, feel or occasionally even understand. What was wrong with a life-giving, shining god that casually blinds people who dare to look him in the eye?

The tree cathedral retains its natural feel through minimal use of signage – it may be a good idea to grab a digital snap of the mapboard at the start and use that to find your way around. Without these few signs, the tree cathedral could be just another anonymous patch of woodland, albeit an

Whipsnade Tree Cathedral

---

[*] Perhaps Britain's red squirrels should have tried to claim sanctuary here.

inexplicably well-kept one. Blyth made provision towards its upkeep when he donated the cathedral and the land to the National Trust. The Trust is lent plenty of helping hands by local Girl Guides, who act as uniformed Wombles,* keeping the cathedral litter-free for the everyday folk in return for the exclusive use of Windy Sayles, a neighbouring camping field.

The creation and triumphant preservation of the Whipsnade Tree Cathedral is a fitting memorial to Blyth's three friends who, like anyone, would have been honoured to know that it was dedicated to their lives. It is a monument to Blyth too, and to the ongoing work of his family. Make a donation in the National Trust's online collection plate, and pay your respects to your own peculiar god if you visit.

Whipsnade Tree Cathedral, Whipsnade, Dunstable, Bedfordshire, LU6 2LL

01582 872406

www.nationaltrust.org.uk

---

* Wimbledon is to Womble as Whipsnade is to Whopsnle.

Salt Museum

Its smallness is not petty; on the contrary, it is profound.

Jan Morris, *The Matter of Wales*

Poor old salt has had a bit of a hard time lately. It's currently dietary enemy number two, beaten only by unsaturated fat. Suddenly, salt is bad news. Yet it has been around for millions of years, and we've been refining it, according to the earliest record, since the Xia dynasty, who were the big thing in China about four millennia ago. It's difficult to stomach that our briny friend might be a brutal hooligan trying to boot our blood pressure to new and giddy heights. Never mind. We can live without crisps. Salt has plenty of other uses: it's a great preservative; it removes rust; it's an ingredient of soap, bleach, glass and countless pharmaceuticals; and, for the sake of brev-

ity, does about another 13,994 things according to Britain's salt chiefs.

Northwich's Salt Museum is easy to find. Just look for the only building in town with a big wooden saltcellar standing outside. Northwich has been a salt town since those far-off days when you could tell places apart by what came steaming out of them on barges. In its industrial heyday, municipal festivities were marked by spanning the road with big archways, constructed using the fruits of the region's key trades. The museum has pictures of arches made of bicycles, chemical barrels and, particularly impressive, a great towering igloo of salt blocks, a proud and seemingly everlasting symbol of civic identity. Sure enough, Northwich still produces salt for use in everything from dialysis machines to cheese.

Salt-making in Cheshire dates back over 2,500 years. Early Brits were fairly cack-handed at it, but admirably patient. They'd patiently pour brine onto patiently heated coals, then patiently wait for them to cool before patiently scraping the salt crystals off the coals. Then the Romans arrived and proved what time-wasting twerps we were by putting brine in big lead pans and boiling all the liquid off instead. The first pan-evaporated salt in England was made at Hellath du, now known as Northwich. 'Wich' means 'salt works' in Anglo-Saxon, so no prizes for guessing what was made just up the road at Nantwich and Middlewich.★

The manufacturing process – almost unchanged since the Romans streamlined production – is graphically illustrated on the first floor of the museum. Photos and scale models show brine being evaporated in vast, glowing pans, while lumpmen stoke coal furnaces and rake the salt, scooping it into wooden tubs called 'dogs' and smoothing them off with happers. The language of salt-making is stacked with blunt, lethal-sounding terms: lofting spike, cotter patch, mundling peg. They could almost be murder weapons from the Industrial Revolution version of Cluedo. It was Colonel Salt, in the hothouse, with the chipping paddle.

A remarkable 1966 film of Murgatroyd's Salt Works looping on a monitor shows shirtless men sweating and mopping themselves down with towels in a scene from Dante's *Salt Inferno*. Until the 1920s, workers toiled in their civvies, their home clothes and clogs soon rotting in constant contact with the salty air and corrosive brine. Female salt-workers spent their working day in their undies, a practice that outraged Victorian sensibilities when revealed by gobsmacked factory inspectors. Salt had long been associated with lust – giving us the word 'salacious' – and twelfth-century women were known to salt their husbands to reinvigorate their virility (ouch). There was even a rumour going around for a couple of hundred years that mice could reproduce just by being in salt. (Don't laugh. Other patently wool-headed myths about the life-giving properties of crystals still haunt the groaning Mind, Body and Spirit shelves of your local bookshop.)

The British diet has long had a salty flavour. Traditionally, the meat and vegetables we slaughtered and harvested would be salted for the winter,

---

★ Having said that, the suffix means lots of other things too (homestead, farm, dairy, hamlet) so it would have been a disappointed Anglo-Saxon who turned up at Ipswich or Norwich looking for something to put on his chips (though some kind soul could have pointed him down the coast to Maldon).

so we'd have something other than snow and earwax to eat when the nights drew in. The demand for salt, therefore, was high and places like Northwich worked hard to satisfy it. However, drawing so much brine from underground reserves came at a price. This price was first paid in 1533 near Combermere, and continued demanding settlement for a further 400 years. A rich description of it can be found in a newspaper article reproduced at the museum.

ON TUESDAY MORNING CONSIDERABLE EXCITEMENT WAS CREATED IN NORTHWICH BY THE DISCOVERY THAT AN IMMENSE GAP HAD OPENED IN THE ROADWAY IMMEDIATELY OPPOSITE THE DANE BRIDGE INN, LONDON-ROAD. THE OCCURRENCE TOOK PLACE AT ABOUT HALF-PAST SIX IN THE MORNING, AND SO QUIETLY DID THE EARTH SINK THAT THE INMATES OF THE HOUSE WERE ONLY MADE AWARE OF THE FACT WHEN THEY CAME TO OPEN THE DOORS IN THE MORNING AND FOUND THE BOLTS ALL JAMMED FAST.

The ground was collapsing beneath Northwich.

Industry's effect on the environment is now a hot topic but, to our ancestors in Northwich, this subsidence came as a nasty surprise. Land collapses had already formed lakes, or 'flashes', up to a hundred acres in size, but the effects in the town were, if anything, even more dramatic. Photographs at the museum show buildings leaning drunkenly this way and that. In one, a fishmonger stands in his shop doorway handing a parcel to a customer on the pavement three feet above him. In another, a two-storey office reclines at forty degrees, as if it had very publicly nodded off. Even the original Salt Museum, which opened in 1889, fell down a hole in the ground. With admirable, if questionable, spirit the subsidence was exploited; photographers did a nice line in

Just some of the salt on display at the Salt Museum.

souvenir postcards of the tumbledown town, and fanatical preachers arrived to stand at the edge of the newly emerged craters, loudly comparing them to the bowels of hell, no doubt with plenty of references to Lot's Wife.

If the fire-and-brimstone mob were right, the sin that British salt towns like Northwich were being punished for was probably greed. A staggering world market for British salt had been created by simply prohibiting or supertaxing regional salt production elsewhere in the Empire. The stricter the controls, the more demand kept rising, so the people of Northwich kept hollowing away. In India, the British salt monopoly was so tight that Oscar-winning star Mahatma Gandhi was driven to protest by walking 240 miles to make a tiny but hugely significant protest. At the end of his journey, which had attracted thousands of followers, he bent down on the beach at Dandi and picked up some local salt crust, thus breaking the British salt law. By restricting access to a naturally occurring substance, the British government had handed Gandhi a potent symbol of oppression, one he could exploit to undermine British rule. Soon the Raj would be listing as hopelessly as a Northwich fishmonger's shop. Salt can lay claim to being the condiment that freed a continent.

Perhaps the grooviest corner of the Salt Museum is the 'Made From Salt' exhibit, the scope of which gives you a taste of the massive impact of salt upon our lives. As anyone who's ever tipped up a cellar with a loose lid can tell you, salt gets everywhere. You can tan leather with it, glaze pottery, even use it as currency, such is its intrinsic value (it's certainly more useful than gold). Here, you'll see an experimental 1957 batch of pink salt for use in sausage manufacture, a salt-encrusted shoe and some complimentary soy sauce. And, naturally, there's a cabinet full of salt and pepper pots, of which, strictly speaking, half shouldn't be on display. That, though, would mean separating Salt Laurel from Pepper Hardy, which might be answerable to a charge of cruelty to cruets. If anyone ever opens a Pepper Museum, maybe they could give the Salt Museum a ring and agree to split the collection.*

It's good to report that Northwich's unassuming museum is regularly overrun by cackles of delighted children. This place makes a real effort to

engage the smaller visitor: the photocopied map given away at the door is better illustrated than a lot of kids' books, scattered with smiling little figures having a lovely salty day out. There's a Victorian smells exhibit that, unless you've sniffed it, simply defies words. Scores of scraps of paper left pinned up in the coffee shop by visitors blossom with childish fascination: 'Salt = Happiness', 'I lick the Mueseum', 'Salt is very helpful for us', 'Quizz was fun I won priz' and 'Your hot chocolate is the best ever Love Kit Kat'.

This wide-eyed response to everyday objects may seem sweet, but it's also more honest than an adult's. Growing up is a process of learning to

---

* At the time of writing, nobody has spotted this gap in the market, although there is a Dr Pepper Museum in Waco.

insulate ourselves from the relentless overstimulation of everything ('Look! A door!') so we can get on with the important stuff like buying a new sofa or worrying about which mobile-phone company offers the best peak-hour minutage. It's a practical approach: if you turned up late at work every morning because you'd got distracted for an hour and a half by a beetle that lived under your bus stop, you'd get in terrible trouble. Although thinking about salt is probably fairly low on your list of priorities, give it a go.

There's so much more about salt than can be done justice to in these few paragraphs, which is why it's so impressive that the Salt Museum manages to be that rare creature, the Museum That's Exactly The Right Size. Salt is in your clothes, your windscreen, your cup of tea and every one of your cells (about 250g of you is salt), as omnipresent and important as a thing could be. A museum of salt could easily spiral out of control to become a museum of absolutely everything, but Northwich's potted (or cellared) history of this mighty mineral and its own domestic industry is as humble, small and moreish as salt itself.

The Salt Museum, 162 London Road, Northwich, Cheshire, CW9 8AB
01606 41331
www.saltmuseum.org.uk

Fitzpatrick's Temperance Bar

Damned alcoholics. They can't hold their drink, you know. They just drink it.
Vivian Stanshall, *The Eating At Rawlinson End*

In the eyes of the Victorian temperance movement, the world was all brimstone and no treacle. Hell-feeding businesses produced the demon drink that led to damnation of souls under dark blood-fringed clouds. Blimey. Better just make that a half of bitter shandy then, please.

In the late summer of 1832, seven Preston men were the first to take the pledge, or The Pledge as it is sometimes pronounced. Inspired by Joseph Livesey, a cheesemonger who definitely wouldn't have wanted you to enjoy a glass of port with your Stilton, they started a craze for total abstinence

from alcohol that faintly lingers to this day. The pledge could be taken short or long: short was for personal abstinence, long meant that in addition you would offer no alcohol to others. Lancashire was the pure beating heart of the temperance movement, and despite temperance bars having spread like an alcohol-fuelled fire across Britain throughout the following century, Fitzpatrick's in Rawtenstall is now the last remaining example.★

At one end of Rawtenstall's main drag, the bar stands, humble as a corner shop, understated enough not to disgrace the austere Methodist movement from

---

★ The Rochdale Pioneers (see the chapter on them) were contemporaries of the Preston seven and similarly unfamiliar with the whiff of the barmaid's apron.

Parsley, sage, rosemary and thyme (approximately).

which it sprang. The chapel next door (to which the bar still pays rent) will never have a drunk slumped in its doorway on Fitzpatrick's account. It's not the kind of bar where you'd find either spit or sawdust, but as bright and wholesome as a fairytale sweetshop. Clean clay jars and tubby, hooped casks resplendent with medicine-show lettering stand heartily along the walls like ornaments on a mantelpiece. A darkly regal marble-fronted bar is topped with a gleaming malted milk pump and studded with a tantalising set of no-longer-functional fat white buttons promising automatic dispensation of cream soda, lime juice and something called 'Wino' (which presumably had as much to do with proper drunk-people's wine as the gums do). The staff stop short of wearing bow ties and jauntily tipped straw boaters, but there's a golden-age charm about the whole enterprise that makes you suspect that they might burst into harmonious song at any moment.

Back in the heyday of spontaneous boatered singing, the grim uncertainties of The Great War gifted convenient reasoning to backers of the cause. David Lloyd George claimed that Britain was fighting against Germany, Austria and drink – and this supposed scourge of the masses was described as a social Zeppelin. Lord Kitchener sent his men out to battle with a note warning them off the bottle, desperately likening Dutch courage to a German spy. Lloyd George's Liberal Party was fiercely in favour of temperance, particularly as the drinks-trade monopoly was held by Conservatives. He also came up with the bright idea of imposing a tax levy on booze purchases. (Swine.)

In the abstemious old days, the Fitzpatricks owned and ran a chain of temperance bars all around East Lancashire. One by one, they closed down, leaving Malachi Fitzpatrick as the last temperance barman standing. Almost 120 years after the Rawtenstall business was established, owner Chris Law props up the business side of the bar, and he can clearly remember his grandfather taking him there when Malachi was the main man.

Law serves effervescing cordials in his very wooden shop, with names that carry a stimulating aroma of the past: dandelion and burdock; black beer and raisin; the raspberry-flavoured blood tonic, sarsaparilla; and the excellent winter warmer, lemon-and-ginger punch. In terms of soft-drink dispensary, this is so far from clanking an orange Tango out of a vending machine or popping the lid on a cinema cup of Pepsi that it might as well be happening on another planet. Okay, so it's got some sugar in it, but you'll be drinking a moderate glassful poured straight from a barrel and topped up with fresh soda, not wolfing a super-sized beaker of it through a straw the circumference of a hosepipe.

Because a temperance bar requires no licence, Fitzpatrick's can serve customers of all ages, even if only a handful can squeeze into the (very) snug at any one time. The two-seater wooden bench inside and the chairs outside are sat upon by everyone from kids on the way home from school to pensioners taking a well-earned shopping break, all enjoying drinks based on the original (and secret) family recipes.* The biggest seller, sarsaparilla (with the liquorice kick), is traditionally made from the roots of the *smilax* family of vines, one of the key ingredients of the occasionally non-alcoholic American-favourite root beer.

Appropriately, Fitzpatrick's also has a sideline in traditional herbalism.

* The word 'bustling' comes to mind, there were that many people coming in and out of Fitzpatrick's on the day that we visited. One of the customers was buying bottles of sarsaparilla to send to her Rawtenstall-born son now living in Australia, who pines after it as much as the Marmite that was also on its way over. Another of their customers misses the point rather by recommending sarsaparilla mixed with vodka as an excellent tipple.

The staff use reference books and files stuffed with years of first-hand experience in order to help those seeking alternative remedies. Camomile is informally recommended for skin complaints, eyebright is alleged to do exactly what it says on the jar and raspberry leaves in a hot bath ease an approaching childbirth by doing things to the cervix that won't be gone into here without the assistance of a very stiff drink. For the more serious cases they will of course refer people just up the road to the handily situated Boots the Apothecarists. The Temperance Bar, not content to double as a herbalist, also trebles as a proper old-fashioned sweetie shop. If you're

looking for jars sticky with cinder toffee, aniseed balls, winter nips or cream soda sold as a sherbet-like powder, this is the place. A visitor to Fitzpatrick's feels as if they have stepped into a Dylan Thomas paean to an ever-receding childhood.

Early temperance was built on moderation. Spirits were the primary enemy; beer was mildly tolerated. But it wasn't long before everything alcoholic was thrown out with the bathwater, and teetotalism became the watchword. Scientific proof of the dangers of drink was offered in 1839 by a Dr John Percy, who unsurprisingly discovered that injecting neat alcohol into dogs' stomachs killed them instantly. The cruel so-and-so didn't even administer the lethal dose with a mixer.

Like all countries with a history of puritanism, we take guilty pleasure in feeling bad about drinking ('I was so naughty last night …'), but luckily we've never gone the whole hog and let ourselves suffer a period of alcohol prohibition. Governments still preach moderation at us, and advertisers exhort us to drink responsibly. Fair enough, though car adverts don't yet feature a 'please drive carefully' message and you aren't urged to 'try not to catch fire' when being sold a hairdryer. These are the mottos your parents were supposed to pass on.

Perhaps it would help if Britain's round-buying pub culture (one that's always glugged down pints of water-weak bitter and schooners of rubbish nine per cent plonk) wasn't suddenly having its big glasses filled with strong continental lager and grown-up European wine. There is, nevertheless, a light ale at the end of the tunnel – two per cent ABV pints were recently introduced so that we can now binge drink responsibly; by the time you're ready for a fight, everyone else will have gone home, had a good night's sleep, be showered and breakfasted and on their way to work.

The seven Preston campaigners who started Fitzpatrick's understood that, even without booze, the pubs and bars of Britain are the traditional hub of our communal social life. So they made one of their own. Having a drink with neighbours, friends and strangers is an important way of breaking down barriers, forgetting your troubles and getting along. Maybe it's time to make a truce between the drinkers and the abstainers and really get the community together. If your local had a saloon, a public *and* a temperance bar, it might do a better job of giving everyone somewhere to go. Move to the temperance bar for quiet conversation, to the public bar for a stand-up row or to the saloon for a pointless, looping argument about West Ham's chances in the cup. Something for everyone.

You never know, whether it's for health reasons, fashion or a desire for cultural inclusion, temperance may find itself in the ascendant again. In the meantime, though temperance bars may seem as unimaginable as smoke-free pubs seemed a few years ago, Fitzpatrick's is both a fascinating relic and a possible glimpse of the future. Just as it was for the young uns of old, grabbing a dandelion and burdock on the way up to the Astoria ballroom, or a recuperative black beer and raisin on the way back down, chugging down a Fitzpatrick special at this tenacious Rawtenstall establishment remains a sobering tonic.

Fitzpatrick's, 5 Bank Street, Rawtenstall, Rossendale, Lancashire, BB4 6QS
01706 231836
www.fitzpatricks1890.co.uk

Fitzpatrick's Temperance Bar

National Coracle Centre

I shall teach you the ways of the river. Another year in that awful suburb and you would be past saving.

John Boorman, *Hope and Glory*

Ah! National Centres. Push your nose against the gleaming dome of a National Centre and you expect to glimpse a temple of idealism, the air

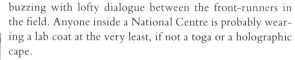

buzzing with lofty dialogue between the front-runners in the field. Anyone inside a National Centre is probably wearing a lab coat at the very least, if not a toga or a holographic cape.

Usually, you'll find that between the weighty words 'National' and 'Centre' live equally ponderous words, like 'Asthma' or 'Hurricane' or 'Atomic World-Exploding Robot Submarine'. But then, along with the really big things, there are those things upon which it's impossible to improve, like the knife, the door and the coracle. And while we're lacking anything as beautifully basic as a National Door Centre or a National Knife Centre we do have the National Coracle Centre in Cenarth.* And it's hidden behind a shop. Not in the way things are usually hidden behind shops, but in the way the Hair Bear Bunch's bachelor pad was hidden behind their cave. Owner Martin Fowler has to unfasten an entire wall of his craft boutique and swing it open to let you in. But this secret room is in perfect keeping with the scale and spirit of the coracle, Britain's oldest, hardiest, humblest boat.

Fowler, a theatrical stage manager, hadn't planned to start a National Centre for anything, least of all coracles. Cenarth was his wife's hometown, and the couple had retired here to renovate the beautiful old mill on the River Teifi (a location so pretty it was used for a Timotei ad). In 1989, a local fisherman asked if Fowler had anywhere he could use to build some coracles. Before this, Fowler hadn't picked up an oar in his life. Yet within

---

* There is a National Knife Collectors Association in Chattanooga, obviously.

two years he would find himself proudly opening his old pigsty and potato-boiling room as the National Coracle Centre.

Coracles are Boat Version 1.0. They are the sort of boats that would grow on a boat tree. If there existed a scale of things that float on water, with the vulgar jet-trash of the Earl's Court boat show at one end, then the coracle would be at the other, just slightly up from the bread you throw to ducks. The coracle is an anti-gadget, the water-borne equivalent of a hammer. It's a practical, hand-crafted, round-bottomed workhorse whose design predates the triglyphs of Stonehenge. Jeremy Clarkson wouldn't be seen dead in one.

A prehistoric speedboat.

National Coracle Centre

A bent hazel or willow frame, covered in stretched animal skin, flannel or canvas, traditionally waterproofed with pitch, the coracle is a design classic. And here, in a long Welsh shed, there are more of these endearing one-man bowls than you ever dreamt existed.

Our islands' love affair with the coracle goes back a long way. It's hard to think of many other forms of transport that have enjoyed such continuous use into the modern age.* An excavation in Fife turned up some 4,000-year-old fishermen who were so attached to their little boats that they'd been buried in them. Though it might look like a schoolboy has just cracked it in half to remove the conker, the coracle is a masterpiece of evolved design.

Each river's coracle was different, perfectly adapted for local use; the Teifi versions were designed for fishing with a net dragged between twin coracles, scouring the

---

* Even evidence for horseriding doesn't go back much further than evidence for coracles. It seems likely that before the coracle the only means of transport were walking or doing roly-polies down hills.

river for salmon. Disease and commercial trawling have left salmon stocks dangerously low, so the normal catch these days is sewin (sea trout). Fowler will show you how, and for this he requires one plastic sea trout, a typical hand-made Teifi coracle, a bit of floor space in the corner of the centre and a willing volunteer from the tour party. Go on. You know you want a go.

The tireless standards setters of the European Union have helpfully classified the coracle as 'BASIL' (Buoyancy and Stability Inherently Limited), and even here on the Coracle Centre floor – where, if you overbalance, the worst you'll get is a carpet burn – it's obvious that this boat has an unfor-

giving learning curve. Sir John Hawkins (editor of the 1760 edition of Izaak Walton's *Compleat Angler*) noted that 'the instant you touch it with your foot, it flies from you'. And Sir John's fictional almost-namesake Jim Hawkins had an equally tricky time not drowning in Ben Gunn's lop-sided homemade model in *Treasure Island* (which you can read about in an extract pinned to the wall). The coracle is the nautical world's plucky underdog and, like any dog, it likes splashing about in shallow water and leaving its owner soaking wet.

Students of Tom Rodgers, who ran a coracle school on the Severn in the nineteenth century, would take their lessons in the nude to avoid ruining their clothes. Formidable twenty-stone Tom, scion of a great coracle-making family, was not a man to be messed with. Legend has it that when he won a four-and-a-half gallon barrel of beer in the town regatta, Tom finished his prize before the end of the day, sold the empty cask back to the pub, and drank the proceeds.

After you've made an idiot of yourself trying to paddle, held your net and clobbered your plastic fish with a stubby rolling pin all at the same time without falling arse-over-trout, you can have a proper look around. But, first, Fowler will grab the coracle from you and unexpectedly turn himself into a tortoise. You may be tempted to applaud.

The coracle is designed to fit over its owner like a shell. The carrying strap is thrown round the shoulders, the weight of the hull counterbalanced by hooking the oar under the seat. The change from boatman to wicker beetle is seamless. Coraclemen go with the flow, drifting downstream with the current of the river. They may have to walk miles back up the riverbank after each catch, in which case it's nice to be out of the rain.* You only get a design that good by refining it continuously for generation after generation. *Vorsprung durch Grandad*, as they say in Wales.

Another neat feature is the coracle's flattened bottom, which allows it to carry heavy loads in shallow rivers impassable to keeled craft. A good Teifi coracle can transport forty rabbits in six inches of water, a measurement that implies some secret scale of standard poachers' measurements ('one Snaffle is equal to six brace of eel per vessel'). Coracle fishing is a quiet, dark pursuit, undertaken at night, to disguise the shadow of the boat on the face of the water, a necessity for a successful catch and a great cover for unscrupulous coracle users. One poacher, Nacky Brathern (whose picture on the wall of the centre appears to have been made by sticking chewing tobacco around a photograph of a hat) dined on nothing but a single endless stew made by throwing whatever he'd snaffled that day into a never-emptied pot. Even the majority of honest coraclemen seem to have been regarded as a lawless menace by the nineteenth- and twentieth-century legislators who sought to regulate rural habits, unwelcome bureaucracy flowing downstream from the big new cities.

Licences for coracle fishing first arrived in the 1860s. The new railways meant salmon-hungry Billingsgate Market was only hours away, and the Teifi was suddenly choked with eager coraclers hoovering fish out of the waterfalls as fast as they could leap, which wasn't good for the river's stock

---

* The Coracle Society advises that you never walk near the water's edge with a coracle on your back in high winds, for reasons they hardly need to elaborate.

levels. It was also obvious that tourists with rods and lines brought far more money into the area than coracle fishing ever could; the little boats simply got in the way. The days when every home in Cenarth had a coracle hanging outside were over (though the pub's still got a few on the wall). Up to 300 coracles would once have fished this stretch of river; today only twelve pairs are permitted to do so.

A visit to the National Coracle Centre is a little like visiting a protected enclosure where the last few examples of a venerable species are preserved. Examples of each breed are kept in controlled conditions for study and comparison by experts, maybe in the hope that someone may come up with some radical breeding programme that means our great-grandchildren will be able to see these things in the wild. Reading display boards about dwindling numbers of coracles and dwindling stocks of salmon, one begins to blur into the other.

But, though endangered, coracles pop up everywhere. The centre has an impressive collection of remarkably similar craft from all over the globe; a round Tibetan yakskin boat, a parisal from India, a Vietnamese version that carried refugees 500 miles to Hong Kong, even an Iraqi water taxi called a guffa.* Wellington and Julius Caesar took coracles with them on campaigns in India and Spain respectively, spreading the design. The inhabitants of the Missouri River plains used buffalo-skin bullboats, chaining them together by their buffalo tails to make articulated coracle caravans. There's an impressive one of these standing in a position of honour at the end of the centre like a big Wild West ashtray. Either the design of the coracle is hardwired into all human brains (like rudimentary grammar, a fondness for the three-chord trick and laughing at farts), or the Celtic prototype has been borrowed worldwide.

Coracles these days tend to be built more for leisure use rather than anything as practical as fishing, but the spread of recreational coracling means that this Great British Boat has begun to be spotted on waterways far from its usual Celtic strongholds. There are now Essex and Lincolnshire models, and it can only be a healthy sign that the current chairman of the Coracle Society lives not in Wales but Norfolk. Yorkshire even has its own unique model constructed from a whisked, oven-baked and varnished mixture of milk, eggs and plain flour. And every year, at Brawby, there is a thrilling coracle race where grown adults hare downstream in these gigantic

---

* The guffa at the centre was designed to withstand heavy Baghdad use, but baulked at the heavy Welsh weather. It sits, melted in a small, sad heap, like torched roadkill.

waterproof Yorkshire puddings.* Sadly, the centre doesn't have a Pudding Coracle on display, only a photo gallery of the event. If an example could be found that had survived the race without turning into cake mix, it would make a star exhibit.

You'd have to have a heart of batter not to be excited by the thought of a Yorkshire Pudding coracle. The eccentricity, the smallness, the hand-built charm, the sense of continuity with our distant past, whatever it is that makes these tiny boats so appealing, it worked on Martin Fowler like it has worked on centuries of fishermen and craftsmen, and the passion is infectious. You arrive at the National Coracle Centre a busy, modern person. There are emails to Podcast, ringtones to call, downloads to upload. What time have you got to think about coracles? But a brief spell behind a secret door in a false wall with a collection of little round boats slows you, refocuses you, recalibrates your priorities and leaves you in no doubt: small things deserve a National Centre too.

The National Coracle Centre, Cenarth Falls, Carmarthenshire, SA38 9JL
01239 710980
www.coracle-centre.co.uk

---

* The Brawby race is organised by Simon Thackray of the Shed Theatre, who also runs the North Yorkshire Elvis Bus Tour, in which a busload of Elvises drive around North Yorkshire singing the King's hits to the tune of 'On Ilkley Moor Baht 'At'. In a sane world, we like to think, Thackray would be Prime Minister at the very least.

Museum of Brands, Packaging and Advertising

Lord, what things I lie here and remember.

George Browne Macdonald, last words

Robert Opie is a folk hero: a writer, collector, photographer, curator, philosopher and self-styled 'supermarket archaeologist' who has made his

reputation by assembling the contents of the nation's dustbins into the Museum of Brands, Packaging and Advertising. If he wanted to save himself a bit of money on sign lettering, he could rename this staggering collection the Museum of Stuff.

Visit most historical collections and you're likely to see things you've either never seen before, have only ever seen a picture of before or have never even heard of before: unusual, rare things of lofty significance. Here, you'll see everyday, seemingly insignificant things for the first, tenth, hundredth or thousandth time; things that are seldom kept, let alone archived, displayed and celebrated: boxes, bottles, tins, leaflets, games, cartons, cans, annuals, dolls, coins, packets, clothes, postcards, wrappers, books, puppets, piggy banks, sheet music, comics, bags, pots, tubes, models and promotional material – almost anything with a name or a logo on it. Stuff. Lots and lots of stuff.

The 12,500 chronologically arranged exhibits knit together to form a vivid picture of British life from the Victorian era to the present day. The older you are, the longer it takes you to get round the museum. You stroll through the collection, quietly engaged, until you reach the bit where you were about five years old, at which point you slow to a complete stop, gasp and crawl the remaining decades at a snail's pace, the doors to the less frequented corners of your mind blown wide open and flapping in the breeze.

Even a ten-year-old will end up gawping at some item here. We all have a past, and, though we'd like it to be signposted with medals and great achievements, most of it's mapped out in labels, lids and litter. At the back of every larder, there's a little piece of history – be it a tin of tongue, a jar of pickled chestnuts or a fading bottle of cochineal – that should have been thrown out long ago and which has acquired that air of dusty otherness that, when you stumble upon it again, makes it seem, momentarily, unbearably poignant.

The museum has had two previous incarnations, in Gloucester and Wigan.* But the collection's first public outing took place in 1975, when Opie showed a small part of it at the Victoria and Albert Museum. Great things were not expected from the exhibition, so you can imagine the management's reaction when the queues grew so long that, for the first time in its history, the V&A had to close its doors to punters. Opie had proven that a Sunlight Flakes soap box or an Eggo advertisement was an even bigger crowd-puller than a mediæval reliquary or a Raphael cartoon. For a moment it seemed

people were more interested in a real can of condensed soup than a painting of one.

Walking through the collection is like being struck by cultural lightning. Imagine a trip to a supermarket where, instead of the shelves being stocked with sixty of everything you can buy today, there's one of everything you could buy in the last couple of centuries. Let's say, for instance, you're a child of the 1970s.† Blundering blithely into the section for that decade, suddenly things that you never even thought would cross your mind become the subject of embarrassing fascination.

---

* The Wigan incarnation was due for inclusion in *Bollocks to Alton Towers*, but it closed while the book was in preparation. We can barely conceal our delight that it relocated in time to make it to these pages.

† Like us, obviously. Forgive the indulgence, but the passions stirred by the Robert Opie Collection are best done justice by example.

You want to rush out and tell the world the mildly surprising fact that Quavers pre-date Hula Hoops. You desperately need a T-shirt made of the three-colour atom burst from the Wavy Line washing-powder box or the clumsily groovy Tab logo. You baulk at the horror that was Co-op Jubilade (a fat little tin filled with strawberry-flavoured drink) yet you revel in the crude, sunburst-coloured glory of a packet of Best potato

crisps (made by Goal products, with George Best's delighted face beaming from its 3p bag). Your larynx even involuntarily tightens at the sight of a packet of Lem-Sip, as you relive slow, rainy days off school with a nagging throat.

Somewhere along the way you may, quite reasonably, ask yourself, 'Why have I been staring at a thirty-year-old packet of Polos for nearly two minutes?' That's the moment. The moment that driving instructors call 'the bite' – when you raise the clutch enough for the gears to engage: the moment you cede control to the thing

Clockwise: pop, pop, booze, pop, pop, booze, pop.

you're in. Robert Opie likes to watch his visitors for that moment. Here you are, wandering through an elegant museum collection in West London, when, bang! You're being shot back in time, poleaxed by the mundane wonder of the past – colds, holidays, chores, Sundays, grazed knees, birthdays.

The bigger picture is equally compelling. You can trace the history of how you've been sold things and how you've bought things and how you've adopted things and how you've stuck with things – and how certain things have become part of the ambient hum of your existence, no more worthy of conscious consideration

than your lymphatic system or your skirting boards. Packaging design changes almost imperceptibly and it's fascinating to view the subtle variations in a brand's identity over time. When exactly did Pop from the Rice Krispies pack start wearing a baseball cap backwards, or Tony the Tiger undertake a rigorous fitness regime? The butterfly lifespan of fashion is exposed in all its cruelty, whether represented by the shoddy Neville Brody hipness of a can of Quatro, or the way that a box of Cadbury's Spice Girls Chocolate Assortment now looks more dated than a die-cast Corgi Beatles Yellow Submarine. Similarly, those products that borrow web-age cachet by sticking a lower case 'i' or 'e' before their names will soon seem as charmingly dated as 1920s bandwagon chasers like Garnett & Sons' Radio Toffees or Macfarlane Lang & Co.'s Broadcast Cake.

Sometimes you squirm in wonder. There's a can of Mock Turtle Soup in one cabinet. You know the stuff, it's mentioned in *Alice's Adventures in Wonderland* (and is made from mutton broth and the meat from a calf's head, in case you were momentarily tempted to get the hob on). So, your mind asks as you stare at the pyramid of cans, what's this Heinz Real Turtle Soup then? Surely people didn't eat liquidised turtle in the 1950s, did they? It's unspeakable. Yet here it is – just below the Oven Baked Beans With Tomato And Pork Sauce (the What Sauce?).

Just as alarming are the TV tie-in board games. How did one play (let alone win) the *That's Life* board game, the *Jim'll Fix It* board game or – the mind struggles to boggle – the *Crossroads* board game? More importantly, why? Was there nothing on the telly? There is one question the museum definitively answers, and that's the well-worn conversation-stopper, Did Monster Munch Used To Be Smaller?★ Well, there's no need to spoil it for

---

★ Up there with Did Pizza Express Pizzas Used To Be Bigger?, Did Mars Bars Used To Be Smaller? and Does Terry Wogan's Hair Come Off?

you. Go and find out if you want to know.

Although this is an extraordinary collection of the thoroughly ordinary, there are some one-offs, peculiarities and esoterica. The Colman's Mustard Zeppelin Raid Indicator, for instance, or the dutifully patriotic Hovis Coronation Periscope. And, of course, Bland & Van Voorst's Delicious Taste Sauce. (Was it the sauce with the delicious taste of a delicious taste? If it was, the word Bland can't have helped sales much.) An inventory of what's on show at the museum would fill several volumes – and there are another half a million items in storage, none of which is catalogued. Opie knows what he's got, and that's good enough for him. He also knows what he's still looking for. So, in case you're routling in the near future, keep an eye open for a wartime can of Spam and an early Barclaycard. Robert Opie will happily take either off your hands. His tentacles are widely spread. His reach is such that he's even had a private audience with Her Blue Peterness Valerie Singleton. She invited him round to take a look at her not inconsiderable carrier-bag collection. And there's not many of us can say that.

The museum has cemented Opie's position as a folklorist in the mould of Cecil Sharp – the chap who trundled around the country about a hundred years ago getting people to sing him folk songs (then writing them down) and getting people to do their Morris dancing routines (then notating them). All those My Bonny Boys and Winster Garlands were things that were in day-to-day circulation once but would have faded forever in the face of progress if Cecil hadn't preserved them. Likewise, Opie saves cans and boxes that would otherwise be rotting in landfill, and with each item preserves its potential to stir long-forgotten memories of any hue.

If Memory Lane can be said to materially exist anywhere, this is it. And it's as much brickbats and shithouses as it is blue skies and hollyhock. The Museum of Brands, Packaging and Advertising is a depository of the underwhelming on an overwhelming scale that confounds and delights at the same time: a skein of contradictions in which things that once meant nothing can mean so much. The American comedian Stephen Wright tells a joke about reminiscing with people he doesn't know: here, Robert Opie does that for real – and to great effect.

Museum of Brands, Packaging and Advertising, 2 Colville Mews, London, W11 2AR
02079 080880
www.museumofbrands.com

Chiltern Open Air Museum

Don't clap too hard – it's a very old building.

John Osborne, *The Entertainer*

At forty-five acres, the Chiltern Open Air Museum easily qualifies as the museum in this book with the most floor space. Unusually for a museum,* it has no walls or roof, giving it unrivalled headroom and, on a sunny day, enviable natural lighting. Since it opened in 1976 this home for homeless homes has rescued over forty local buildings from demolition or neglect, hauling them to its site in the Chilterns, then renovating and restoring them to their former glory.

Bogs.

If you're entering into the spirit and having a proper day out, you'll have had a good few cups of tea from your tartan flask on the way to the museum, so the first thing you'll be looking for is the loo. At Chiltern, this is an exhibit in itself. The Caversham Public Convenience, a tramshed toilet originally constructed in Reading in 1906, celebrated its centenary with a well-aimed two-day piss-up, courtesy of the museum staff. There aren't many hundred-year-olds with their waterworks still in fully functioning order, bless it. It's a mark of the care and attention lavished on each building here that even the lavatory gets star treatment. The original Twyford's Adamant urinals in the Gents look sturdy enough to stand another full century of high-pressure punishment and the toilet cubicles are

---

* Although usually for an open air museum.

tiny iron fortresses, each capable of containing a small atomic blast. They just don't make khazis like these any more.

As you can tell from the toilets, the Open Air Museum isn't a retire-

ment park where unloved buildings go to die. The reclaimed structures, where applicable, are still hard at work. They're either given their old jobs back, or smart lick-of-paint demob suits and new careers. The gift shop at the museum's entrance was once an outbuilding from the Post Office Savings Bank. The restored cottage opposite now doubles as the museum's office. And the tennis pavilion has been reinvented as a charity shop. In a small amount of space, three disparate buildings from not too far away – Hammersmith, Astleham and Maidenhead respectively – have taken a short walk in the brisk country air, sat down and found a new lease (or freehold) of life.

Without purpose, these restored buildings could easily become fancy, empty show homes – all pristine plasterwork and faultless flashings. Reconstructing them out of reach of the wrecking ball is the first stage in their preservation, but the key to restoration here at the Chiltern Open Air Museum is repurposing. The downfall of many historic structures is disuse. The pretty ones, the Gothic wedding-cake castles and timber-clad Tudor houses, can usually drag enough cash through the turnstiles to pay for their upkeep, but a plain-Jane building can't flutter its eyelashes and hope some-one will buy it dinner. When the beauty of a stately home starts to fade, there's always plastic surgery (install a train, a zoo, a theme park), but when the congregation stops coming to a corrugated iron Victorian church, it's left to rust. A functional building without a function isn't an historic monu-ment, it's the architectural equivalent of an abandoned car. The Open Air Museum gives these buildings much more than new foundations and a lick of paint; it gives them back their soul.

The sixteenth-century Northolt Barn, subject to three arson attacks in its previous life, looks far happier and a lot less on fire in its fresh location. A sign pinned up inside the barn apologises for the mess caused by nest-ing kestrels. There is, of course, no need to apologise. The kestrels' sloppy white seal of approval is proof that, despite all the upheaval, the building has retained its inherent barn-ness, and is still a good place for a nest. There's more barn-and-bird-of-prey action at Skipping's Barn, which has found new purpose as the Hawk and Owl Trust National Conservation and Education Centre. The wildlife exhibition here has some useful buttons which, when pushed, make the pant-wetting screech of a barn owl, which is handy if your kids need frightening.

Now that they've all ended up in the same place, each building's history has an interesting coda. Some were actually built to be moved and reassembled, like Lego houses. The Victorian prefabricated Thame Vicarage Room on the museum's mock village green has been moved a holy trinity of times throughout its life, a tribute to the original structure's durability and portability. Long before IKEA sailed here in their easy-assembly pine longboats, the estimable Norwich firm of Boulton & Paul produced mail-order catalogues full of flat-pack buildings; anything from a shed to a glass exhibition hall the size of Crystal Palace could be sent to you by train. The Henton Mission Room at the far side of the green is a great example of one of their  pop-up parish churches. Its simple red iron sides are so austere that, if you stuck a prefabricated farmer and wife in front of it brandishing a pitchfork, it could be a Grant Wood painting.★

Although most of the adopted buildings are fairly basic in construction, it's inevitable that some structural tinkering may have occurred during their lifetimes. Unlike many restoration projects, the museum makes no attempts to take its exhibits back to some idealised fresh-off-the-drawing-board state. Over time, porches move, doorways widen, and extensions are added to suit changing tastes and usage. The guidebook laments the prohibitive expense of full restoration, but preserving a building's battle scars can be interesting, and is certainly better than no preservation at all.

The juxtaposition of salvaged buildings from different eras can be slightly disconcerting, especially if you were expecting one of those reconstructed heritage villages that attempt to recreate a specific bygone age ('see the blacksmith milk a horse …'). Besides, it's only what happens naturally in most towns: rooflines of all eras jostling for supremacy. Unlike most

---

★ Boulton & Paul later became famous for even more lightweight structures, producing aircraft such as the Sopwith Camel in the First World War, and the Defiant in the Second World War.

towns, though, plenty of thought has been put into the layout: community buildings around the halcyon village green, agricultural buildings sequestered in their own farming quarter and an industrial area that includes an old furniture factory (now the café). Like the distance between Amersham's Old and New Towns down the road, there's enough space between the museum's zones to allow the diverse architectural styles to breathe.

A good example of this is the 1940s Universal House Mk.3, a prefab which lives cosily alongside its Victorian grandparents round the village green. Designed as a cheap and cheerful house kit to deal with the postwar housing crisis, it's a striking building for something so grey and utilitarian. In summer, when the roses are blooming up the garden path and round the front door, it looks positively chocolate boxy.* The interior is perfectly proportioned: two bedrooms on the left, one each at front and back, indoor toilet, narrow hall, large lounge and kitchen. And the Anderson Shelter next to the Mk.3's vegetable patch has such a warm, friendly glow that it could have been recently struck by an incendiary device.

---

* Not Milk Tray. No, not Terry's All Gold either. We mean that enormous chocolate box with the faded magenta flower on the lid that's been sitting above the spirits and fags at your newsagent's since 1977.

Even the fittest legs will sooner or later appreciate the museum's aesthetically designed benches. Each unique perch (created in 1996 by students at the Chilterns University College) is a subtle art installation. Stop and marvel at the majesty of the bench encircling the village green's gargantuan lime tree. If, after all the walking, your kids' batteries need further draining there's a modern mini adventure playground, hidden away on the woodland walk, as if embarrassed by its lack of heritage. In an ideal world the playground would also be filled with reclaimed vintage equipment: a creaking witch's hat, a gigantic wooden roundabout that takes four grown men to set spinning and a two-ton seesaw that could take a finger off. But, there you are, you can't have everything.

The Chiltern Open Air Museum is an organic attraction, growing as the staff and volunteers reassemble more buildings. There is stacks of room left on site and, with eleven buildings in storage and more on the way, only reconstruction costs keep its expansion in check.* Who knows, with enough money the museum may eventually become a small town in its own right. Visitors won over by the slower pace of life and picturesque setting may decide not to leave and could take up residence in the barns, like the kestrels. It may even lead to a group of smaller satellite museum towns springing up on the perimeter with green 1930s buses carrying commuters to and fro. The campaign against the reclaimed flyover starts here.

Chiltern Open Air Museum, Newland Park, Gorelands Lane, Chalfont St Giles, Buckinghamshire,
HP8 4AB
01494 871117
www.coam.org.uk

---

* The disassembled buildings are stored, recursively, in the Glory Mill Store – a reclaimed paper-mill store from High Wycombe that was reassembled on site.

Forbidden Corner

It's absurd to call it a maze. You keep on taking the first turning to the right. We'll just walk round for ten minutes, and then go and get some lunch.

Jerome K. Jerome, *Three Men in a Boat*

Go and stand in the Forbidden Corner.

Hampton Court Maze doesn't burp at you when you enter it.* Nor did Lancelot 'Capability' Brown plant a tree in the folly-filled gardens at Stowe that rears up and widdles water on you as you approach. Still, had the master landscape artist been aware of such novelties, who's to say that Brown wouldn't have got his kicks by leaving peeing privet hedges where least expected? The Forbidden Corner, a modern folly in Leyburn, North Yorkshire, is full of such unapologetic dirty tricks. Equal parts maze, grotto and garden, it's a silly, scenic and stylish day out that leaves a smile on your face and a wet patch on your trousers.

---

* Although Hampton Court Maze does laugh and sing at you at various points, thanks to a recently added sound installation. The idea may be better than it sounds (as it were).

There are few clues to the rude delights of the Forbidden Corner before you go in, and much of the fun comes from being kept in the dark.* The leaflet handed to you on entry is cryptically entitled *Your Guide?* and there's nothing on sale in the shop as dully practical as a map. Once through the gate, you're on your own. A tip: let the people in front of you disperse into the trees before you set off, so they don't spoil the excitement of triggering the prankish traps yourself. And don't be put off by their screams.

There's no wrong way round the attraction, but the best way to discover what's on offer is by making mistakes. There's always something eye-catching peeping out from the other side of a hedge, although trying to reach it by any method other than chance will take you on an hour-long wild-goose chase. And, if you're trying to outwit the tricks, don't; they're smarter than you. Any attempt to go the clever way round will trigger immediate retribution in the form of a good old-fashioned soaking.

The Forbidden Corner obeys the first rule of follyhood: it's the brainchild of an eccentric millionaire. In 1990 Colin Armstrong, a businessman

in the agrochemical industry, instructed his architect Malcolm Tempest to dig a very deep hole on his Tupgill Park Estate. The two men were going to create a grotto. Towers, walls and mazes soon followed, creating a private playground for Armstrong and his family to enjoy. In 1994, giggling behind his hand, he opened it to an unsuspecting public. The locals kicked up quite a fuss, not least because Armstrong had only obtained planning permission retrospectively, setting a dangerous precedent. Disappointingly, though the gauntlet had been thrown down, and the council were

---

* This chapter will avoid giving away the attraction's show-stopping moments, which would be as spoilsportsmanlike as handing you the blueprints of David Copperfield's massive industrial flying rig on the way into one of his gigs.

obviously napping on their watch, the Forbidden Corner failed to inspire an outbreak of similar follies springing up all over the Yorkshire Dales.

To get himself in the right mood, Armstrong visited the legendary hand-built village of Portmeirion* in Wales in the summer of 1991. Its influence on the Corner's architectural styling is clear. Like Clough Williams-Ellis's mad Italianate Utopia, so much is packed into such a small area that the site feels a lot larger than it actually is. The Forbidden Corner is an idea that swiftly outgrew its original plot of land, the architectural equivalent of a pad of intricate doodling where someone's gone off the edge of the page and started drawing on the table. One-way trails coil around forest paths like a turf maze, forcing you to cover a much greater distance than first appeared necessary. Hidden doors lead to underground chambers with ceilings formed from the bases of things you've already seen above ground. While the Portmeirion touches, the Corinthian pillars and the scattered statuary give the Corner a sense of weird entrapment that is pure *Prisoner*, it's more like an episode of *The Avengers in Wonderland*, with tricks, riddles and nursery-rhyme imagery lurking round every corner.

Young children either love the Forbidden Corner and dart in and out between your legs eager to uncover its secrets, or are terrified by it and spend the visit with their eyes shut asking when they can go home. It's all harmless fun, though. Kids can be seen running to their parents after being freaked out by something, then secretly sneaking back in for another scare. It's a place to regress. Grown adults rediscover their sense of wonder as

they wait nervously by entrances to darkened tunnels, hoping someone else will go in first. If Blackgang Chine† is the fairytale theme park's jolly uncle, then the Forbidden Corner is its sinister aunt.

The trick here is to accept misdirection like a volunteer at a magic show. The weary soul who finds a fiendish two-way gate between perpendicular paths a bloody nuisance instead of a magic barrier is not really entering into the spirit of the thing. For those seeking a moment's relief from the countless japes, dead ends and darkened corri-

---

* See *Bollocks to Alton Towers*.

† We said, 'See *Bollocks to Alton Towers*.'

dors, the Corner's low-level yew maze (on a plateau overlooking a swathe of Wensleydale) turns out to be rather calming. The inevitable sting in its bushy tail? Occasional bursts of holly sprout from its sides preventing you from solving the maze using the trusty keep-one-hand-on-the-same-wall method.

Keep a close eye on members of your party. If a loved one disappears through a door, there's no guarantee you'll be able to follow them through. Mobile phone coverage is deliciously patchy, so desperate texts of 'Where R U?' won't help. One part, the Eye of the Needle, involves entering a dark tunnel that plays similar perspective tricks to an Ames Room. Without giving too much away, the apparently long and short of it is that children will find it significantly easier to navigate than adults.* Those of a larger build may wish to seek an alternative route to avoid embarrassment.

The blend of modern technology and traditional folly building makes the Corner befuddling and timeless. Sepia-tinted Edwardianisms and classical ornamentation abound, with the figures of Caliban and Ariel popping up as an architect's nod to the play that shares his stormy name. Sporadic sound effects lurch unexpectedly from the attraction and do their best to part you from your skin, loudspeakers concealed under stone slabs and in darkened corners disguising the whereabouts of the brouhaha. It doesn't help that most of the noises are downright creepy; the last thing you want to hear whilst navigating a darkened corridor is what appears to be the sound of the Pope delivering his Easter message while devouring an unbuttered

---

* Oh, all right then. An Ames Room is an optical illusion featuring an irregularly proportioned room with sloping ceiling, raked floor and four different-sized walls. When seen through a fixed viewpoint on the near wall, the room appears regular in proportion, but identical objects placed against the left and right walls appear to vary wildly in size. As we are sure every reader is aware, the effect features memorably on the cover of Status Quo's *On the Level*.

wholemeal cheese sandwich. And there's a song about a cat and mouse that thumps along with the single-minded ferocity of a techno 'They're Coming To Take Me Away, Ha-Haaa!' which should leave you with a good month or so of Tom and Jerry nightmares.

For the couple of hours you're here, your mind slowly adapts to the peculiar surroundings until the garden becomes your home. You'll stop to ask someone the way out, fully expecting to be told that they've been lost there for the past ten years and survive by stealing clothes and satsumas from passers-by. For those planning a midsummer visit to the Forbidden Corner, it's reassuring that the hilariously off-kilter British weather can't piss on their parade. Our traditional August rains and snows only add sparkle to the foliage and help to conceal the water traps (flagged by telltale puddles in dry weather). If the weather does get persistently inclement, there's always lashings of fun (and a chance to dry out) undercover too.

Follies fulfil their creator's desire to have their own castle, while side-stepping the draughty, cold reality of actually living in one. Had the golden age of castles coincided with the vogue for follies, all castles would have been designed as impregnable M. C. Escher fortresses, attackers unexpectedly finding themselves upside down, firing arrows into their own back. Likewise, when you eventually emerge, panting, damp and wonky of head, back at the entrance of the Forbidden Corner, you'll feel like you've been on a mental and physical workout. It's exhausting being hoodwinked for such a prolonged period, but a network of these follies across the country would make a fun alternative to the soul-destroying experience of watching banks of silent televisions from a gym treadmill. You'd definitely want to return for a workout the following day and attempt to find all the bits you'd missed. And try to avoid getting showered by all the bits you didn't.

Forbidden Corner, Tupgill Park Estate, Coverham, Middleham, Leyburn, North Yorkshire, DL8 4TJ

Entrance by appointment only: 01969 640638/640687

www.yorkshirenet.co.uk/theforbiddencorner

Poldark Tin Mine

Work is of two kinds: first altering the position of matter at or near the earth's surface relatively to other such matter; second, telling other people to do so.
Bertrand Russell, *In Praise of Idleness*

British holidaymakers love Cornwall. If you want to get away from your worries, you can't get much further away from them without falling into the sea. A burglar-pleasing number of the pretty cottages on Cornwall's roads and harboursides lie empty for much of the year because they're for holiday use only, rat race bolt-holes for escapees keen to be as far from the sodding crowd as possible. Not for nothing do the Cornish refer to a trip east as 'going to England'. Cornwall is a peninsular apart.

But only a century or so ago, a Yorkshire woman who'd been forced to decamp to Cornwall for her husband's work described her new home as 'the most disagreeable [place] in the whole country. The face of the earth is broken up in ten thousand heaps of rubbish and there is scarce a tree to be seen.' You can see the Cornish Tourist Board beating her door down for a testimonial.

The woman's husband was industrial entrepreneur Thomas Wilson, sales agent for James Watt's celebrated steam engines. The Wilsons had wound up here for one reason: Cornwall was where the money was, and the money was in mining. It's sobering to contemplate that the only reason this area (and so many other tourist hot spots) is so lovely to look at today is that its chief industry has collapsed, leaving a clearer view of the greenery behind. The soaring ruins of the engine-house chimneys, the tumbledown workers' cottages and the foam-spouting cavities in the Cornish cliffs are all by-products of a dead industry.* Even that verdant geodesic oasis, the Eden Project, is built in an abandoned china-clay quarry.

To a nineteenth-century tin miner, it might seem odd to spend a relaxing day out in what was once a backbreaking workplace. It gives you hope that

---

* The smugglers' caves frothing picturesquely on Cornish beaches are very often man-made 'adits', tunnels used to siphon the water that floods into mine workings safely into the sea. The cost of running a steam engine to pump water out mechanically was often so high, and the price of labour so cheap, that it made economic sense to dig adits anything up to two miles long.

in the future our grandchildren will be able to ride an educational steam train round the scoured husk of the Tiscali Customer Service Call Centre and that every branch of Asda will have a landscaped leisure jungle grown over its staff room.

If it weren't for tourism, though, the Poldark Tin Mine may have remained utterly forgotten. In 1972, ex-Royal Marine Peter Young bought this site, with its abandoned forge, at auction for £100 (outbidding

his nearest rival by a clear £90). He'd come for a wardrobe, but obviously had an eye for a bargain. Opening it as a public attraction, Young displayed his collection of steam engines in the forge grounds. After neighbours complained about the relentless chuntering of the engines' compressors, he dug a cutting to deaden the noise – and nearly fell into the old Wheal Roots mine, which had lain undisturbed since 1860. Not one to look a gift mine in the head, he simply included the tin workings as part of his attraction, Halfpenny Park, alongside the air hockey tables and twopenny falls.

Then, in 1975, Robin Ellis arrived back from the American War of Independence over a sweeping television hilltop, and the nation went Cornish tin mining mad. The BBC's high-gloss adaptation of Winston Graham's Poldark novels drew in massive audiences (eventually being export-

Wish you were down here.

ed to twenty-two countries worldwide) and, quicker than you could doff a tricorn hat, Halfpenny Park was rebranded as the Poldark Tin Mine. They've got a keen eye for the value of a 1970s TV drama tie-in round these parts; the nearest village has even got a *Flambards* theme park. They've stopped short of naming the local garage after *The Duchess of Duke Street*, or building a Sweeneydrome in Carharrack, but you wouldn't put it past them.

Poldark justified its claim on the name by maintaining good relations with *Poldark*'s makers, who would occasionally pop by for one promotional reason or another. Guides here proudly state that the underground scenes of the series were filmed on location at the mine. Back in the 1970s, the BBC would normally have weighed up all their hefty cameras and lights, taken one look at the shiny wet stone tunnels here and opted for a nice safe White City studio full of varnished polystyrene. But a quick check of the DVD reveals that *Poldark* does feature some spectacular clambering about in a genuine tin mine, actors excitingly trapped 200 feet down, their felt hats and tallow candles drenched with authentic mine water. At a time when so much TV drama was studio-bound, a claustrophobic tin mine must have felt like a breath of fresh air.

A trip down the mine today feels thrillingly authentic – at least, as authentic as a twenty-first-century visitor with lily-white hands and a straight back can be expected to bear. The tunnels were not dug for public access, so Poldark is still covered by the Mines and Quarries Acts – and it feels that way. Though it's perfectly safe – a ninety-two-year-old woman was recently taken into the bowels of Poldark without tumbling down a whinze* – it is wet, cramped and steep, and you will, no matter how many times you're warned, repeatedly whack your head.† The wide passages you walk down were originally cut as economically as possible, no bigger than was needed for a man to pass through – broad at the shoulders, narrow at the feet – and known as 'coffin tunnels'.

Working life in the mine was indeed short (in the hardest mines a man

Poldark Tin Mine

---

* A tunnel that connects levels of a mine without ever reaching the surface.

† We kept a tally, cheering every time our hardhats rang dully against the roof. You may wish to have a competition with your friends to see who can hit their head the most, the loser having to carry the winner out and buy them a reviving pasty.

would be usefully finished by twenty-five). It was considered bad luck to send a woman underground, and there was no child labour as such, but women worked the stamping machines on the surface, and boys as young as ten could be seen toiling at the lode, learning the trade at their uncle's or father's side.*

Cornish miners' working conditions were skewed hard in favour of the employer. Men who'd often started their day with a ten-mile walk looking for work wouldn't be allowed to unpack their shovels until they'd underbid previous employees' wages in a topsy-turvy auction (deductions were also made for tools, candles, explosives, equipment, the cost of hauling rock to the surface and accident insurance). Skilled miners were paid by commission, which meant that once they hit a profitable lode, they were hard to stop. The temptation was to scratch out every scrap from a rich seam, often going almost to the surface, weakening the ground above. Thanks to this, Cornwall has more 'derelict land' than any other county, and the evidence of frenzied hollowing is all around you on the tour. There are stopes† in coastal mines where the digging stopped just in time, and you can hear the waves a few feet above you. A few more strokes of the pickaxe and the seawater would have poured in.

Down in Poldark, there's a constant rushing sound and, as you pick your way delicately down the dripping steps into the deepest shaft of the tour, water gushes past you on all sides, finding its way unerringly down the collar of your jacket. Occasionally, a guide wanting to scare the living daylights out of hardier-looking tour parties might turn off one of the two

---

* The child in the queue whom we heard nervously ask 'Do we have to dig?' had no idea how lucky he was.

† Stopes are big caverns within the mine. Remember them, along with adits, whinzes and lodes, and next Christmas you'll kick your family's arse at Scrabble.

pumps so the water suddenly overflows halfway up the mine. It livens up the day underground.

In a county with enormous mineral riches but no coalfields, the hunt was on for anyone who could get all that water out using as little fuel as possible. It was local boy Richard Trevithick who refined James Watt's enormous, expensive stationary engines into the revolutionary 'puffer-whims' that would eventually make Cornwall the world leader in state-of-the-art mining technology. Trevithick's engines used high-pressure steam in a way that Watt had dismissed as impossible, and were so compact that they could be dragged about on farm wagons. They made economical pumping feasible, would be exported worldwide as Cornish Engines and really, really got on James Watt's nerves.*

As you moistly leave what we might call the mine's 'dampening chamber', a broad and impressive wall looms above you. It's here that the scale and repetitiveness of the operation becomes clear – the ore was trawled up the face of this shaft by horse-whim, and the surface has been worn marble-smooth by the action of thousands of buckets bumping their way to the surface, day after day, for decades. As you contemplate the grimness of the miner's life, the last thing you expect to see round the next corner is a jolly red antique postbox. The owners boast that it is Britain's deepest, and will happily frank your holiday postcards to prove that they were mailed underground. The chamber is also licensed for subterranean weddings for anyone who fancies forgoing their topper and bridal veil for matching hard hats.

As you leave, the guide encourages you to throw a coin into a wishing-well pool cut into the rock. The money from this well goes towards the keep of a Cornish Cemetery in Real Del Monte, Mexico. From 1861 to 1901, one in five Cornish males emigrated, going where the work was – and that meant the silver mines of Central and Southern America. As Methodists, the miners couldn't be buried on Catholic ground, so were given their own cemetery, every headstone of which faces Britain. Mexico still produces its own version of the Cornish pasty (with chillies in it), and the town clock in Pachuca's Independence Square tolls with the chimes of Big Ben. Returning migrants could sometimes be seen walking the streets of Camborne and Redruth in colourful sombreros.

They had a better time of it than local hero Richard Trevithick. When

---

* The Trevithicks had been getting on Watt's nerves for many years. When Richard was five, his father, a mine captain, went to see Watt's pioneering new invention in London, and was later forced to return, shamefacedly, having 'accidentally' slipped the blueprints under his coat on the way out.

his inventions were exported to the Peruvian silver mines, Trevithick followed them, imagining he'd come back laden with South American riches. Instead he returned beanless eleven years later to discover George Stephenson had pinched his idea for a steam locomotive and puffed off to a fortune. He was buried in an unmarked grave.

If Poldark's current owners (a mining heritage trust who bought it in 1999) have their way, Cornwall's mining past will get a slightly more honourable monument. The free-to-enter attraction, with its friendly family amusements and well-tended floral borders, is in the process of changing from a funpark with a nice mine attached into something that more specifically honours the region's industrial history. The displays of assorted bric-a-brac are being replaced by whopping great wheels and massive chunks of engine: examples of the industrial ingenuity and technical skill that made Cornwall's miners and engineers world famous. Four millennia of Cornish tin production may have finally ended in 1998 with the closure of the South Crofty mine, but by going down Poldark you're getting, in the opinion of the chairman of English Heritage, one of the two most atmospheric mine tours in Europe.* Impressively, in 2006, thanks to the efforts of Poldark's owners, the Cornish mining landscape was granted World Heritage Site sta-

tus – the same designation as the Great Wall of China. The transition from dead industry to live tourist attraction will soon be complete.

Poldark Tin Mine, Wendron, Helston, Cornwall, TR13 0ES
01326 573173
www.poldark-mine.co.uk

---

* The other one's in Poland, so we'll take his word for it.

Brownsea Island

There are no countries in the world less known by the British than these self-same British islands.

George Borrow, *Lavengro*

It's early September and you, a fascinating personality holidaying alone in a wind- and rain-lashed Cornish holiday flat, have been playing the same eight gramophone records repeatedly since your arrival. Your furious neighbours are already banging on the thin walls, not caring that you, together with your copies of the Bible and the Complete Works of Shakespeare, have come away to escape exactly this sort of thing. This is the reason that Roy Plomley didn't choose to call his long-running wireless show *Peninsula Discs*.

The idea of relocating to a distant island will always be seductive to wistful souls. The chance to approach one's life afresh without being hindered or judged by the outside world appeals to anyone struggling to avoid being lapped in the rat race. The British, despite already living on an island, aren't immune to the romantic notion of discovering their own offshore lump of unfettered Utopia; it's why so many of them retire to the Isles of Man or Wight, those islands fringing an island.

500-acre Brownsea Island, the largest by far of a series of secluded landmasses encircled by Poole Harbour, would appear as the main thought bubble emanating from the Dorset heathlands to Brownsea's south-west (linked by the smaller bubbles of Furzey and Green Islands) in the unlikely event that the Dorsetshire heathland was to feature in its own comic strip. Brownsea is now maintained by the National Trust and normally populated only by a few staff, but down the centuries the isolated island has been passed from owner to owner like a hot offshore potato that no one could decide whether to bake, mash or roast.

The Romans are known to have enjoyed the ancient charms of the island, but by the time of the Domesday Book, Brownsea was considered so worthless that it failed to make the cut. Tide-bothering monarch Canute had enjoyed a decent little south-coast pillage earlier that century, spoiling much of the surrounding area, and doubtless making off with any of Brownsea's eleventh-century goodies worth a farthing or two. In Domesyear it was known as Bruno's Island, after the lord of the local manor, the name eventually corrupting to Branksea. Monks from Cerne Abbas ran it for the entire mediæval period, building themselves a chapel, and a hermit a hermitage, pleased to leave the site of that embarrassing chalk dude with his crown jewels on display a significant walk behind them. Complete with its tiny castle, originally built by Henry VIII to help defend England from some crosspatch Catholics, Brownsea today would be

pretty familiar to any 500-year-old former island residents allowed out of their retirement homes for the day.

To get to Brownsea you'll need to catch one of the day-return boats from Sandbanks or Poole – unless it's November, in which case you'll need to patiently stand in the queue with a flask of hot tea waiting until the crossings start again in March. Staffed by friendly but unnecessarily glowing types who have probably surfed to work all the way from Newquay, the most remarkable thing about this five-minute boatride is likely to be the unexpectedly high number of woggles.

Brownsea Island was home to the first ever Scout camp, arranged for twenty boys in August 1907 by Robert Baden-Powell, already a national hero for his siege-winning role in Boer War hit, Mafeking. Today scouts of all sizes and flavours are highly visible on the island, making the pilgrimage to the location of their movement's birth, where regular camps still take place throughout the year. A hundred troubled years after the inception of these ging gang goolier than thous, there's something rather stirring about the thought that there the bracken is still trodden by intrepid young bods erecting tents, lighting campfires and earning their survival badges if they see the night out.

Once part of the kingdom of Wessex, Brownsea Island is quite definitively far from the sodding crowd. The kind of people that visit are the National Trust's kind of people: seeking a quick fix of getting-away-from-

it-all, escaping the pressures of the mainland to a place where the only traffic hullabaloo comes from yacht motors or the odd passing jet-ski. ASBOs aren't issued on Brownsea, hoodies are rarely worn; the disdainfully prowling peacocks wouldn't allow it. They won't even fan their tails at humans, making it quite clear that they don't fancy us in the slightest. How rude.

The island has not always been such a magnet for daytrippers. In the 1850s Colonel William Waugh had snapped Brownsea up for a cheeky £13,000 on the information (kept from the seller) that the clay around the island was of such fine quality that it would be worth a far cheekier £1m. Waugh set about establishing a pottery works with a view to manufacturing top-quality porcelain, installing a clay-transporting tramway to further muddle Brownsea's organic natural character. A couple of hundred workers were employed and Waugh built Maryland village here, cosy enough to house those keen to avoid the daily nautical commute.* Unhappily for the colonel his clay inexpert had failed to correctly assess the quality of the resource so he (and his customers) quickly found themselves in deep doo-doo. The clay turned out to be fit only for drainpipe manufacture, a discovery made when the supposedly top-of-the-range sanitaryware produced at Brownsea turned out to be too fragile for the job. Best not to think about that too much.

Matters came to a head when a party of Poole traders nipped across to the island to ask Waugh to stand for parliament; Waugh was away, so they were received by his wife. On recognising the shop owners, a panicked Mary chose not to wait to hear the reason for their visit, instead launching an impassioned plea for them to be patient with regard to the non-payment of bills. Scratching their heads, the traders returned to Poole where several pennies finally dropped – an untidy amount of money was owed. Legal proceedings were instigated against the Waughs who, unable to come up

---

* Once boasting its own grocery store, pub and skittle alley, Maryland lived on in body if not in spirit until its use as a decoy in the Second World War. The Luftwaffe attacked a cunningly disguised Maryland, believing that they were having a pop at Dorset proper. Thanks to the assistance of two toilet cisterns, some paraffin and the Ealing Studios pyrotechnics department, the German attacks on Poole and Bournemouth were only sparingly effective.

with the necessary, promptly legged it to Spain, blazing a trail for future generations of British fraudsters. The pottery ceased production and the abandoned workers and villagers were forced to move on. The Waughs' splendid butler decided to stay on alone at Brownsea, having the renovated castle as a bolt-hole all to himself. Until he was noticed and kicked out, the canny butler survived by coming ashore and flogging off some of the remaining clay drainpipes in Poole whenever he required funds.

Despite all his attempts to turn Brownsea into a steaming industrial crater, Waugh still couldn't ruin it for the animals. Sika deer survived only to be killed off by one of the several fires that ravaged the island during the twentieth century, then recolonising when more hardy Sika managed to deer-paddle their way across from the mainland. Disappointingly AWOL from practically the whole of the rest of the country, red squirrels still go nuts for Brownsea. Their dingy American cousins have so far failed to make an appearance (although your bags aren't checked on arrival for smuggled-in greys). At around 0.5% of the current English population, there are just 200 or so reds here even in a good year, so don't get your hopes up that you will actually be seeing any.★ The undergrowth doesn't help matters by being a predominant reddish-brown (useful for the squirrels, rubbish for animal spotting). Why not enjoy lying to your kids instead? They've probably never seen a red squirrel, so try explaining that they are roughly the size of a woolly mammoth and leap silently on their prey from the trees. Nervous-backward-glances box ticked.

Fetching heathland and cloud-tickling pines encourage you to breathe in great lungfuls of fresh English Channel-scented air, and remind you that you forgot to take any hay fever tablets this morning (there are no branches of anything on Brownsea, especially Superdrug). It was exactly this kind of stupidly healthy environment that led Baden-Powell to start Scouting the island. Brownsea owners Charles and Florence van Raalte gave permission for that first 1907 camp, having met the impressive Baden-Powell on holiday in Ireland and heard of his plans to involve Britain's youth in the defence of the nation. Today a slightly dry stone memorial stares out to sea commemorating the site. Even with keen scouting eyesight, it's impossible to read the inscription on the seaward side, but the thumping great menhir looks substantial enough to carry 'BE PREPARED' on the rear in massive let-

---

★ Road safety bore Tufty spent years teaching red squirrels how not to die, so it's surprising that grey squirrels were the ones to survive. Why did the reds and greys have to fall out so spectacularly? If they had managed to successfully cohabit, how lovely Britain's parks and gardens would be, home to a new strain of rosé rodents.

ters, a suitable tablet for Baden-Powell's one commandment.

Charles – who was completely unprepared for the kidney infection-assisted pneumonia that finished him off in Calcutta the next year – officially rechristened Branksea as Brownsea. He had grown tired of his invited guests turning up late after a round trip to the similar-sounding Branksome railway station further back up the coast towards Bournemouth. Charles's enforced name change didn't quite stick with the locals; bloody-minded pensioners were steadfastly calling it Branksea until the late 1980s.

The faint whiff of scouts along with the mostly invisible red-squirrel presence are reminders that, like all proper getaway locations, Brownsea has somehow managed to escape the ravages of progress. Cut off from the rest of civilisation, time dawdles forward at a mercifully half-hearted pace – for which its final private owner should take much of the credit. From 1927, Mary Bonham Christie took control of the island with single-minded purpose. Brownsea was to be returned to its natural state of wilderness. Estate workers, domestics and their families were all shipped out, with a mere four out of 270 people remaining to oversee Bonham Christie's well-meant intentions. Everyone else became trespassers – the sole exception being a 1932  Scout trip she let in to celebrate their silver jubilee (and she even regretted that one). She chose to live in the now deserted Maryland, in the furthest cottage from the castle.

There was plenty of gossip and nonsense doing the rounds back in Poole concerning the lady's lonely island life, no matter how unlikely it was that she only took the air at the stroke of midnight to feed her gigantic wild rats. Grumpy at not being allowed onto 'their' island, locals spread rumours that Bonham Christie was hiding German spies on Brownsea. She wasn't, of course; she just wanted her wilderness campaign to keep making unkempt advances, and this was only interrupted when she agreed that Brownsea could be used as a temporary clearing centre for Dutch and Belgian refugees fleeing their Nazi invaders. She moved into the castle for the first time during this period, living in just one room surrounded by crates stuffed with her belongings, although she was happy to mix with the refugees and offer

Spot the red squirrel.

support where she could. Even when it was being used as a wartime decoy, Mrs Bonham Christie refused to leave the island, enjoying a spectacular view of the aerial bombardment from an unlit castle window.

When she died in 1961, the Bonham Christie family were left with crippling death duties and reluctantly gave up the island to the Treasury. The National Trust was encouraged to purchase Brownsea and it did so, having managed to raise a speedy £100,000. The substantial sum donated to the fund by the John Lewis Partnership explains their logo bafflingly stuck to the wall as if the castle were the most exclusive branch of the chain. In return, the company secured an arrangement giving it unique use of the castle as an ultra-secluded holiday home for its lucky staff. The Dorset Wildlife Trust now cares for the part of the island set aside as a nature reserve – Mrs Bonham Christie must be at the very least partially delighted.

With its castle, open-air theatre and church lending it an air of permanency and grandeur, a trip to Brownsea Island in the twenty-first century retains a distinctly *Swallows and Amazons* charm. Wandering by the daffodil field or the Scout post, it would come as no surprise to be confronted with a plum-faced chap wobbling a shotgun at you, or a Hurd of John Majors* chuntering about the joys of drinking a warm pot of tea in the middle of a cricket pitch on a balmy bank holiday Monday. There is nothing about Brownsea, as the Reverend Theophilus Bennett wrote of the place, 'that furrows the forehead with lines, and ages men before their time'. This is Little Britain, this island within an island – you need search for it no further.

Brownsea Island, Poole, Dorset, BH13 7EE
01202 707744
www.nationaltrust.org.uk/brownsea

---

* If that's not the correct collective noun then it should be.

Brownsea Island

British Commercial Vehicle Museum

What is this that roareth thus?
Can it be a Motor Bus?
Yes, the smell and hideous hum
Indicat Motorem Bum!

A. D. Godley

If there's one thing the British produce in lorry loads, it's vintage-vehicle enthusiasts. This Sunday, grab a pair of binoculars, throw on a sensible cagoule and go out to collect the set: from the Green-Capped Military-Vehicle Aficionado, through the Midlife-Crisis-Faced Sports-Car Collector, to the Common Greatly Spotted Train Enthusiast. Our love affair with these classic machines is such that people still yearn to return to the day (often well before their time) when they could take a choking steam train to the coast for a day's paddling and return, well and truly braced, with soot-caked lungs and confused hair.

So it's strange that, as a nation of plane, train and car lovers, we rarely champion that hero of Britain's transport heritage, the commercial vehicle. Because these machines are built to do the unglamorous somebody-has-to-do-it jobs, the idea of operating one doesn't conjure the same rush of pride as flying a Spitfire or stoking Mallard's boiler. The nation's walls may be adorned with paintings of classic vehicles that helped shape its history, but little is made of the unsung work-horses that toil behind the scenes. Imagine finding granny cross-stitching a sampler of a thundering Leyland T45 Roadrunner bearing the legend, 'the

The old vans' home.

toughest truck on two wheels'.*

The British Commercial Vehicle Museum occupies one building on the old Leyland site, so it's fitting that little touches remain preserved as they were in the manufacturer's heyday. The tiny outbuilding at the corner of the car park was once the gatehouse for the whole plant, the broad factory floor makes a perfect open-plan gallery for the large vehicles and the blacked-out glass panes in the museum's roof (painted during the Second World War to shield the plant from vicious Heinkels) help the museum's discreet lighting.

The walls are peppered with painstakingly restored radiator grilles scalped from the bonnets of dead trucks and buses and mounted like stags' heads on a grand staircase. These burnished chrome frontispieces, once hidden behind grubby soft toys, ossified insects and years

---

* Do look at the exhibition of paintings at the far end of the museum by long-distance lorry driver-turned-artist, Alan Spillett. You've never seen trucks and cabs more lovingly rendered in oils – and not a dirt-smudged 'clean me', 'also available in white' or 'I wish my wife was this dirty!' graffito in sight. When Alan took a shortcut through a picturesque village, he wasn't taking in the scenery like the rest of us, he was committing it to a mental canvas.

of exhaust grime, remind you that British vehicles used to have proper faces, like Thomas the Tank Engine or the Morris Minor (the car which Lord Nuffield – aka William Morris, the big twit – derisively dubbed 'the poached egg'). In another life, the polished grimace of the Thorncroft Nubian would have made a striking fireguard.

Thorncroft Nubian. Seddon Atkinson Omnibus. Massey Ferguson Tractor. Big vehicles need big names. No one in their right mind would want to be spotted emptying a ton of manure from a Toyota Picnic. (Over it, perhaps.) You could pack most of a provincial town into the AEC Mammoth Major 8 Mk III lorry and get the bugger halfway up Everest before the Mammoth showed any inkling of weakness.

Given the thrashing most of the examples here took during their lifetime, it's nothing short of a miracle that so many of them have survived. Things were built to last back then, you muse wistfully – even if you never lived through that halcyon era and every mechanical device you have owned has expired three days after the warranty. Because these vehicles are usually left rusting in bus graveyards rather than fed into merciless car crushers, you can pretty much guarantee that enough dismembered buses and trucks are available worldwide to strip for spares. Many of the display vehicles' bonnets prop up Before and After boards documenting their journey from single crumbling nut found in a field to freshly painted delivery lorry. The

worse the state of initial repair, the more apparent the restorer's glee. These miracle metal workers take no glory in buffing up paintwork scratches; they want to be ankle-deep in a slurry of rust by the middle of the job.

Wandering around the British Commercial Vehicle Museum, you're overcome by the shame that these hardworking vintage vans are in far better shape than your own set of wheels. Pristine lorries, trucks, buses and fire engines all conspire to embarrass you. You might almost have stumbled into a 1950s car show-room, with volunteers polishing so scrupulously that you can see your moustache or hatpin reflected in the scintillating sheen of the brake pedal. With many of the engines restored to full

roadworthiness, you have to fight the temptation to nip into the driver's seat and take one of them for a spin down the A65.

The tempting colours – all racing greens, mustards, pillar-box reds and navy blues – attract the wandering eye like jars of sweets, a proud historical snub to the current car industry diktat that you can have any colour you like as long as it's silver.* The cream interiors of the vintage trucks make them particularly homely. It's a cosier environment to sit in than the cold, slate-grey, plastic trim of most modern vehicles. Once upon a time, manufacturers respected that their drivers were going to spend a lot of time behind the wheel and were entitled to a few home comforts. It isn't hard to imagine the door mirrors festooned with flower baskets.†

To give you a taste of the trucker's high life (avoiding low bridges), you can board some of the vehicles and play in them. There's a Leyland DAF lorry cab into which you can haul yourself and pretend you're trucking a load of vital gromits from Portsmouth to Glasgow and hogging the middle lane. When you've finished admiring the fantastic Thatcher-era decals, try pressing the accelerator. BrrrrrrRRRRM! Real engine noise! Now try the lights. Now hide, wait for someone to walk in front of the bonnet and hit the lights and the throttle at the same time. Your victim will dive for the nearest wall. It rains on Grand Theft Auto's parade from an enormously satisfying height.

If, after that, you're let back into the museum, it might be time for some loud, relaxing music. Something in the small print of the paperwork for setting up a vintage-vehicle museum stipulates that a minimum of one steam organ must be on display at any time. The BCVM's contractual obligation comes in the form of a splendid Earl of Warwick Concert Organ – and it's

---

* Silver, according to car salesmen, is so popular because it is the colour on which dirt and damage show up least. Black and white, so the wisdom goes, are the best showcases for filth and dings.

† The car we inadvertently killed off while researching *Bollocks to Alton Towers* had beautifully cultivated window boxes of moss growing on the rear doors.

a doozie. Sadly its predecessor, a 1930s Franz Decap Dance Organ, is no longer with us. A picture shows it as a resplendent, unforgiving leviathan, a noisy art deco monolith: part jukebox, part castle.

The organ isn't the most over-the-top item on display. That accolade is reserved for the Popemobile. Yes, *that* Popemobile. Or, more accurately, one of *those* Popemobiles, since two were made for the pontiff's 1982 visit to Britain – one each for the Scottish and English legs of his papal gadabout. The English one is on display here and it's a monster.* In the flesh (as it were), it's far from the bumbling Papal ice-cream van you may have been expecting. This twenty-four-ton, six-wheeled, bullet-and-bomb-proof behemoth is built around a Leyland Constructor 6 chassis – chosen 'because of its renowned off-road performance'. Quite what His Holiness was planning on doing with such terrifying hardware after greeting his hordes of acolytes isn't specified, but we can only guess that the answer was 'anything'.

After such prestigious commissions, it's sad that countless buy-outs, mergers and acquisitions have led to the disappearance of the famous Leyland badge under an avalanche of capital letters. The Leyland Trucks factory, now part of PACCAR, still makes DAFs but, regretfully, no Leylands. Leyland used to build Foden trucks, but the last one rolled off the production line in July 2006. The only other big independent British truck manufacturer, ERF (a Foden spin-off) was scooped up by German-based MAN in 2000. The last scraps of the industry may well be swallowed – hook, line and adjustable, electronically controlled, four-bellows air suspension – by the Original Mississippi Steamboat Co. any day now, so the chances of seeing a truly British commercial vehicle in the wild are rapidly thinning. The expert conservationists at the old Leyland works have stuffed, polished and mounted the finest examples as a service to the nation. Long may the British Commercial Vehicle Museum mark the passing of its glorious marques.

British Commercial Vehicle Museum, King Street, Leyland, Lancashire, PR5 1LE
01772 451011
www.bcvm.co.uk

---

* The Caledonian Popemobile belonged to the late Mick Hayton, who bought it in 1998 for his Albion Truck Museum in Dumfries. It was sold at auction in September 2006 for an alms-busting £37,000.

National Fruit Collection

So I go to my apple-store like an acolyte to the shrine of Pomona and, if I do not wassail her, I mean to praise her on this autumn day.

H. J. Massingham, *An Englishman's Year*

An apple a day (or five, according to government guidelines) keeps the doctor away. Pop down to the National Fruit Collection at Brogdale in Kent at the right time of year and you could potentially enjoy 2,300 different types of apple a day, enough to keep a doctor the size of Godzilla away. (Watch it, though. This runs contrary to most healthy eating advice.) In this Braeburntastic chapter we'll be counting down the nation's top 1,000 apples, so sit back and crack open a can of scrumpy, all right, apple-pickers? Not 'alf.

Well, perhaps not, only it's difficult to stop reeling them off, so poetic are their names: Nutmeg Pippin, Scotch Dumpling, Bloody Ploughman. Schoolmaster, Chorister Boy, Kosmonaut. Greasy Pippin, French Crab, Golden Knob. Gavin, Wayne, Polly Prosser. Missing Link, Extraordinaire, Climax, Ballyfatten, Red Army, Dick's Favourite, Improved Cockpit. Now, how do you like them apples?

Apples might form the bulk of the collection, but Brogdale also hosts hundreds of pear, plum and cherry strains, and a fair smattering of fruit

you've only ever heard of in nursery rhymes. Before you've set foot through the turnstile, seek out the quinces and medlars growing next to the car park. If your fruit education stalled at the University of the Front Bit of the Supermarket, you might as well toss a coin to decide which one is which.

The National Fruit Collection originated in the early nineteenth century in the (not yet Royal) Horticultural Society's back garden in Chiswick. It was supposed to be a living record of Britain's fruit family tree. The absence of some sort of ancient knitted internet and the consequent lack of provender discussion boards had led to fruit-flavoured pandemonium; an apple known as a Granny Smith in one county might have been called a Prince Albert's Magnificent Royal Bum in the next.* Taxonomy was the hippest

game in town at the time, and the National Fruit Collection was an attempt to pin down each variety and give it a proper designation, not a folk name. It still isn't absolutely clear whether all of the duplicate identities have been spotted amongst the varieties new and old, popular or semi-retired, and some apples and pears may still be carrying multiple passports.

By 1921 the collection, now dubbed the National Fruit Trials, moved to Wisley in Surrey, remaining there for thirty more years until it was shifted lock, stock and apple, to Brogdale, the very core of the Garden of England. The fields of Kent didn't always heave with plump fruits. Richard Harris, gardener to Henry VIII, grew the first significant imported fruit garden a tiny hop up the A2 at Teynham. With the exception of crab apples, Britain has no native apples; most originated in Asia and were imported by Roman and Norman invaders amongst others – yet more immigrants making a valuable contribution to British culture.

The Trials ticked along placidly in Kent, watched over by the lazy eye of the Ministry of Ag, Fish and Food until the end of the 1980s when the government seriously started to lose interest. Brogdale's protected fruit would have disappeared completely, but a trust created by the local council, the Duchy of Cornwall and the Worshipful Company of Fruiterers saved

---

* Obviously we've invented this particular example. The Granny Smith wasn't introduced to Britain from Australia until the twentieth century.

the collection from a fate exactly the same as death.* There had been some muttered suggestions that the trees could be moved to another location

but Brogdale's favourable soil conditions and low susceptibility to frost made it the perfect place for growing fruit. The weather suits the trees down to the ground; the highest-ever recorded UK temperature (38.5°C) was registered at Brogdale's weather station in August 2003. Its balmy orchards are even sheltered by fringes of black alders whose leaves grow back as soon as the cold wind has whipped through for the sixty or so days necessary for the trees to bear fruit successfully.

Your tour around Brogdale will be shaped according to the whim of your guide. Ours started with a brisk march towards a tree bearing a fabulous pear, the Santa Maria.† After one has been picked, quartered and stuffed in your mouth, you'll know what you've been missing. It doesn't matter if you usually buy your fruit from a greengrocer or a supermarket, what this pear does to your mouth will probably never have happened before. The Santa Maria is fabulously crisp and flavoursome, with a crunch far more akin to the bite of an apple than the slightly soggy, grainy pears we are usually fobbed off with. If properly grown fruit used to taste this sexy, the lascivious way characters eye the plums and greengages in mediæval paintings might not be elaborate symbolism after all.

The sad truth is that supermarket fruit is grown for travel, rather than taste. The lovely sweet softness of a Fondante de Cuerne would be a mush by the time it got onto the shelf at Sainsbury's, pummelled about by thick stalks and a victim of the annoying way fruit refuses to tessellate neatly. Straight from the tree, that's the natural way to enjoy them. Few national collections can offer this; the Tate Modern won't let you stroll around its national collection with a paring knife, eating bits of Kandinsky's *Cossacks*.

---

* These Worshipful Companies are everywhere. On our travels writing this book we have tripped over fruiterers, fanmakers, salters, bakers and clockmakers. There are 107 of these City of London livery companies so it's going to take us a while to collect the set.

† Actually it's a pair of pear trees. The trees at Brogdale come in twos so that they can, well, get fruity and make plenty of fruit babies. It's like a Noah's Basket.

At Brogdale, the fruit never disappoints; your guide will have wandered the 150-acre site earlier on, creating a bespoke tour based on which fruit is the perfect ripeness to be tasted on that particular day. Do not, repeat DO NOT, spoil your appetite before you visit.

Tutti fruity.

The nation's favourite plc, Tesco, recently entered into a sponsor partnership with Brogdale. The sum involved, though substantial, is the sort of money Tesco make in the time it takes the average human being to fart satisfyingly, but the raised profile and interest generated by the deal has been extremely helpful to the trust. Brogdale was keen to involve itself in a long-overdue scheme to introduce more unfamiliar varieties of British-grown fruit to our supermarkets, thus breaking the stranglehold of those rather bland Mr Men apples (perfectly round, perfectly red, perfectly green) that fill our fruit bowls, bravely struggling to ripen.

Tesco marketing heads came up with Heritage apple variety packs, gleefully including the alluring film-star looks of the dusky Pomme Noire in its advertising campaign while giggling up its sleeve at the admittedly aesthetically-challenged Knobby Russet. Although Knobby is all dimples and mottles, a dead ringer for Charles Laughton in *The Hunchapple of Notre Dame*, beauty is in the tastebuds of the beholder, and the Knobby Russet is a belter. Perhaps some enlightened fruiterer might like to take advantage of its funny name and wonky looks by bottling it as a novelty juice. Waitrose has begun to sell lower grade fruits at cheaper prices, ideal for cooking and especially for jams. It's an admirable move, as many UK growers are being priced out of the market by our perceived demand for only the prettiest food. Let this go on and we are but a small step from checkout bag-packers making choo-choo train noises and asking if we need our purchases cut up into little bits.

In December 2006, Defra, owners of the Brogdale trees, announced that they were inviting single bids for a new contract to jointly maintain and curate the National Fruit Collection. Citing a desire to get best value out of the project, Brogdale has its back to the wall again. Hopefully Brogdale will see off this challenge as it has fended off several potentially fatal blows over the last half-century. The collection survived fiscal trauma in the 1990s, and its future hung in the balance until a property developer's intentions for the land were curbed by the denial of planning permission. Now that the trust's financial situation has become more stable, helped by takings at the gate, plant centre and gift shop (do go home with an absurdly delicious jar of something or other), perhaps the decades of hard work already put into the conservation of those thousands of varieties will weigh heavily in Brogdale's favour.

A sedate inspection of the National Fruit Collection makes for a majestic day out. Follow the drunken wasps, never happier as they dopily buzz around the cider apples and perry pears, filbert bushes and cherry blossom of this tempting garden of paradise. Generations of Costard-apple-hawking costermongers, Richard Cox (the Bermondsey brewer who gave us Britain's most widely grown dessert apple, the orange pippin) and old Granny Smith herself will join you in spirit. Eat well, and no scrumping.

Brogdale Horticultural Trust, Brogdale Road, Faversham, Kent, ME13 8XZ
01795 535286/535462
www.brogdale.org

Anaesthesia Heritage Centre

Sleep hath its own world.

George Gordon Noel Byron, *The Dream*

Tucked away near Harley Street, in the left ventricle of the heart of London's Operating Theatreland, is a museum dedicated to a subject you probably won't have lost much sleep over: the history of anaesthetics. The Anaesthesia Heritage Centre is easily overlooked in the basement and shadow of 21 Portland Place, an imposing mansion block owned by the tongue-twisting Association of Anaesthetists of Great Britain and Ireland (or AAGBI, which is easier to say with your mouth forced open by tongue forceps).

The Heritage Centre's scalpel-neat topiary and clean hospital-white porch frame the entrance to a very exclusive club, at whose arcane pleasures the rest of us can only marvel. This isn't a Museum or a Collection, it's a Heritage Centre, and Heritage Centres are all about nostalgia. For a very thin slice of the population, the artefacts on display here are rich with bygone resonance. You can imagine veteran surgeons and ageing anaesthetists rolling out of the doors, giggling and punching each other in the arm, swaggering into the pub to reminisce about the Brady and Martin Spirometer and the Cardiff Penthrane Inhaler, going on about how the  tube mountings on the Newcastle Bang Ventilator are a total blast from the past, like ordinary folk do about people they went to school with. One of the staff talks with faintly embarrassed relish about watching 1960s-set TV hospital drama *The Royal* and shouting out the names of the equipment as it appears on screen.

The centre's collection of objects grew from an initial hoard of seventy items belonging to Charles King, an engineer and medical equipment salesman trading to Harley Street at the beginning of the twentieth century.

Through his daily contact with surgeons, King became a prime mover in anaesthesia technology. He's the man who, with Dr Robert Minnitt, co-created a device capable of administering an inhalation-regulated blend of nitrous oxide and oxygen to the patient. This invention is directly responsible for the gas-and-air systems in maternity wards today (and in no way responsible for the grin behind dentists' masks).

If some of King's prototypes on display in the museum look as if they're cobbled together from scrap valves and pieces of car engine, it's prob-

ably because this is exactly what they are. Like many great men, King had a history of tampering with vehicles. A heavy smoker, he installed an oxygen pipe in his car, just in case he ran into trouble breathing while driving. This is not the combination of gas and air that he's most associated with, perhaps, but it does give an insight into the resourceful mind of the inventor, and would be a great pick-me-up for interminable motorway drives.

A video monitor in the centre's central hall plays a short film introducing the collection, hosted by Dr Peter Wallace (Lord Mayor of Anaesthetist Town and AAGBI President 2002–4). A second screen opposite is reserved for showing reels of historic films on anaesthesia. If you're at all squeamish at the thought of watching (a) footage of surgical procedures or (b) Dr Peter Wallace, you may want to close your eyes and hum quietly. If you can stomach the archive footage of anaesthetic pipes being forced down volunteers' throats, you'll appreciate the boon that pain relief has been for modern surgery. We're so mollycoddled by present-day operating techniques that it's easy to forget how recently the anaesthetic revolution took place and how different things might have been.

Until the 1840s, the process of surgery was nasty, brutish and sharp, dependent on speed, luck and alcohol (for all parties). A lot of patients didn't make it through their surgery and, in the case of amputation, a lot of surgeons didn't make it through their patients. The only alternatives to alcohol were suck-it-and-see treatments such as ice, opium and dwale. Dwale, a pungent fourteenth-century brew used as a sleeping potion, was cobbled together from hemlock, opium, henbane, bryony root, vinegar, lettuce and bile★ and would have been the type of drink to ask a few serious questions on the way down before forcing its way up again in order to answer them.

The race to find something slightly more sophisticated than a glass of dwale on the rocks followed by an opium chaser heralded the birth of modern anaesthesia. The new patient-relaxants included nitrous oxide (fast and funny), chloroform (potentially lethal) and ether (safer than chloroform, but highly volatile, risking the patient waking up at the precise moment they were blown out of the window). Anaesthetic technology was moving quickly, yet still dogged by the ever-present nightmare of patients coming round mid-operation and seeing how it all worked. More refined drugs followed, as did the development of specialised equipment such as rubber tubes, syringes and valves designed to ensure a constant and safe dosage, examples of which are on display in the centre.

Smaller items of equipment can be viewed in drawers beneath the main displays, temptingly labelled *Airways/Tongue Forceps* or *Mouthgags/Mouthprops*. Depending on your level of expertise their contents will resemble either landmarks in the development of medicine or that stuff that's kept in the gap between your cutlery tray and drawer. Unfortunately space constraints demand that the bulkier apparatus and the rest of the 2,000 item-strong collection is relegated to storage (although a catalogue of the oversized overstock reveals contraptions that bear startling similarities to black-and-white-era *Doctor Who* robots). There are some large oddities on display, one of

Vintage anti-ouch equipment.

★ Yes, lettuce.

the largest and oddest being the electro-cardiogram machine used during George VI's treatment for lung cancer in September 1951. This was the last operation to be performed at Buckingham Palace (not counting the removal of a benign Michael Fagan from the Queen's bedroom in 1982).

In 1939 Britain suffered a severe outbreak of Second World War, and suddenly Fritz was Blitzkrieging his way across Europe, creating an urgent need for mobile medical equipment. If anaesthesia technology was moving at a fair old lick before the 1940s, then the war gave it a jet-propelled boot up the fundament from which it's still benefiting today. Soon chloroform-inhaler backpacks were shipped out to troops desperate for portable, durable apparatus. After the war many field anaesthetists found their way into roles within the newly founded NHS.

No potted history of anaesthesia would be complete without mention of Edgar Pask, widely regarded as the bravest man in the RAF never to have flown an aeroplane. Pask was employed at the Nuffield Department of Anaesthetics at Oxford University under the guidance of Sir Robert Macintosh – Britain's first professor of anaesthetics. During the war the two worked together at the Physiological Laboratory of the RAF. It was here that Pask tested different survival methods that could be employed by airmen in case of emergency. One of Pask's tests saw colleagues dropping him in the deep end of a swimming pool while anaesthetised in order to discover whether his self-designed lifejacket would keep his head above water. Simulating the floppy dead weight of an unconscious airman involved a lethal cocktail of drugs and potential drowning. Sixty-a-day smoker Pask liked to push his body to its limits. It's possible his sheer balls would have kept him afloat even if his jacket failed. A slightly less-than-essential deployment of Pask's talents occurred when Winston Churchill requested that Macintosh's team develop an oxygen mask that might allow a person to simultaneously breathe oxygen and enjoy a trademark cigar at high altitude. Unsurprisingly, the whole thing went off like a joke-shop cigarette.

The development of anaesthetics, like all branches of medical science, is a perpetual work in progress, refined by unsung experts who really know what they're doing with all these cylinders, masks and rubber tubes. The Anaesthesia Heritage Centre is the only place we've got dedicated to this vital practice's history and continued research. Next time you stumble to the bathroom first thing in the morning and blearily mistake the tube of Deep Heat for the toothpaste, spare a thought for our many wonderful analgesics and anaesthetics, and give praise to this branch of medicine that touches our lives and leaves us comfortably numb. Flicking back the operating-theatre curtain and taking a peek into this hitherto unimagined cabal, with all its secret language and bizarre machinery, is a mind-broadening bit of fun. Just relax, breathe deeply and count backwards from a hundred.

Anaesthesia Heritage Centre, Association of Anaesthetists of Great Britain and Ireland, 21 Portland Place,
London, W1B 1PY
02076 311650
www.aagbi.org/heritage/heritagecentre.htm

Anaesthesia Heritage Centre

Bressingham Steam Museum and Gardens

... better men than we go out and start their working lives
At grubbing weeds from gravel paths with broken dinner-knives.

Rudyard Kipling, 'The Glory of the Garden'

Nothing could be more British than the words 'Steam Museum and Gardens'. For an uncommonly British day out, just one of these would more than suffice. If, however, by the time you leave Bressingham, you think they accurately encompass the scope of this attraction, you've missed something. This isn't just a Steam Museum and Gardens. By gum, no. In fact, it is – although this probably wouldn't fit nicely on the signs or stationery – the Bressingham Steam Museum, Gardens, Dad's Army Museum, Smallest Cinema In The World, Garden Centre, Vehicle And Fairground Ride Collection, Fire Museum, B&B And Del Boy Experience. Truly, this is a giant of a day out.

It was Alan Bloom's idea. He bought Bressingham Hall in 1946 and turned some of its 220 acres into a farm and nursery. He turned a pond into a lake. He turned the nursery into the largest in Europe. And then he did what any self-made man does when he has run out of things to transform into other things: he bought a steam engine. Then another thirteen. And laid a narrow-gauge railway. Then another three railways. And built a locomotive shed. And bought a fairground merry-go-round. And bought the official Dad's Army memorabilia collection. And so on. You get the picture.

One of the great pleasures in taking a day out is to be surprised:

and you're seldom treated to as many surprises as there are at Bressingham. You're greeted by the sunny sight of Blooms Garden Centre, which distinguishes itself from your average B&Q or Homebase by filling its car park with soothing chuff-chuffing. On the other side of a low picket fence, Bressingham's 0-4-0 Locomotive No. 1 – aka Alan Bloom – can be spotted building up a gusty head of steam.* Built by the museum's own workshop staff from scratch, it's a highly polished, burgundy-and-gold beauty that loops around the splendid gardens at a genteel pace. It's stoked, driven and maintained by volunteers – as you can tell from their big smiles. Knowing that you're somewhere on your own time by your own choice, if possible wearing a train driver's hat, is the key to happiness in the workplace. Even so, these chaps have to work their way up to the lofty heights of engine driver. The rigid railway hierarchy is part of the fun – they're living out their boyhood dreams.

Chuffed to bits.

The Alan Bloom is one of eight narrow-gauge locomotives that live here with their fourteen bigger siblings, all of which have magnificent monikers like Ivor, Oliver Cromwell and King Haakon VII. They share the grounds with the many traction engines (Bessie, Bunty, Bertha, Boxer, Beulah, Buster, Brutus and the others) and the assorted engineering marvels that make up the rest of the

---

* You may, like us, have wondered what those three numbers mean. Well, we can far from exclusively reveal that they're the Whyte Notation classification system. The first digit refers to the leading wheels (unpowered, helpful with curves), the second, the driving wheels (powered) and the third, the trailing wheels (unpowered, supporting the cabin). If you're ever attacked by a man in an anorak, you'll know how to distract him.

steam collection. The biggest of these is the 'Gallopers' merry-go-round. Its hearty organ pumps out selections from *Jesus Christ Superstar* and the theme from *The Wombles* – proving that calliope rolls were being made as late as 1973 and making you wonder if you can get any Deep Purple for it. It's a blindingly colourful bit of kit, and, given that it's over a hundred years old, in terrific nick. Again, it's maintained by volunteers.

You'll probably be quite machined-out by now, so take yourself off to the gardens – which could fill a book themselves (perhaps lovingly pressed). Alan Bloom was one of the greatest horticulturists of the twentieth century, and the many gardens here – among them the delirious Dell Garden and the unreal hues of the Snake Bed – are a fitting memorial for a man so dedicated to flora. The detail and variety in his many innovative 'island beds' is breathtaking. Bloom – a man who could only have been more appropriately named if he'd been called Alan Steam-Museum-and-Gardens – introduced over 200 perennials himself and, to this day, Bressingham will help anyone who's discovered or bred a new strain of plant to develop and market it. It's the politest imaginable way of playing God.

Saunter from the Elysian blaze of the gardens with nostrils full of invigorating pollen, and walk towards a low hangar to step happily into the cool blue shadows of the Dad's Army Museum. Inevitably, at this point, a voice in your head will be asking, 'Why is there a Dad's Army Museum here?' Well, much of the location shooting for the TV series and film was done around Thetford, a few miles away, and Boxer and Bertha (see above) had puff-on roles in the show but, to be honest, it's best to simply accept that if you're having an uncommonly British day out, sooner or later you're going to wind up in a Dad's Army Museum, and lap up the atmosphere.

Set dressing, vehicles, props, photos, scripts, albums★ and Perry and Croftian assortimentia all live in this warehouse; it could be the clutter of a cinema soundstage. Indeed, stretching the full length of the shed is an indoor recreation of television's very own Walmington-on-Sea, complete with post office, Swallow Bank (manager: George Mainwaring), Jones the butcher's shop, Frazer's funeral directors, the town fire engine and even a Jeep signed by the cast (beat that, autograph hunters). This must surely be a British first – a tourist attraction dedicated to a sitcom. There's no sign of a Fawlty Towers World (especially since the building used as the hotel's

★ Trapped tantalisingly behind glass is *Bless 'Em All! Arthur Lowe Sings The Songs Of World War II With The Richmond Orchestra & Chorus Under Malcolm Lockyer*, an album that we've been scouring eBay for ever since.

exterior was destroyed by a combination of fire and property developers in 1991) and there's certainly no Only Fools and Horses Museum.

Oh, no, hang on, here it is. At the other end of the warehouse. Yes, that's the Trotters' living room, all right, down to the plastic pineapple ice buckets on the magnolia home bar. And that's a yellow Reliant Regal Supervan (looking quite terrified and very, very small next to Bertha, of whom etc.). And that's a yellow double-decker bus, the Mobile Only Fools and Horses Museum, which has had a close shave with a low bridge at some point. You think Bressingham can't pull anything more out of the bag, and then it does, in spectacular style. You're at the height of your stupid-boy-ing and don't-tell-him-Pike-ing, when suddenly you find yourself lovely-jubbly-ing and Rodney-you-plonker-ing.

By this point, you'll have realised that this isn't, as it seemed from the road, a garden centre with a steam railway amongst the flowerbeds: it's something a great deal more ambitious. Bressingham is Britain World, a memorial to the things we deem precious: flowers, steam trains and situation comedies about underdogs of all breeds. It may be a delirious kedgeree made of everything in the cultural fridge, but it's a more accurate reflection of Britain than the top-down planning of the Millennium Dome could ever offer, because it grew from the ground up.

As if frightened that all this might not be enough, Bressingham stuffs every other spare corner of the site with small delights designed to tickle various other national passions. Elsewhere you can stumble upon model trains, a collection of railway uniforms and ephemera (oh, look, it's a horse-measuring gauge) and, of course, the Smallest Cinema In The World – an elaborate roco-co caravan with a tiny silver screen and a handful of plush seats (a great deal smaller than the Smallest Cinema In The World in Nottingham, and pos-sibly smaller than the Smallest

Cinema In The World in Radebeul, Germany – not that we'd wish to start a fight, because they're all no doubt excellent in their own smallest ways).

There's nowhere quite like Bressingham, because nowhere could Catherine-wheel off in quite the same directions. It's as if John Betjeman had been left in charge of the Eden Project: a shrine to unassuming pottering. It's pretty and personal. Even the tannoy announcements have a charm about them. 'Hope you had a nice day here at Bressingham. The weather's been lovely. But we are closing in five minutes …' Bressingham is one family's portrait of what Britain might fancy doing on its days off, done with a flair and wit as individual as their personalities. Were he still alive today, Alan Bloom would be chuffed to know that his vision is blooming.

Bressingham Steam Museum and Gardens, Thetford Road, Bressingham, Norfolk, IP22 2AB
01379 686900
www.bressingham.co.uk

Alderney

I know that's a secret for it's whispered every where.

William Congreve, *Love for Love*

Small, as you may have heard, is beautiful. Less often mentioned – but increasingly obvious – is that big is rubbish. Big gives you a ticket number and tells you to wait until your name is called; big insists that your call matters even though you're being held in a queue; big makes you shuffle between ribboned barriers in a switchback-laden line of unbreakfasted travellers at an airport. Big treats you like a goat. Small, on the other hand, treats you like a human being.

Three miles long and two wide, the island of Alderney is extremely small. Luckily, the population of 2,300 Ridunians* is itself small enough to fit on the island and still leave enough space to be terribly charming to each other. Everything about the island is intimate. Flying there, from Bournemouth, Southampton or Shoreham, slams this home. You're in a plane narrower than a car. There are about ten of you, practically sitting in each other's lap. You're called to join the flight by your first name. At maximum altitude (which you can check by peering at the altimeter over the pilot's shoulder), you've barely got the clouds in your hair and could probably give some-

one lounging on a yacht below a hand with their crossword. You're likely to bump into your fellow passengers several times during your stay on Alderney. When you land, the airport is about the size of a provincial infant school. At the entrance is a peep of chickens pecking and scratching around the gate. Alderney is one of the few

Alderney

---

* Pay attention. 'Which island's inhabitants are known as Ridunians?' will be a million-pound question on *Who Wants To Be A Millionaire?* one of these days, mark our words.

places where you can give someone directions to the airport using poultry as a landmark.

British, but not British, Alderney was first attached to the English crown in 1066, when William the Conqueror (trading as Duke William of Normandy) became King of England. To this day, the island remains loyal to the Duke of Normandy – who, at the time of writing, is HM Queen Elizabeth II. And, although it's not part of Britain, Alderney is part of the Bailiwick of Guernsey, which is a crown dependency – in other words, the British Crown owns it, but doesn't run it. Like all the Channel Islands, it is not subject to the British Parliament, but has its own legislature, the States of Alderney, comprising a President and ten States Members (none of whom is paid for the job). It's not part of the EC (i.e. it's Duty Free, so bring a shopping trolley), but maintains relations with the EU via the UK. If this all sounds rather tangled and complicated, it is. Think of it this way: Alderney is one of Britain's nieces – cherished by Auntie Brit, but seldom answerable to her.

The Alderney Odeon.

You've probably either lived or visited or holidayed somewhere small, but when it's this small and it's an island, you may as well be in an Enid Blyton adventure, somewhere just different enough to be exciting, but seemingly safe. The shops you see today – Richards Stores, the Albert House café – are the same ones you'd have seen forty, fifty years ago. (Photos at the award-winning museum attest to this.) The interval at the cinema (open three nights a week) scatters the audience towards the local pubs until an alarm sounds in the street, so everyone can hear it, sending the filmgoers scuttling back to their velvet-covered seats for the dénouement. Alderney has steadfastly refused to stop doing the improbable things twinkle-eyed grandparents insist to disbelieving grandchildren were done back in their day.

Motoring on Alderney is similarly one of the Experiences That Time Forgot. If you drive around the island (barely bothering third gear) and the bairn in the back dares to ask, 'Are we there yet?' the answer is probably, 'Yes.' You're never far from anywhere – indeed, you can go quite mad passing the same things again and again and again. Alderney registration plates bear the letters AY followed by up to four numbers. The game is to spot the lowest number. AY1 and AY2 are  trucks. AY8 is a Triumph Herald estate. AY999 is – good guess – the police car. The speed limits (35mph and 15mph in built-up areas) are disconcerting since they don't end in noughts. There are three speed humps and one parking attendant on the island. Some of the roads disintegrate before your eyes: a metalled stretch turns into a barely-trodden track in an instant. And people don't just leave their cars unlocked here – they leave the keys in the ignition.

In case you're thinking of rushing over there to nick some cars, think again. There's a reason you can leave your keys in the ignition here: there's no crime. Where are you going to take the car you nick? At most, three miles. And, after that, nowhere. The police wouldn't need to chase you – they could just stand still and wait until you drove past again. If you mess about here, everyone, but everyone, is going to know.* Small places have secrets, but they're open secrets. Just as the quietest Agatha Christie village had bodies piling up in the vestry, and the cosy afternoons of the Famous Five always peeled up at the edges to reveal unshaven, child-coshing smugglers, the sweetest-looking places can hide the nastiest surprises.

The grassy, picnicky area north of Telegraph Bay, near the airport, is a blackberry picker's wet dream, a tangled riot of brambles heaving with fat fruits. Tuck in. You probably won't even notice the concrete gate posts that part the thorny branches, let alone wonder who built them and why. But you've just stumbled upon Alderney's open secret. This was the entrance to the only SS concentration camp on British soil.

---

* On our visit, dozens of shop windows were displaying a home-printed page asking for help solving the case of a local pensioner who'd had her jewellery box stolen. The notice didn't end with the usual blurb about a reward being offered for information leading to the arrest and conviction of anyone etc., but the emboldened, underlined question, 'How could anyone be so cruel?' Such simple humanity is enormously humbling.

Alderney played an extraordinary part in the Second World War. Hitler saw the Channel Islands as unsinkable battleships, logic that crumbles on closer inspection: unsinkable, yes – but also immovable. And, if your enemy's advancing at you and you can't run away, you are, in military argot, fubar. Still, a hopelessly ill-thought-out idea never stopped the Nazis doing their thing, and in the summer of 1940 the island was invaded, all but a few residents having got out before the German forces turned up and started turning it into a fortress. Naturally, the army didn't do this conversion themselves; instead, they shipped in a 4,000-strong work party of prisoners and forced labourers.

The prisoners (deludedly labelled 'volunteers' by the Nazis, as if that might help) were stationed in four camps: Helgoland, Norderney, Borkum and Sylt. They slaved for twelve hours a day, seven days a week, with a lunch break that could be as short as ten minutes, and a half-day off once a month. Fortifying Alderney was a back-breaking slog, yet they had no clothes issued to them (so when their shoes wore through, they worked with rags tied round their feet), no access to medical care and no right to complain about their duties. Their daily diet was a pint of coffee-substitute for breakfast, a pint of cabbage soup for lunch and another for supper, this time with a slab of bread thrown in. No meat. No fruit. No milk. Some prisoners came so close to starvation that they scavenged through the slaughterhouse bins for rotting entrails to eat. Others accidentally killed themselves by eating nightshade berries. The death rate was two or three prisoners per camp per day. Men were garotted, hanged or shot for rule breaking or being hungry or just too weak to build bunkers.

Though there is a memorial to the prisoners, festooned in flowers, at one end of the island, the least spectacular but most affecting monument on Alderney is the blurred, overgrown footprint of Lager Sylt. This labour camp was handed over in March 1943 to the SS, who ringed it with extra fortifications and turned it into a concentration camp. Those blackberry-covered concrete gateposts are twisted with grim history. This is where the SS brought their prey to be shot. A few yards down the road, at the top of the Val de l'Emauve, was the site of the chalet built for camp commandant Maximilian List. A tunnel into Sylt's heating block gave List a handy back door into his domain and, though the chalet was dismantled and recon-structed elsewhere on Alderney after the war, the secret tunnel is still there, its entrance heavily bearded in ivy and gorse.

Peering down a concrete passage into the pitch darkness of a disembow-elled basement isn't far from terrifying. Though Sylt wasn't a death camp, it was run by the same SS Death's Head unit[*] maniacs who were in charge at Auschwitz and Buchenwald. Reminding yourself this tunnel led to noth-ing more sinister than a boiler room is little consolation; Sylt is a sobering place: the wreckage of a horror we probably prefer to think only happened in some unvisited corner of Eastern Europe. But here it is, just down the road from a quiet British pub with a portrait of the Queen swinging jaun-tily outside draped in bunting. It seems like a scene from *Went the Day Well* – the vile machinery of the Third Reich left on a village doorstep.

What is interesting about Alderney today is the way it handles this dark episode in its history. Little or nothing is either fenced off or signposted, so it's all there to be seen, if you can find it. The inhabitants treat the upsetting detritus of invasion and slavery in the same way an Ancient Briton might have grown vegetables up the side of a Roman guardpost. Successive waves of defensive structures have bristled from the cliffs of Alderney ever since the Middle Ages, so a gun emplacement or a radar bunker doesn't seem out of place, no matter who built it.

Sensitively, Alderney neither dines out on its wartime past, nor hides it from you. Many of the Second World War fortifications still stand, simply because the amount of explosive needed to blow up these gaunt, reinforced concrete blocks makes it wildly uneconomical; they were designed to with-stand a bigger battering than peacetime is usually willing to provide. And, since these structures are not going anywhere in a hurry, the islanders have just got used to them being around. Mobile-phone antennae are strapped to a Luftwaffe telecommunications tower that now belongs to the water board.

---

[*] The *Totenkopfverband*. We would pepper this chapter with lots of multisyllabic German words, but all those *Unterscharführers* and *Festungskommandanturs* take forever to type. Besides, 'Flak' is far easier to spell than '*Fliegerabwehrkanone*', and German typos in a book of uncommonly British days out might well cause certain readers an excess of Schadenfreude.

The massive five-storey concrete lookout shrugging its round shoulders on top of Mannez Hill has been christened The Odeon, after its likeness to one of Harry Weedon's modernist cinemas. If you fancy looking inside this deserted direction-finding post, pop into the homely shop of the Alderney Wildlife Trust in St Anne, borrow the key (for a small consideration) and get a first-hand, unguided tour. Looking out towards the mainland through one of its blustery observation decks is chilling in more ways than one. This is how scarily near the Third Reich came to Britain.

The soldiers marooned here for five years (many of whom thought they were on the Isle of Wight) called it 'the arsehole of the world' and treated it with a mixture of contempt and efficiency. When the islanders returned in December 1945, they found a mess. Their former homes and workplaces had been ransacked, looted and – in some cases – completely destroyed. Street lighting wasn't working and manhole covers were missing, so rats were everywhere. (One poor woman nearly expired when a rodent jumped out of her harmonium.) Birds had abandoned the island, so the native snails and slugs had become worryingly large in size and number. Some islanders, quite understandably, turned round and went straight back to Britain. But those who stayed were optimistic. The Germans had, after all, left them resurfaced roads, improved electricity and water systems, mains drainage and a new bakery.

The history is remarkable, but Alderney is one of those remarkable places. The wildlife (including the native Blonde Hedgehog, as championed by *Literary Review* Bad Sex Award runner-up Alan Titchmarsh) is exceptional, the granodiorite rocks are pink and purple, and a warm Franco-British culture perfuses the island. St Anne's High Street becomes Le Huret. The supermarket is LeCocq. Yet it's got pound notes and the Coronation pub and a proper Giles Gilbert Scott phone box (painted a fitting other-side-of-the-tricolore blue).* Eccentricity thrives. The train, which makes three (short) return journeys per day at the weekend, is a diesel locomotive called Elizabeth pulling two 1950s London Underground carriages. The locals see in the New Year by being hosed down by the fire brigade in the town square. There's an annual sandcastle competition. And a daft raft race. And homemade biscuits in the rooms at the Georgian House Hotel. And the slim chance of bumping into the fifth Beatle.† And all that VAT-free shopping.

It's such a seductive, quirky island that it's hard to imagine it strafed with 30,000 landmines and 60,000 yards of barbed wire. Happily, there's nothing ghoulish about Alderney because its open secret is so well handled. It's enough to make you feel – well, human.

Alderney

---

* Not the only bit of Gilbert Scott on Alderney: Giles's grandfather George designed the parish church of St Anne, which Betjeman thought 'quite the best of his work I have ever seen'.

† National treasure George Martin chose to live here, joining an elite that includes Duncan Goodhew, Julie Andrews, Ian Botham, John Arlott and Elizabeth Beresford, creator of the Wombles.

Sharmanka

If it weren't for those pesky Normans, Huguenots, Saxons, Vikings and all the other settlers, invaders and conquerors, and all the stuff they did after they'd turned up, it's likely that Britain would have stalled at Quite Ordinary without ever quite reaching Great. Our island needed all those fresh pairs of eyes and, as Sharmanka shows, it's not just the longboatmen, longbowmen and fugitive French Calvinists who can make a difference. When someone is denied artistic freedom under the terms of their own country, they can come here and be embraced, appreciated and recognised.

Mechanically minded Russian sculptor Eduard Bersudsky is just such a

someone and, with the assistance and encouragement of Tatyana Jakovskaya, he has set about establishing a cast of clanking and spinning contraptions at Glasgow's Sharmanka Kinetic Theatre. A darkened room has been stuffed to bursting with performing machines that meld Russian and Scottish folklore with an understated social and political commentary, all to the accompaniment of an eclectic musical soundtrack. It is as unusual as it is unnerving, a mysterious toymaker's midnight workshop.

A Sharmanka show begins with Jakovskaya briefly recounting the history of the exhibit, before the room lights dim and coloured spotlights direct your gaze, one by one, to the dozens of automata, or kinemats, with their countless human, animal and devilish animated figures. Fashioned from wood and metal, otherwise unwieldy items of abandoned furniture and salvaged scrap dance gracefully around: lawnmower parts, fan blades, old sewing machine treadles all given mechanical life. You wouldn't want to get into a fight with one of these babies.

Earlier works are made from Russian rubbish, newer ones from Scottish. The older pieces often feature fragments of intricately turned antique furniture, rescued when Russian families modernised their homes, putting their heirlooms out for the glorious party binmen. Thirty years on, this furniture is too expensive to get hold of as scrap, so Bersudsky now favours modern cast- offs such as washing-machine extractor hoses and bicycle wheels. He still prefers to employ items that appear to have lived a little, as if their story helps him tell his. Each kinemat is thus touched with an imagined patina of history, no matter how recently it was constructed. Some of Bersudsky's sculptures appear to have been created hundreds of years ago. Fair enough. Parts of them were.

The action flits to and fro around the room; apparently random but obviously carefully choreographed. Each mechanism creaks slowly into action, powered by vintage technology remotely operated from an unobtrusive control box. The promenading spectators feel like supporting players in a Jan Svankmajer animation, never quite sure where the next surprise will come from, charmed and confused at the same time. Bells toll and tinkle, bicycle wheels whirl, and knives slice air. Each piece packs an allegorical punch however you choose to approach it. Kafka and Bulgakov make appearances in spirit, while Stalin and Marx are physically represented. Sharmanka may be built from junk but it's bolted together with shrugging, Eastern Bloc philosophy: its many characters seemingly insignificant cogs that the larger cogs couldn't do without. This is the unpredictable stuff of dreams, and not necessarily

nice ones, the sort that keep you clutching the sheets, wide eyed, nervous of what sleep might bring. It's definitely not somewhere you'd want to spend the night.★

Sharmanka is the Russian word for a barrel organ, and it was the name given to the first key piece constructed by Bersudsky. Inspired by the music-making beggars of his childhood, this sculpture shows a carved fellow with a finely chiselled beard wearing a jaunty hat and sporting a big bird atop his head. He winds the titular barrel organ to the accompaniment of a bell-ringing monkey and a cymbal-playing marionette. Oh dear. It's all gone a bit Pinky and Wonky. Things aren't right when the puppet has a puppet.

For almost two decades Bersudsky created these ingenious kinetic sculptures for his own amusement, living amidst them with a broken-winged pet raven in his small St Petersburg home. Nobody saw them except for especially invited visitors. Under Communist rule it was impossible to display them, as only artists who were also party members were permitted to exhibit. Even if Bersudsky had wanted to become a member (which he didn't at all, thank you very much for asking) the political subtext of his work would have been suppressed.

From the Brezhnev era until the onset of Gorbachev's ground- and Berlin Wall-breaking reforms, the only Bersudsky creations seen by the St Petersburg public were the wooden carvings he made for the playgrounds in the city's parks. Habitually misguided in everything that they oversaw, the Communist Party had decreed that art wasn't art if it was in such a location (try telling that to the Serpentine Gallery). Most of these child-friendly figurines have now been removed or have simply rotted away. There is a photograph of a proud pair of Bersudsky's carved lions on the Sharmanka website; their world-weary eyes full of character, their faces cartoonish – quite unlike the staid, bronze Landseer creations that guard the base of Nelson's column in London. Perhaps for Trafalgar Square's next Russian New Year celebrations, the appropriate embassies could arrange a cultural lion exchange and cheer the place up.

★ Some members of a Russian dance troupe did kip amongst the automata for a couple of weeks when they came to Scotland to perform with Bersudsky's sculptures. The temptation for the security guard to flick the 'on' switch at three in the morning must have been unbearable.

Bersudsky narrowly escaped the Siege of Leningrad as a child, and was so affected by his traumatic memories of national service and encounters with survivors of the Gulag system that he ultimately lost all inclination to speak. Art became his chosen method of communication. His quiet thoughts on the nature of the human struggle permeate Sharmanka in flashes alternately brilliant and dark, while still allowing each individual audience member space for their own interpretation of the experience. Pieces like *Babylon* and *Time of Rats* and the semi-translated *An Autumn Walk in the Belle Epoque of Perestroika* will send out distinctly different messages to pessimists, optimists and whateverists.

Shadowplay.

It was Tatyana Jakovskaya who spotted the potential of Bersudsky's self-imposed scrap-heap challenge. Jakovskaya, a critic and theatre director, visited the private collection, decided it was the best theatre she had ever seen, and abandoned her own career forthwith. Sharmanka needed to be seen by the outside world. The first public display of the collection took place in 1988, but it was only by using a subtle piece of misdirection that they were able to entice anybody to come to see it at all. Assuming that it would be far too difficult to convince people to watch piles of reclaimed metalwork swinging about, it was decided to advertise it as a mime show – not a strategy particularly likely to work over here, but St Petersburgers go wild for a spot of mime. This wasn't so much a white lie as a black truth: there was mime, but only as an introduction. Then the mime artists stepped back and Sharmanka physically – and as a theatrical concept – burst into life.

227

By the following year, Sharmanka's reputation was enough to help secure their first proper display space: a former nursery. From there, via Utrecht, Leipzig and international acclaim, Sharmanka eventually fetched up in Glasgow. The glory of the current incarnation results from an equal partnership between the kinemats and the lighting and music. Jakovskaya's son Sergey has been part of Sharmanka's creative process since 1993 when he was barely a teenager. Now training as a lighting designer, Sergey has lit each of the sculptures to their better than best advantage. From pitch blackness, coloured lamps suddenly hurl dramatic shadows against white walls, as integral to the show as the machines themselves. Every piece has its own musical accompaniment: funky bagpipes, hurdy–gurdies, sad strings and snatches of speech, all complementing the movement of each piece with eerily familiar tunes.

Bersudsky rarely knows how one of his sculptures is going to turn out when he begins working on it, giving them an improvised, jazzy feel. Some are dedicated to lost friends such as Tim Stead, a sculptor and furniture-maker who offered encouragement and assistance when Sharmanka first came to Scotland. Bersudsky joined forces with Stead to build a striking millennium clock tower for the entrance hall of the Royal Museum of Scotland in Edinburgh. Stead died, far too young, in 2000. He is much missed at Sharmanka, where you can sit on his fine rustic seats at his fine rustic table. The two artists obviously had a direct influence on each other's lives, as well as their carving styles.

Sharmanka still wanders off on the occasional tour. Bits of it have holidayed in Jerusalem's science museum and spent fifteen months at the somehow more fitting Theatre Museum in Covent Garden.* But Glasgow has been its home for over a decade, and the show adds a welcome rich-ness to the already full-bodied 1990 European City of Culture. Picture a carefully stage-managed world-record domino-topple that can be reset at the flick of a switch, and you're somewhere near the mechanical brilliance of Sharmanka. This junk show is anything but rubbish. If anyone else creatively brilliant but neglected in their own homeland is out there, rest assured: our country needs you.

Sharmanka, 64 Osborne Street, Glasgow, G1 5QH

01415 527080

www.sharmanka.com

Sharmanka

---

* R.I.P.

228

Cheddar Crazy Golf

I happen to live about eighteen inches from the clubhouse. It's a long, long, long walk at my age, so I tend to stay overnight.

Peter Cook, *Peter Cook Talks Golf Balls*

Please spare a thought for the golfing widow, not to mention the golfing orphans and the ever-increasing number of golfing widowers. Nearly-whole families sit round dining tables every Sunday watching unclaimed plates of lovingly prepared roast growing slowly tepid. Before long, gravy congeals, crackling struggles to live up to its name and roast potatoes go figuratively and literally to the dogs. The Nineteenth Hole has a lot to answer for, although not nearly as much as the many hours spent playing the other eighteen that led there. There is a far more genteel alternative that takes up less time, involves no uppity dress codes or caddy tipping and doesn't rudely appropriate broad swathes of countryside during its construction. It's smaller, better behaved and, in Great British tradition, mainly enjoyed by amateurs who don't take it all that seriously. When was the last time you heard of a miniature-golfing widow?

The sport of small golf encompasses three disciplines – minigolf, crazy golf and adventure golf. Minigolf, the purest of the three, involves a few simple obstacles and lipped fairways, and relies on the art of the rebound.

Crazy golf opts for spinning windmills and mild peril. Adventure golf is often showy and usually themed – cowboys or space, that sort of malarkey – and, like most themed things, really needs to be done by Americans to not look completely ludicrous.

Cheddar Crazy Golf is not particularly crazy. It is, truth be told, more like minigolf but, according to owner Malcolm Scard, minigolf just can't bring the punters in like the promise of craziness. British craziness tends to be different from the craziness of other nations, anyway. Shouting 'let's go crazy!' to a crowd of Britons won't start a frenzied carnival but a burst of embarrassed shuffling. The closest most of us get to crazy is the paving on our drive. (Come to think of it, the Cheddar course does look a bit like a series of little suburban driveways.) The craziness here is on a tight, polite, British leash. Malcolm has plans to crazy-up the course, but thankfully this will not involve the construction of a purple robot King Kong that shoots

hot balls out of its eyes, but rather the addition of a discreet loop-the-loop to one of the holes. Cheddar craziness is building-a-tiny-Swiss-funicular-railway-in-your-garden crazy, not picking-strangers-off-a-water-tower-with-a-high-powered-rifle crazy. Perhaps you could think of it as Mildly Eccentric Uncle Golf.

But the real joy of Cheddar is its handsome setting. Golf courses attract the cream of the niblick set by offering glorious vistas. The best ones run attractively along the sea edge, command breathtaking views of heather or lounge in the landscaped grounds of stately homes. But no full-size golfer is ever going to get the chance to drive down the fairway in the narrow wonder that is Cheddar Gorge; the course wouldn't fit. Holiday brochures have worn thin the cliché of a windblown chap hacking a ball into the big sky above some awesome cliff-top links. State your independence by putting your small way quietly round an equally awesome cleft.

The course's stone construction is sympathetic to the natural landmark that towers on either side, and tips a dignified cap to both the gorge and Glastonbury Tor in the shapes of some of its obstacles. Aside from gentle chattering and the occasional ebullient cheer from other players, the loudest sounds are the wind riffling through the trees and a busy waterfall laughing splashily somewhere in the distance. Once merely a scruff of wild land behind a small parade of shops, it took Scard fifteen weeks in 1995 to transform it into this place of unexpected serenity, and it's substantially calmer than miniature golf's usual squawky seaside home.

A leisurely round at Cheddar tees off with a relatively straightforward first hole, lulling you into thinking that the game is going to be a breeze. Don't rush it. Cocky shots are frequently punished, and one man's doddle can easily become

A golfgoyle.

another's downfall. The fearsome yips can suddenly set in and before you know it you're carding the worst score since course records began.* Seasoned eight-year-

Cheddar Crazy Golf

---

* We came close. One of the holy commandments of minigolf is that you are only permitted a maximum of seven shots on any one hole before admitting defeat and moving on. It was a nice day, so we foolishly ignored this rule. By the time we eventually finished, it was dark, and we'd forgotten to find a hotel. We nearly had to sleep in one of the obstacles.

old minigolfers in polyester plus-fours stand patiently in lines behind you, wincing and yawning as you red-facedly skip your little coloured ball over the yoghurt-pot hole yet again. You step back and let them pass, but ten minutes later you're no further on, sixteen over par, glancing nervously out of the corner of your eye as the course pros whip round the holes a second time to lap you. Whatever your minigolfing ability, take time to savour the setting. Besides, leaning back and shading your eyes to gaze admiringly at the cliffs above is a good cover for having taken too long on your putt.

Unlike groups of giggling holiday duffers, top minigolfers treat their sport with real gravitas. There are British Opens, Nations' Cups, and European and World Championships with tidy cash prizes for the winners (but no Ryder Minicup as yet). There are practice days before tournaments: a chance to work out the lie of the land and to observe the regulars who already know all the course secrets. Minigolf stands apart from traditional golf, a proud sport with its own rules and its own champions. The game's leading practitioners play with state-of-the-art putters and choose specific types of ball for individual holes. Some have personalised golf balls. (Hopefully, they stop short of Tipp-Exing their signatures on the side of their cars.) A proper sense of fun pervades their mini world and a genuine camaraderie seems to exist between them as a result.

Minigolf isn't conkers or tiddlywinks (admirable games though they both are). There is significant prize money at stake here.* Sort of. European paydays don't match up to the six-figure US dollar sums that can be won across the water. Tim 'Ace Man' Davies, the top ranked British minigolfer at the time of writing, has accrued career earnings of around £4,500. Yet he's a key member of Planet Hastings, his home team, which once held the Albert Steptoe Memorial Cup – first prize, 20p. And competition was fierce.

---

* Unless you're Michael Webb, a high-ranking Brit and member of the London Minigolf Club. Playing strictly as a gentleman amateur, he is always respectfully referred to as Mr Michael Webb throughout the UK minigolf scene.

Like that naughty Auric Goldfinger in the film of the same surname, the urge to cheat at minigolf comes as an annoyingly comfortable second nature. Gamesmanship is rife, even in a mild Cheddar contest, with distracting coughs par for the course amongst the ultra-competitive. Poor show? Hard cheese. Warnings are routinely dished out at major competitions for such indiscretions so it's clearly a recognised part of the sport. Nudging the ball in a discreetly advantageous fashion probably isn't, but there are no umpires scrutinising here so shh.*

No matter how uncompetitive you attempt to appear at the beginning, by the third hole you will be flashing jealous glances at your companions' scorecards, holding a wetted finger in the air and cursing the wind (or lack of it). You'll be doing well to hit the mini-leaderboard. Scard reckons that a Cheddar round of under sixty is good going, and as far as he is aware the course record is forty-five. It's fast, fun and has loads more concrete gargoyles than Wentworth. Why crazy golf isn't a televised sport is anyone's guess. The longueurs would disappear and broadcasters wouldn't need to employ half as many cameramen. Surely millions of viewers would have tuned in to watch Jack Nicklaus repeatedly failing to chip through a tunnel running through a knee-height fairytale castle while Tom Watson waited patiently on the other side sucking on a Lemonade Sparkle.

A relaxing session at Cheddar, soaking up the pleasant grounds as you potter round with your putter, is a most agreeable way of letting time roll by. The most stressful thing that could happen to you here would be getting a hole-in-one. It's an unadorned, small pleasure that, if more of us regularly participated, could unwittingly lead to an outbreak of more civil behaviour in other areas of our lives. Above all, like the relationship of pool to snooker, it's the classlessness of minigolf that truly makes it the people's game.

Cheddar Crazy Golf, 7 Queens Row, The Cliffs, Cheddar, Somerset, BS27 3QE
01934 743661
www.cheddarsomerset.co.uk/spon/cheddarcrazygolf.htm

---

* You may well look disapproving. Our combined final tally added up to 326, an average of eighty-one-and-a-half strokes each (that's beyond hopeless). Without cheating by occasionally picking the ball up when no one was looking, we'd still be there now.

Rushton Triangular Lodge

It is quite a three-pipe problem.

Sir Arthur Conan-Doyle, *The Red-Headed League*

The prow of Rushton Triangular Lodge.

In *The Observer's Book of Sensible Numbers of Sides for a Building to Have* there is no chapter three. Chapter one deals with industrial chimneys, chapter two is more of a story and chapter four is absolutely huge, dealing with most of the buildings ever put up. But the third chapter had far too few entries to warrant inclusion. Such is the fate of triangular buildings: though they can do almost everything a normal building can do, they usually find themselves in the category marked 'follies'.

There are exceptions to this rule. The Fuller, or 'Flatiron', Building in Manhattan has three sides and is far too serious to be a mere folly. Perhaps it's because it does something useful: filling a gap at an acutely shaped road junction with office space. Or maybe, because it was one of New York's first skyscrapers, it's large enough to conceal its unreasonably acute frontage within a reasonable curve. The building also seems fairly sensible because its floor plan is a right-angled triangle. Stand at the squared-off back of the Flatiron and you

234

could be outside any number of normal buildings, two walls appearing to zip off at ninety degrees as if nothing were out of the ordinary. A proper triangular building should pull no punches, corner-wise. And Rushton Triangular Lodge in Northamptonshire is a proper triangular building.

Pre-dating the Georgian fad for tricorn follies by a good 150 years, the Triangular Lodge is a building designed to intimidate, confuse and confound.★ Its creator, Sir Thomas Tresham (Father of Francis, one of the Gunpowder Plot conspirators), lived in neighbouring Rushton Hall, and supposedly built the lodge to house his rabbit breeder.† Sir Thomas was a clever and well-to-do fellow who, after his conversion to Catholicism around the end of the markedly Protestant sixteenth century, spent a great deal of his time in prison. During one particularly long twelve-year stretch in Ely clink he gradually covered his cell with symbolic, devotional art. On his release from jail in 1593, like a man who spent twelve years spinning round on the spot, then tried to stand upright, he dizzily returned to Rushton and became obsessed with the unbalanced idea of building a symbolic and devotional lodge house. Within two years it was finished.

Although the building looks like the work of a madman, it needed a stable brain for its construction. It is immaculately crafted (sharp corners and edges emphasising its irregularity) and terrifically well preserved: the masonry is good as new and puts buildings a quarter of its age to shame.

★ From Hoober Stand in Wentworth (1748) to King Alfred's Tower in Stourhead (1772) and Severndroog Castle in Eltham (1784), three-sided buildings were once springing up like weeds. Check out the corners, though: towers and curves all over the place. Pretty, yes, but a real triangular building should have corners you can part your hair with.

† This is a moot point: Tresham may also have used it for banquets (at which he presumably served three-course meals finished with those triangular Quality Street chocolates wrapped in green foil. Or Dairylea and biscuits).

Perhaps the geometric strength of triangles is the key to its longevity; the pyramids have lasted a fair old while (even if they are built on a square base).

For something so hidden – and you might easily drive past without noticing it – the lodge is no shrinking violet. Tresham designed a building that was so unusual it would elicit triple-takes and act as the perfect canvas for his message, which he scrawled in bricks and mortar across its outside. What his message was is entirely up to you. The external walls are decorated with numbers he considered significant.★ Some of them make sense, others are open to interpretation. The big iron 15 and 93 on two walls refer to 1593, the date of the building's conception, and the initials 'TT' stand for 'Thomas Tresham' or 'Terrific Triangles'. It looks like a puzzle because it's meant to be a puzzle. Numerologists will note that both 15 and 93 are divisible by three, and that $1 + 5 + 9 + 3 = 18$, and that $1593 \div 3 = 531$, and that $5 + 3 + 1 = 9$ and so on. Non-numerologists will already be glazing over.

With three side elevations but no front or back, the original plans for the lodge must have bamboozled its masons. Designed as a place for contemplation, the sheer weight of symbolism and cryptic imagery gives visitors headaches to this day. The three external walls are each thirty-three feet three inches long (thirty-three being Jesus's age at his death) and rise to three gables on each side, all topped with heraldic trefoils, inscriptions and religious imagery, restlessly allusive and offering no easy answers. It's the kind of place that would give Dan Brown a best-selling thrill (or thriller): a three-dimensional Sudoku house full of encrypted religious clues, equal thirds Kit Williams's *Masquerade*, Marillion album cover and Rubik's Cube.

Tresham may have been inspired by the first syllable of his name to construct a celebration of the number three, but it was more likely that it was his passion for the Holy Trinity that set him off. Christianity wasn't the first religion to embrace the mystique of the number three: there are trinities of gods in Babylon, Greece and Egypt. In Greek mythology there were three Fates, three Furies and three Graces. Hinduism has the Trimurti. Buddhism has the Trikaya doctrine. Oaths are traditionally repeated thrice: Peter denies Christ three times in the Bible. Muslim men can divorce their wives by saying 'I divorce you' three times. Bad luck comes in threes. It's said to be unlucky to light three cigarettes with the same match. On the

★ 1580, 1593, 1595, 1626, 1641, 3509, 3898 and this week's bonus ball, 5555.

other hand, it's third time lucky. And this is just the superstitious stuff. We won't even get started on the mathematics. Three, as the well-known threesome De La Soul observed, is the magic number.

The Triangular Lodge is wildly disorienting to walk around. It's large enough to blind you as to where you are, and fool you into perceiving its three equally sized sixty-degree corners as four ninety-degree ones. To get back where you started, instead of turning your body through 1,080 degrees (4 x (360° − 90°)), you're only turning through 900 degrees (3 x (360° − 60°)) – which really messes with your internal calculator. In a world where buildings have at least four sides, the friends that you left waving to you from the entrance will pop back into view one wall (or 180°) too soon. Your brain will make the quite reasonable assumption that the building must have another entrance and all your friends' twin siblings have just come out of it, as if that were more likely. In triangles doth madness lie.

High-concept symbolic buildings died out with the fad for follies in the nineteenth century. These days, architects wouldn't dare design a bus shelter that attempts to explain the periodic table or a shopping centre in the shape of Buddha's All-Encompassing Love. However, the sixteenth century was a far loopier era and, for Tresham, the concept of the Holy Trinity seemed a sensible, non-controversial thing upon which to base the design of his lodge without upsetting the Protestant neighbours. Had the Catholic faith's doctrine been based on a Holy Duality, Tresham would have been

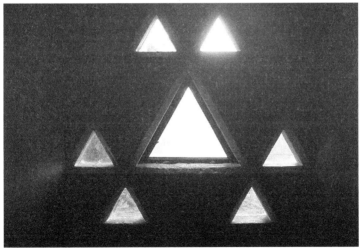

forced to make an ungainly two-sided house,★ but handily the polytheistic-sounding-but-apparently-monotheistic belief in three identical yet differently named gods acting as one god lent him the spiritual and structural support he needed to maintain his folly's integrity.

Inside, to encourage musing upon its mysteries, the Triangular Lodge is austere and contemplative. Impeccably decorated in magnolia with a Victorian cast-iron fireplace, it looks like a newly developed show home on a strictly triangular Wimpey estate. Each floor contains three rooms – two triangular, one hexagonal – and a third triangular space housing the spiral staircase.† Window seats allow you a moment to pause for a long, hard think about your triangular life. Upstairs, Tresham appears to have briefly forgotten himself and put in some lozenge, diamond and hexagonal windows. But peer round the back of the first-floor fireplace and … he's back! A triangular flue. Still, it's a surprisingly relaxing interior for a god-fearing wigwam.

In the 1960s some architects postulated that in the future we'd be living in organically shaped round pods. A nice thought, but impractical as hell. The rooms don't sit back to back comfortably, wasting loads of space; getting your existing furniture to sit flush against the walls would be a nightmare; and how the blazes would you hang a picture? By comparison, triangular houses like Tresham's make a great deal of sense. For a start they're one wall cheaper to build than conventional houses and they would tessellate like a dream into neat hexagonal clusters. Perhaps the future streets of Britain will be lined with triangular houses in gorgeous Trivial Pursuit cheese terraces. Well, they might be if someone comes up with a Hoover to cope with those bloody corners.

Rushton Triangular Lodge, Rushton, Kettering, Northamptonshire, NN14 1RP

01536 710761

www.english-heritage.org.uk/rushtontriangularlodge

★ Like 23–24 Leinster Gardens, Bayswater, London, which are two grand-looking houses that aren't really houses at all. Built in 1868 to cover the hole left after two identical-looking properties were demolished to make way for the Metropolitan Railway, the sham facade is very convincing. The address used to be given to the police by miscreants not wanting to be found at a later date. The fuzz are wise to the scam now.

† Although this sounds like an uncharacteristic lapse, think about the shape of the steps …

Epilogue: The Wicker Man's Legs

His looks do menace heaven and dare the Gods
His fiery eyes are fixed upon the earth
Christopher Marlowe, Tamburlaine The Great

History ruffles your hair when you stand under a blue plaque. Unwrapping a pre-packed sandwich on Handel's London doorstep, it's tempting to think of the composer bustling through you in ghostly time-lapse, day after day, over those same flagstones on the way to the snuff merchant or the harpsichord shop. Surely all that passage has left a little bit of Handel in the air for you to taste on your lips, like sea spray?

Picking your way through the wind-battered caravans of Burrowhead Holiday Village, on the cliffs overlooking the Solway Firth, there's the opposite of that sensation. Absolutely nobody famous ever lived here.* In fact it's unlikely anyone at all's ever stayed here for much longer than a fortnight. But, as you cross the brow of the promontory and spot a couple of wooden stumps driven into a lump of cement, there's that blue plaque buzz – someone was here. In October 1972, a sixty-foot human effigy made from fence-panels was torched on this headland by a freezing film crew. The burning would become one of cinema's most terrifying and enduring images, the climactic shots of Anthony Shaffer's *The Wicker Man*. This, you realise, is where the Wicker Man stood. Come. It is time to keep your appointment with his legs.

You probably know what happens in *The Wicker Man*,† and, if you do, it's testament to almost three decades of word-of-mouth whispering about 'the best scripted film I ever took part in' (according to actor Christopher

---

* The nearest celeb was Gavin Maxwell, author of the ottertastic *Ring of Bright Water*, who was born about ten miles up the road.

† An uptight Christian copper investigates a young girl's disappearance from a remote Scottish island community. The locals, jolly hippies in sturdy knitwear, freak the living daylights out of him with their pagan sexuality, rude folk singing and gleeful obstructiveness. The film ends with an enormous flaming Wicker Man, lots of screaming and a couple of hymns. Nobody wins.

Lee). The studio didn't see it that way and considered it an unmarketable flop, giving it a limited release as a B-feature ('one of the ten worst films I've ever seen' said the head honcho, daring to disagree with Dracula). Even screening the film to religious leaders in America's Bible Belt – in the hope of annoying them and generating some much-needed controversy – couldn't crack the lack of interest in the picture. (The pastors rather liked its brisk theological intelligence and refused to condemn it.) *The Wicker Man*'s following built so slowly that a fan convention at the film's main pub location in 2000 was attended by less than a dozen people – and when the film was shown at all, it was in a truncated version seemingly edited with a knife and fork.

The movie's arresting image of a human sacrifice in a burning wooden giant took nearly thirty years to fully enter the national consciousness, but is now familiar from countless homages. When it was made, much of the film's sense of creeping horror depended on the audience not knowing what a Wicker Man was. The poster art coyly dodged the issue, showing a purse-lipped sun god and some silhouettes of people with antlers on their heads. (It's that sort of film.) Thirty years later, and the full-length uncut

DVD (once the holy grail of horror, these days given away free with your Sunday paper) blows the film's twist with impunity, putting a lovely big Wicker Man on the front.[*] We all know what a Wicker Man is now. He's a British icon, like the Blackpool Tower, or the Angel of the North (who, come to think of it, could be a distant cousin).

The two stumps at Burrowhead are the last remaining parts of the smaller of two Wicker Men built for the film. The legs of the larger prop lasted until 1993 when some holidaymakers had a barbecue slightly too near it. What was left of this Wicker Man did exactly what it was designed to do and caught fire, leaving its partner (the one used for close-ups) alone a bit further down the cliffs.

Finding the legs still here in a remote corner of the western Scottish mainland is an odd experience. It's hard to think of another film prop that's been left in situ for fans to visit. Normally a set is struck, or the location is returned to its former state for everyday use. Here, sunk in concrete, the iconic thighs stand abandoned, as if the crew packed away yesterday and forgot to tidy up properly. It's like taking a wander through the sewers of Turin and finding one of the Minis from *The Italian Job* parked in a conduit.

Art director Seamus Flannery had a 1676 illustration by Aylet Sammes to work from when designing the film's Wicker Man, but the blank-faced leviathan was pretty much entirely his own invention.[†] Shaffer and Flannery's grisly figure has done so much to popularise the idea that our superstitious ancestors burned innocents in wicker effigies that it may come as a surprise that sacrificial burnings of the type depicted in the film probably never happened.

It was O-level Latin favourite Julius Caesar who first put the idea about. In his account of his war against the Gauls, Caesar noted that the druids would burn condemned criminals in human effigies made of osiers (willow-branch baskets). Keen that the Romans back home understood that this wasn't just colourful regional justice, but rather the action of heathen brutes who needed to be civilised at the sharp end of a gladius, Caesar hurriedly added that if enough criminals couldn't be found to please the local gods, innocents were added to the bonfire. It was a brazen bit of black

---

[*] Seeing a decent edit of the film used to be like trying to book an audience with God. Most fans' favourite cut of the film was the one shown in the early 1990s as part of BBC2's *Moviedrome* slot. You can approximate this at home by skipping the exposition-heavy opening of the Director's Cut and starting about six minutes in. Trust us: start with the seaplane.

[†] Flannery intended that the featureless head should resemble a masked executioner.

propaganda, most likely drawn second-hand from an earlier Greek description and tarted up by tossing a few virgins onto the bonfire for good measure (the earlier version makes up the druids' shortfall not with innocents but with prisoners of war – more capital punishment than barbaric sacrifice). The killing of an innocent is a good standby when you want to smear your enemy; Christians have made allegations of baby-slaughter over the centuries against witches and Jews, and the Romans weren't above saying early Christians lunched on babies themselves. We do love the idea that strangers are beasts and we are civilised by comparison. It's one of the reasons *The Wicker Man*'s climax has such dark power. On the other hand, it's also why people watch *Wife Swap*.

Whatever the reason the Celts built them, their descendants did the same, and even as late as the 1890s, folklorist James George Frazer could list plenty of (slightly more benign) wicker men still doing the rounds. The towns of Dunkirk and Douay held annual wicker giant festivals with big osier figures operated by puppeteers inside. The main giant at Dunkirk, called Papa Reuss, was forty-five feet high, big enough for him to carry a small child in his cloak pocket. Coventry had a huge wicker giant who walked through the streets as part of its midsummer festival, accompanied by his huge wicker wife. Belgian wicker giants would go from town to town visiting each other at festival time (except the Antwerp Giant, which was too tall to get out of the city gates).★

The practice of ritual burning has continued too. The Guy we put on our November 5th bonfire is the continuation of a long tradition where a representative scapegoat is burned to rid the community of bad spirits. Paris used to have a midsummer bonfire where they would ceremonially torch a mast topped with a barrel of live cats. In 1648, Louis XIV lit the bonfire himself – like a celebrity switching on the Christmas lights – and did a dance. Cats were associated with the devil, the thinking went, so burning them might bring good luck. The Edenbridge Bonfire Society in Kent takes a similar approach today, choosing a new villain every year. Recent celebrations have seen flames licking happily round effigies of John Prescott, Gordon Brown and a massive wicker Anne Robinson.

Something about building big wooden effigies and setting them on fire stirs us deep inside. Sure enough, every year more and more people make

★ This tradition is continued into the modern day by the Royal De Luxe theatre company. Their 'Sultan's Elephant' show, with its cast of house-sized wooden marionettes, stomped through London's streets in May 2006.

pilgrimages to Burrowhead, to pay homage to the revival of the practice in the modern era. The first Wicker Pilgrim was probably a man called Dave Lally, way back in 1981. Lally had just published a speculative *Wicker Man* fanzine (*Summerisle News*) – in much the same way as a castaway might despatch a message in a bottle to see if anyone else were out there – and decided to make his own tour of the film's locations.

Back in the days before the internet, such fandom required considerable diligence. Even identifying the correct headland was a matter of scouring photocopied magazine articles in archives and asking bemused locals to point out where a film they'd never heard of had been shot. By the turn of the millennium, the film's burgeoning reputation, and the power of the net for putting like-minded fans in contact, has meant a simple Google search will spit out an illustrated guided tour in seconds. Local enthusiasm has grown too, doubtless helped by the steady trickle of tourist pennies it brings. It's hard to believe that the first local reaction to a preview of the film was that it would irreparably damage the area's reputation. Dumfries

and Galloway now host an annual Wicker Man rock festival, and in Creetown (where the film's hero spends a couple of nights at a thinly disguised Ellangowan Hotel) the delightful local history museum has its own locally built Wicker Man in the foyer, complete with tiny soft-toy victim, arms spread in cloth supplication.

This new enthusiasm has its price, however, and the Wicker Man's Legs are paying it. Only a few years ago, the stumps were dusty grey, their surface weathered and rain-soaked. Now the bright, tan interior of fresh wood is exposed on each trunk – evidence of the increasing numbers of pilgrims who have taken a fragment home as a souvenir, breaking bits off faster than the wood can weather.

But here they stand for now on an imposing Scottish clifftop – the finest pair of wooden legs the British film industry has ever seen. They're not easy to find, so there's a compelling thrill about coming across them. It's not often you get to stand at the feet of a giant, especially one whose associations are with a scene so iconic and – this can't be underestimated – so absolutely, what-the-bloody-hell shocking the first time you see it. This is the site of one of the most brilliant plot twists in the history of cinema.

A sign used to sit by the Wicker Man's Legs. An unaffected, memorable reminder of the need to preserve tourist attractions for fellow travellers, it read, 'Take only photographs; leave only footprints.' It has long since gone. Presumably someone took it.

★ ★ ★

And that's how this book would have ended, had some unidentified cretin not sawn off the Wicker Man's Legs from the platform on which they had stood for thirty-four years and made off with them, upstaging our punch line. We visited Burrowhead in the last week of September 2006. Seven weeks later, they were gone.

This is a serious loss to the British film industry, and any heritage potential the film's ever-expanding fan base was dutifully generating. Those legs (or logs), so kindly left standing around by the film crew, were – if you can say this of a pair – unique. They were accruing such a following that it wasn't impossible to imagine them making the leap from curio to fully fledged tourist attraction. Of course, that would have meant fencing them off, and charging the punters a fiver to stand within a dozen feet of them: in other words, you'd have paid to be kept from them. You'd have been herded around them, the Stonehenge way. On the other hand, they'd still be there.

Sadly, they're not. Film is a relatively young art, and its masterpieces are still under negotiation. Things go in and out of fashion from generation to generation. In the case of The Wicker Man, *a brilliant script became a cheap but clever film which became an overlooked little gem which became a cult novelty which became an underground classic which has become, at last, a recognised masterpiece. One poll calls it the sixth best British film of all time. Here, on this commanding headland, amidst the deftly drawn-up threads of Anthony Shaffer's terrific story, the Wicker Man stood. What's more, he burned. He burned against the blood-orange sun and frightened the wits out of us. And then, because the more people there are who like something, the higher the chances that at least one of them will be a soulless moron who prefers his landmarks on eBay than the horizon, what was left of him was nicked.*

There is a lesson here, and it's a salutary one: some of the places we've written about won't last forever. Since Bollocks to Alton Towers *was published, at least two of its subjects have been significantly eroded. These places aren't on the A-list of tourist attractions for good reason: they're not immediately most people's cup of tea. But once you appreciate a tiny bit of what they're doing, you're in – and the cup of tea, at the risk of fricasséeing our metaphors, is easily half full. If you like the sound of anything we've mentioned along the way – or any other oddity that takes your fancy – make the effort to see it, because you may not get the chance again.*

One of the reasons we were able to say bollocks to a big theme park with brazen confidence is that it wouldn't be significantly affected by our attempts to steer its potential visitors somewhere smaller and more distinct. But the intrinsic appeal of the places we've featured is often threatened by the regrettable inevitability that, in the end, too little love will kill them. The Wicker Man's Legs, we're shocked to report, are the first example we've come across where too much love killed them. Just our luck – the sodding crowd turned up.

Burrowhead Holiday Village, Nr. Isle of Whithorn, Newton Stewart, Dumfries & Galloway, Scotland,
DG8 8JB
01988 500252
www.burrowheadholidayvillage.co.uk

Bibliography

'A Man Who Hated Whimsy', *Time Magazine*, 13 Feb 1956

'The German Mouse: Super-Super-Super-Heavy Tank Became Hitler's White Elephant', *Intelligence Bulletin*, March 1946

A Souvenir of the Restoration of the Toad Lane Store to the Care of the Co-operative Movement, The Rochdale Pioneers and the Co-operative Union Ltd., 1931

Alexander, Hélène, *Fans*, Shire Publications, 2002

Amato, Ivan, 'Time 100 Most Important People of the Century', *Time*, 29 March 1999

Archer, Ian, *The Jags – The Centenary History of Partick Thistle Football Club*, Molendinar Press, 1976

Armstrong, Colin and Tempest, Malcolm, *The Forbidden Corner Guidebook*, Forbidden Corner

Armstrong, Colin, *Behind the Forbidden Corner*, Forbidden Corner, 2006

Aslet, Clive, *Landmarks Of Britain*, Hodder & Stoughton, 2005

Atkinson, R.L., *Tin and Tin Mining*, Shire Publications, 1985

Ayers, Tim, Brown, Sarah and Neiswander, Judy, *Stained Glass Museum Gallery Guide*, The Stained Glass Museum, 2004

Barton, Stuart, *Monumental Follies*, Lyle, 1972

Battrick, Jack, as told to Lawson, Gail, *Brownsea Islander*, Poole Historical Trust, 1978

Bender, Lionel, Parr, Peter and Angel, Jon, *Beginner's Guide to Miniature Golf*, Bender Richardson White, 2005

Berridge, Virginia, *Temperance – Its History and Impact on Current and Future Alcohol Policy*, Joseph Rowntree Foundation, 2005

Blythman, Joanna, *Bad Food Britain*, Fourth Estate, 2006

Bobbitt, Malcolm, *Bubblecars and Microcars*, Crowood Press, 2003

Boulton & Paul Ltd., 1898 Catalogue, Algrove Publishing, 1998

Boulton, Tom, 'The Man Behind the Award – the Life and Times of Professor Pask', *Anaesthesia News*, November 1999

Bramah, Edward, *The Bramah Tea & Coffee Walk Around London*, Christian le Comte, 2005

British Commercial Vehicle Museum Official Catalogue, Vintage World Ltd

Brown, Allan, *Inside the Wicker Man*, Sidgwick & Jackson, 2000

Caesar, Julius, *Gallic War*, Project Gutenberg

Carter, Anthony J., 'Dwale: an Anaesthetic from Old England', *British Medical Journal*, 18 December 1999

Caterall, Ali, and Wells, Simon, *Your Face Here*, Fourth Estate, 2001

Chandler, Arthur R., *Through the Shepard Archive: The Man Who Drew Pooh*, Jaydem Books, 2003

Clarkson, Jeremy, 'Fun: the true sign of a good school,' *Sunday Times Review*, 15 May 2005

Comfort, Richard, *The Lost City of Dunwich*, Terence Dalton, 1994

Encyclopedia of Company Histories, Gale Group

Foote, Timothy, 'Bear Essentials', *Time Magazine*, 23 June 1975

Fox, Kate, *Watching the English*, Hodder, 2004

Frazer, Sir James George, *The Golden Bough*, Penguin, 1998

Gander, Terry (ed.), *Alderney: An Introduction*, Alderney Wildlife Trust

Gaskill, Malcolm, 'Witchfinders', *Fortean Times*, July 2005

Gaskill, Malcolm, *Hellish Nell: Last of Britain's Witches*, Fourth Estate, 2002

Geraint Jenkins, Dr J., *The Coracle*, Gwasg Carreg Cwalch, 2006

Gershlick, Janet, *Plaques: The Story Behind the Plaques on Southwold Pier*, Janet Gershlick, 2004

Gilchrist, Jim, 'A Spiritual Healing', *The Scotsman*, 27 July 2002

Girouard, Mark, *Rushton Triangular Lodge*, English Heritage, 2004

Gravett, Paul and Stanbury, Peter, *Great British Comics*, Aurum, 2006

Greater London Council, Department of Public Health Engineering, *London's Main Drainage System*, GLC, 1972

Haran, Brady, 'Stuck in the middle with ewe', BBC News Online, 20 October 2002

Heath, H.W., *Proceedings of the Physical Society of London, Volume 35, Issue 1*, IOP, 1922

Hickman, Trevor, *The History of the Melton Mowbray Pork Pie*, Sutton Publishing, 2005

Howie, Craig, 'Fraudulent Medium or Powerful Psychic: The Trial of a Scottish Witch', *The Scotsman*, 24 October 2005

Jones, Barbara, *Follies and Grottoes*, Constable, 1956

Jones, Neil, 'Oysters are off but soap operas are on for Essex drinkers', *The Guardian*, 27 November 2006

Kennedy, Lady Charles, 'The Logan Fish Pond', *The Scottish Field*, January 1941

Kochmann, Karl, *Black Forest Clockmaker and the Cuckoo Clock*, Antique Clocks Publishing, 1987

Kurlansky, Mark, *Salt: A World History*, Walker/Penguin, 2002

Lacey, William J., *The Case for Total Abstinence*, National Temperance Publication Depot, 1889

Legg, Rodney, *Brownsea – Dorset's Fantasy Island*, Dorset Publishing Company, 1986

Lurie, Alison, *Not in Front of the Grown Ups*, Abacus, 1991

Mantel, Hilary, 'Unhappy Medium', *London Review of Books*, May 2001

Massingham, H.J., *A Mirror of England*, Green Books, 1988

McCann, Nick (ed.), *Papplewick Pumping Station – The Wonder of Water*, Papplewick Pumping Station Trust, 2005

McKie, Robin, 'Hero in a Half Shell', *The Observer*, 22 October 2006

Milne, A.A., *Now We Are Six*, Methuen, 1927

Milne, A.A., *The House At Pooh Corner*, Methuen, 1928

Milne, A.A., *When We Were Very Young*, Methuen, 1924

Milne, A.A., *Winnie-the-Pooh*, Methuen, 1926

Milne, Christopher, *The Enchanted Places*, Penguin, 1976

Monopolies and Mergers Commission, *British Gas plc*, 1993

Ogilvie, Jen, 'Tinfoil Helmets', *Fortean Times*, November 2006

Oldham, Tony, and Oldham, Anne, *Discovering Caves: A Guide to the Show Caves of Britain*, Shire Publications, 1972

Packe, Michael St John, and Dreyfus, Maurice, *The Alderney Story 1939–49*, The Alderney Society and Museum, 1971

Pantcheff, T.X.H., *Alderney: Fortress Island*, Phillimore, 1981

Parker, Dorothy, *The Collected Dorothy Parker*, Penguin, 1989

Pavia, Will, 'My, Christopher Robin, You've Changed', *The Times*, 9 December 2005

Reid, Kennedy, Thomson, Anderson, Deans, *Partick Thistle F.C. – The Official History 1876–2002*, Yore Publications, 2002

Robson, Maisie (ed.), *Arthur Mee and the Strength of Britain – Selections from First World War Pamphlets*, Eynsford Hill Press, 2006

Room, Adrian, *The Penguin Dictionary of British Place Names*, Penguin, 2003

Schwarz, Dr Sharron P., *The Cornish in Latin America*, University of Exeter PhD project, 2003

Searle, Ronald, *The Terror of St Trinians*, Penguin, 1989

Shanahan, Andrew, 'No Razor Fish, We're British', *The Guardian*, 12 May 2006

Skinner, B.F., 'Superstition in the Pigeon', *Journal of Experimental Psychology*, 1948

Spalding, Julian, *The Art and Time of Eduard Bersudsky*, Sharmanka

Steckoll, Solomon H., *The Alderney Death Camp*, Granada, 1982

Steingarten, Jeffrey, *It Must've Been Something I Ate*, Headline, 2002

Stevenson, Robert Louis, *Treasure Island*, Penguin, 1994

Tank Museum Exhibition Guide, Bovington Tank Museum, 2006

Taylor, Arnold, *Beaumaris Castle*, CADW Publications, 2004

Thompson, Janet, *The Scot Who Lit the World – The Story of William Murdoch*, Janet Thompson, 2003

Turnbull, Jean and Southern, Jayne, *More Than Just a Shop – A History of the Co-op in Lancashire*, Lancashire County Books, 1995

Twyman, Mick, 'The Mystery of Margate's Shell Temple', *Bygone Kent Magazine*, October 2006

Uglow, Jenny, *The Lunar Men*, Faber & Faber, 2002

Walker, Ben, 'Library's Overdue Success', *Fresh Produce Journal*, 3 May 2002

Walters, Guy, 'Jackboot UK', *Daily Mail*, 14 July 2004

Walton, Izaak (ed. Hawkins, J.), *The Compleat Angler*, Project Gutenberg, 1760

Wells, David, *The Penguin Dictionary of Curious and Interesting Numbers*, Penguin, 1986

Westwood, Jennifer, and Simpson, Jacqueline, *Lore of the Land*, Penguin, 2005

Wilkinson, D.J., 'Charles King: A Unique Contribution to Anaesthesia', *Journal of the Royal Society of Medicine, Vol 80*, JRSM, 1987

Winder, Simon, *The Man Who Saved Britain*, Picador, 2006

Zeitlin, Gerald L., 'Who Was Sir Robert Macintosh?' *Anaesthesia Record, Vol VII, No. 17*, 27 April 1999

The Mystery of History, BBC, 2005
Panorama: The High Price of Gas, BBC, 2006
Poldark, BBC, 1975
Aldeburgh Moot Hall museum exhibit

www.ashdownforest.co.uk
www.bedsguiding.org.uk
www.britannica.com
www.cardross.org
www.castles-of-britain.com
www.castlewales.com
www.crossness.org.uk
www.davidbryce.org.uk
www.en.wikipedia.org
www.english-heritage.org.uk
www.follies.btinternet.co.uk

www.forteantimes.com
www.georgianindex.net
www.just-pooh.com
www.localhistory.scit.wlv.ac.uk
www.projects.ex.ac.uk/cornishlatin
www.punch.co.uk
www.rcahms.gov.uk
www.statistics.gov.org

Acknowledgements

Thanks are due, firstly, to the many people who own, run and staff the entries in this book. We hope some of their enthusiasm and humour is reflected herein.

A doggy bag of cake and balloons goes to Rowland White, our steadfast editor; Cat Ledger, our increasingly enchanting agent; and the Penguinistas, notably Anwen Hooson and Georgina Atsiaris.

Our gratitude is also extended to the many people who suggested places to go, including Paul and Lin Fermor, Martin Graham, Davy Jones, Denise Mina and Carole Tyrrell.

What up and big shout to the book's first readers, Samantha Mackintosh, John Morris and Jason Whyte, and the many kind souls who put up with us along the way: Beth Gibbons, Jo and Damon Green, Murray Grigor, Charlotte Hazelby, Sue Knowles, Michael Mann, Nathalie Morris, Lisa Randall, James Randi, Julia Raeside, Nikki Reid, Abbie Sampson, Alice Sommerlad, Annabel Venning and, especially, Guy Walters, for efforts far above and way beyond the call of reasonable duty.

Index